MISSPELLED PARADISE

A YEAR IN A REINVENTED COLOMBIA

Bryanna Plog

Book Layout © 2013 BookDesignTemplates.com
Map of Colombia © 2013 Bryanna Plog and Wilma la Paglia

Misspelled Paradise: A Year in a Reinvented Colombia
Bryanna Plog. -- 1st ed.
ISBN 978-1494984021

Dedicated to teachers and travelers everywhere

and

a las estudiantes de la Institución Educativa de Santa Ana

ACKNOWLEDGEMENTS

Many thanks to Bradley Sands for your edits, feedback, and patience and to Jason Sinner for correcting more than a few typos. Thank you to the brainstorming team of Barb, Jacqueline, and Jenny—who also deserves a thank-you for graphic design and transportation help. Thank you Wilma for your patience, help with titles and covers, and for convincing me to get on Twitter, and to Kristin, Manu, Stephanie and all the others who showed interest in the book at its early stages.

Thanks muchísimo to Adam, Rachel, Kassira, TL, Shannon, Alyssa, and Kayla for making my year in Colombia so enjoyable and memorable and for letting me share our story.

To all the Colombians who showed me your country, I am eternally grateful for the chance to live in your beautiful land and for the kindness, joy, and interest you showed me. Gracias for letting me share Colombia with the world.

And thank you Mom, Dad, and Charlotte for all your love and support. You are the three best teachers I know and I salute you.

Finally, a big thank-you to whoever invented electric fans and air conditioning—you are brilliant and should be forever honored for your contributions to society. Sorry I didn't realize it before.

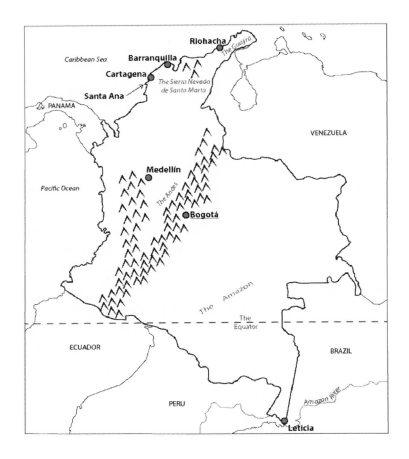

<u>MAP OF COLOMBIA</u>
with cities and regions mentioned in the book

PROLOGUE

The news ticker ran across the bottom of the TV screen: "Prostitution Scandal in Columbia."

I rolled my eyes as the reporter stood in front of waving palm trees, his somber tone not quite disguising his joy at being able to say "prostitution," "secret service agents," and "the president's visit" all in the same sentence.

I wasn't rolling my eyes at the fact that America's 24-hour news networks had brought us another story of drugs, sex, and rock 'n' roll (or, in this case, salsa music). While the ridiculousness of both the secret service agents and the prostitutes was perhaps newsworthy, my inward groan was because of the news ticker itself.

Note to TV stations: it is a good idea when reporting from a foreign country to spell the country's name right.

Because if there is one thing I learned from teaching English for a year in Colombia, it is that the name of that complicated country does not contain a single *u*. Colombia might be named for an explorer we English speakers call Columbus, but his name in Spanish is Cristóbal Colón and in his native Italian he is Cristoforo Colombo (note the lack of *u*'s). That linguistical detail might make Colombia perhaps the most misspelled country in the world, giving Kyrgyzstan and

Liechtenstein a run for their money. The tiny *pueblito* of Santa Ana, on the island of Barú—just two hours away from the ritzy hotel where the secret service agents were getting their Latin on—was my home for a year. My job: to teach English at one of the island's public schools. The fact that I was not an accredited teacher was painfully obvious to anyone stepping into my sparse, sweltering middle school classrooms at the Institución Educativa de Santa Ana, a bumpy twenty-minute motorcycle ride into the interior of the island. But the Colombian government required every student to take English classes, so I took my shiny new degrees in global studies and English and joined thousands of other U.S. Americans heading off, bright-eyed, to teach English in a foreign country.

There was something I couldn't grasp that drew me to Colombia. I think it was the realization of my own ignorance of the place, coupled with a desire for that elusive but strangely tantalizing experience of adventure in a place the media has dubbed dangerous. I hoped to effect positive change in Colombia through well-meaning (read: naïve) sacrifice, so dedicating a year to sit in a 95 degree classroom with middle school students at a public school seemed to fit the bill.

I, along with most of my fellow volunteer teachers from the Harvard-based program WorldTeach, had learned most of what I knew of Colombia from thirty second news bits, *Romancing the Stone*, *Blow*, and Juan Valdez commercials. I knew Colombia "had problems" (as a friend had said before I left), but that was akin to describing Russia as "big" and the Vatican City as "Catholic." I figured there was much more to discover beyond rebel groups, drug running, and the ongoing civil conflict. However, while I didn't envision that the day-to-day life of Colombians involved harrowing escapes from drug lords in the jungle or that every Colombian was mustached, wore a white sombrero, and led his donkey through coffee fields, after dismissing these images, nothing else really came to mind. It was a fuzzy void on the map, with the Caribbean Sea, the Pacific Ocean, the Amazon, and Venezuela framing a region seemingly unexplored by modern cartographers.

And it was that inability to place anything inside that blank part of a map (a part that—let's face it—I labeled as Columbia all too often) that put me on a plane flying south one dark, early January morning.

My time in Colombia filled the void and the country became more than a map of rebel-held territories and tourist destinations. Colombia might still have serious problems with armed rebel groups and drug trafficking, but the country taught me that its spectacular landscapes, thriving cultures, and joyful citizens also made up a country that was tantalizingly close to becoming a paradise.

And, of course, my year teaching and traveling also taught me to spell Colombia with an *o*.

CHAPTER ONE

BOGOTÁ

Although Colombia is known best for its dense jungles, hilly coffee farms, and sweeping coastlines (and yes: cocaine, Pablo Escobar, and armed guerrillas), my year began in a metropolis high in the mountains: 8,600 feet high. That's the kind of altitude that puffs up bags of chips so they look like they just came off airplanes and makes your red blood cells cry out in protest if you so much as think about rushing past a gimpy llama on the street.

When I say I'm going to the mountains on a January day in the United States, I usually mean something along the lines of grabbing some skis, checking to see if I have a good map, and pulling on a lot of long underwear. But instead of rustic cabins or tiny ski chalets, high in the Andes I found myself in the sprawl of seven and a half million people known as Bogotá (to help out certain phonetically impaired newscasters, it is pronounced bo-ga-TA, not bo-GAW-ta).

Bogotá is a city that still has the label of being dangerous or at least a little rough around the edges. Hollywood especially likes to portray it as a war zone. In *Mr. and Mrs. Smith,* for example, Brad Pitt and Angelina Jolie meet in a Bogotá that has spontaneous flashes of explosions going off, Black Hawk helicopters overhead, and everyone in full riot gear. The movie makes it look like a cross between a

WWII bombing raid and anarchists rioting in the street.

I hadn't particularly imagined Bogotá as a war zone, but I wasn't sure what to expect when I took my first steps toward exploring Colombia. I jumped down from the cramped van that had brought the entire group of teachers-to-be into the downtown and looked around, surprised. I certainly hadn't envisioned a Bogotá that included sky-scrapers, sleek cars, and Colombians as white as I was.

In fact, if you had asked me what a Colombian looked like before I set foot on Colombian streets, I would probably describe a *mestizo*, which is what most U.S. Americans think of when they visualize someone from Latin America. The mixed heritage of Europeans and indigenous peoples is dominant in much of Central and South America, and Colombia is no different: mestizos made up almost 60% of the population. However, a full 20% of the population is white, almost 20% is black (or mixed black, white, and indigenous), and a mere 1% of Colombians are indigenous.

As I looked around at the mix of faces passing me on the street, there may have been spies walking around for all knew, though not seeing any Brad Pitt look-alikes was a bit of a disappointment. But on the up side, it seemed like I wouldn't need to be constantly on the lookout for falling missiles every time I walked down the street.

It looked similar to any downtown European or North American city. Even the cooler temperatures of South America's third-highest capital meant that the trees looked more temperate than tropical. In fact, with its brick apartments, gray industrial buildings, and low clouds hanging over the nearby hills, Bogotá felt a little like the neighborhoods in Seattle near where I had grown up.

A horse pulling a cart with thick rubber tires rattled past and I realized how much I had failed to notice during my first glance at the city.

There were vendors under umbrellas (for the frequent rains and high-altitude tropical sun) selling cell phone minutes and haphazardly-arranged packaged snacks, candies, and cigarettes. There were cookie-cutter businessmen in well-cut suits getting out of their Toyotas and Mercedes-Benzes and walking up to tall office buildings, shiny briefcases in their hands. There were women pushing around vats of condiments and tortillas. And there were horse carts clip-clopping on the wet streets (one nearly colliding with a young woman on a shiny blue moped), young boys running around in battered flip-flops, and families of shoppers with their latest purchases in their hands.

Just regular folks going about their daily business.

And that's what we were doing as well. My first Colombian adventure was not hacking through the jungle, escaping para-militaries, or soaking in the sun on a Caribbean beach. Instead, I had to navigate Colombian bureaucracy.

We walked into the immigration (or DAS/Department of Admin-istrative Security) office with the goal of getting at least the first round of paperwork needed to procure a Colombian ID card (the *cedula*) finished. Apparently there wasn't a wave of immigrants trying to move to Colombia that day and the small office was practically empty when we arrived. I gave my paperwork to a light-skinned woman with dark hair pulled back in a bun.

The lady flipped through the abundant—and very specific—documents I had gathered to prove my identity, saying, "Dos fotos" (two photos that had to be on specifically sky-blue background), "tarjeta de tipo de sangre" (blood ID card), "dos copias de su visa" (two copies of my Colombian visa), "pasaporte... copia del pasaporte," (actual passport, plus a copy of my passport ID page), "y su forma de DAS" (the official DAS form filled out in block letters in black ink. No cross-outs or whiteout allowed). She didn't look remotely surprised that a middle class U.S. American was moving to her country, though looked a little surprised all my paperwork was in order.

"Entonces, está bien. Esperase ahí." She pointed to a few rows of chairs and told me to wait.

Apparently I wasn't on any Colombia version of the Terrorist Watch List and another immigration official soon called me back to be fingerprinted. In a back cubicle I was surprised to come face-to-face with not a regular inkpad, but a high-tech reader that blinked at me menacingly. I sat down a bit nervously, unclear as to where to put my hands. I needn't have worried; the assistant lifted up my fingers onto the slightly smudged glass plate, which would apparently scan and record my fingerprints. The glass was cold to the touch and shot out an eerie blue light before popping the image of my prints up on a nearby computer. I felt as if I *was* signing up for spy work (if only I looked as good as Angelina Jolie).

I'm not sure if DAS distrusted their fancy equipment, were just being thorough, or needed to send my prints to every police station in Colombia, but they also rolled out the regular ink and took my prints twice for both hands, and I emerged from the back room with the smudged black fingertips to prove I had passed their tests.

I sat uncomfortably for a while, starting to get worried at the amount of time my passport was hanging out behind the counter. The immigration official finally handed it back, I was told I could pick up my cedula in a week, and it was official: I could stay in Colombia for the rest of the year.

As fun as it was to fill out paperwork and get my fingerprints taken, Bogotá had more to offer visitors than government ID cards. While I was in Colombia to teach (my official edict according to the immigration office), my three weeks in Bogotá were to provide an orientation to the country and help me get to know my new home. So since I wasn't teaching yet, I washed all the ink off my fingers and headed back to the city to be a tourist for a day along with a couple of other almost-teachers who were in WorldTeach's orientation with me.

We hopped on board a bus that brought us to the unimaginatively named #80 Terminal, where we got our first taste of the modern transportation system of Bogotá: TransMilenio.

While many Latin American cities are known for their honking, rundown clunkers of buses, minibuses, and taxis masquerading as a public transportation system, Bogotá is known for its sleek fleet of TransMilenio buses—which add to the traffic of the old minibuses and the like. TransMilenio began in 2000 and the subway-like system of stations and bus lines (termed bus rapid transit—or BRT) covers most the city and outlining areas.

After getting the fare for the round-trip from #80 Terminal to downtown Bogotá and back loaded onto a throwaway paper card, we made our way downstairs, up to another platform, and with the help of a man wearing a bright yellow "Amigo de TransMilenio" vest, ended up at the area where the J95 bus would stop. We waited on the raised platform and watched a bright red articulated bus (with an accordion-like middle section allowing the bus to be twice as long as a normal one) stop a few yards before the spot where we were standing. It let everyone off, then drove ten feet to and lined up the doors with the stripe of yellow painted on the platform. The doors opened, I got inside, and stood with the flexible middle section on my right and about a dozen people squished against me on every other side. TransMilenio was obviously a popular choice for getting around— 1 million to 1.5 million passengers rode it each day. A sizable percentage of them seemed to be on the J95 bus with us.

We passed rolling green hills, expansive greenhouses growing roses, and a few shopping malls. When we got off, the gray morning was drizzling a bit and we were back in the middle of the metropolis. Tall office towers were mixed with 18th century buildings and rows of stark concrete blocks lacking architectural finesse, which likely meant they were built in the 1960s.

The mixture of buildings revealed that while Bogotá's prominence started in colonial times, most of its growth happened much more recently. The city was founded in 1538 by Spaniards traveling to the interior from the Caribbean coast. First known as Santafé de Bogotá, it grew in importance for the next few hundred years, so when Gran Colombia (which included today's Venezuela, Panama, and Ecuador in addition to Colombia) achieved independence from Spain in 1819, Bogotá was named the capital. Much of its population growth happened in the second half of the 20th century, when rural poverty and violence caused thousands to move to Bogotá, increasing the population by more than six million between 1950 and 2010. Most *Bogotanos* live in the sprawling foothills in the valley, but all the prominent businesses, government offices, and tourist attractions are downtown, which is where we started our explorations.

We navigated around the large construction project in the middle of the road, and walked up the avenue toward our first touristy stop: the Botero Museum. It was surprisingly difficult to find considering it was one of Bogotá's most popular museums, so we eventually asked a couple of policemen and a security guard who were outside a McDonald's (apparently tasked with guarding hamburgers). The guard gave us directions, we thanked him, and then realized we were now required to walk across the street. This resulted in our first life-threatening Colombian experience: navigating a busy Bogotá intersection.

There seemed to be no rhyme or reason to Bogotá's traffic with its mixture of cars, trucks, buses, motorcycles, bicycles, horse carts, and TransMilenio buses and the lights and signs seemed to serve as suggestions rather than helping to enforce traffic laws. Horses, motorcycles, and bikes weaved between trucks and around puddles and potholes, making me question how much I really wanted to cross the street. Of course the sheer volume of traffic meant it was more stop than go at times, which is likely the main reason pedestrians are not an extinct species in Bogotá. The other reason is that cars (and horse carts) are banned on dozens of Bogotá's streets every Sunday, which opens up the thoroughfares for bike and pedestrian traffic. Unfortunately, though, we had to cross the busy intersection before enjoying the peace and quiet of the car-free side streets. But despite our poor navigational skills—amid a thousand cars and bikes whose main reason for being out on the street was to see how many pedestrians they could hit—we finally succeeded in arriving at the museum of Colombia's most famous sculptor and painter, Fernando Botero.

The museum's most prominent feature was Botero's own works, where all his subjects are obese: large-bodied sculptures and portraits of fat characters such as chubby Colombian farmers and puffed-up military leaders (even Botero's still lifes of fruit were on the fat side). The museum also housed much of Botero's private collection, which included pieces by Renoir, Monet, and Picasso. While it was exciting to admire these masterpieces, looking at serene scenes of sunny 19th century French parks was a bit surreal after we had walked through the honking traffic of the cloudy Colombian city outside the museum walls. And I am sure few people have actually thought, "You know what, honey? I'd like to take a vacation to some place to see great art, maybe some Renoirs and Monets. How about... Colombia?"

Unlikely.

A few days earlier, we had been introduced to the other famous museum Bogotá offered: the Museo de Oro, or the Gold Museum. There with our whole group we got a good English-language tour, consisting of an hour and a half of exploring the museum's renowned pre-Columbian artifacts (the Columbian with the *u* refers not the country, but to the period of time before Christopher Columbus arrived in the Americas).

Colombia was another stop off for conquistadors trying to find El Dorado. The conquistadors famously failed to find a gleaming city of gold, but at least in Colombia there were a few indigenous tribes who *were* making things out of gold (just not buildings). There is a legend of a chief who covered himself in gold dust and dove into a lake in the Bogotá area as an initiation ceremony and homage to the gods. So maybe instead of tramping through the Andes and the Amazon, treasure hunters should be looking for layers of gold underwater—a sort of Colombian Atlantis. Because while the Bogotá airport might be called El Dorado, the gray buildings we walked by certainly didn't seem to be the lost city everyone was looking for.

That didn't mean the intricate designs of the ancient gold work displayed in the museum didn't draw me in. The workmanship was excellent and the prominent displays were a good way to honor the Muisca, Quimaya, Tayrona, and other indigenous groups living around Colombia before the Spanish plowed in. The 55,000 pieces of metalwork, pottery, and other artifacts were not all laid out for the public, but there was a lot to see.

I was glad my introduction to my new home included part of the history of pre-colonial Colombia, but the hot and dim museum did not lend itself to the rapt attention of its visitors, especially visitors like us who had been on our feet all day.

"The sun is represented by gold," our tourist guide droned on with what I am sure was interesting information. It was crowded as we all shuffled past lit displays, straining to hear our guide's voice, and the humid interior was stifling. Being herded along as part of a gaggle of tourists wasn't exactly the reason why I had moved to Colombia, although I suppose it did give me an idea of what it would have been like to stand next to smoldering coals while the original inhabitants of Colombia smelted gold and fired pottery. I pulled out a bandana and wiped sweat from my face.

After going back outside, we found that a heavy rain had started. We stepped over puddles in the sidewalks, maneuvered past couples with umbrellas, and skirted by the occasional cart selling grilled *arepas*. A few fellow teachers and I looped around looking for an early dinner and decided on a cozy-looking restaurant with a worn-looking wooden sign. I ordered something called *changua* for only 5,000 Colombian pesos (about $2.75), and we enjoyed getting out of the rain, sitting cozy and warm in the restaurant while we waited for our food to arrive. Two elderly Bogotanos sat at a worn wooden table behind us, slowly sipping tiny coffees while across from us the waiter flirted with a young lady eating rice, chicken, and an avocado the size of a small watermelon. My dish—a chowder-like soup—arrived, I breathed in its aroma, and gave it a quick stir with my spoon. I was surprised to see large chunks of bread already soggy from the soup floating around with a hard-boiled egg and eyed it warily. But despite this strange assortment of ingredients, the changua was delicious. Without even trying, I had ordered a traditional Colombian meal (though I later learned that changua was usually eaten for breakfast).

But Bogotá was full of less-traditional eateries as well. Though I wasn't exactly expecting cruise missiles, watching upper middle class Colombians walking out of swanky coffee shops carrying cappuccinos surprised me. Still, coffee shops charging five dollars for a latte was something only the very richest of Colombians could afford. Perhaps because the best Colombian coffee beans are shipped overseas, Bogotá doesn't advertise a world-famous coffee culture. Instead, Bogotá's main plaza is a much more iconic symbol, and it was there we headed after our late afternoon meal.

La Plaza de Bolívar is an expanse of stone in the center of Bogotá, flanked on one side by the imposing Catedral Primada and surrounded by the Congress building, the Supreme Court, and the mayor of Bogotá's office. The "First Cathedral" was finished in 1823 and built on top of a foundation laid when the Spanish first set up shop in Bogotá in the late 1530s. While the outside is a gold color with two sculpted towers rising proudly into the gray clouds, the cathedral was made from cut stone rather than the actual gleaming metal. Both the interior and exterior of this seat of Bogotá's archdiocese was impressive, though perhaps the most impressive part of the cathedral was the official name of the building, which was Catedral Primada Basílica Metropolitana de la Inmaculada Concepción de Bogotá. It might take half the service just to welcome people to Mass.

Colombia may have been named after the Italian explorer who inadvertently "discovered" two new continents and brought the Spanish speeding over to new lands, but the name of Bogotá's main plaza paid tribute to the country's actual founding father. General and politician Simón Bolívar, known as the Liberator of South America, led the armies of what he named Gran Colombia against the Spanish, organizing independence for the northern half of the continent in 1821. Of course, like any prominent man of Spanish descent of his day (and like prominent cathedrals), his full name was a bit more of a mouthful: Simón José Antonio de la Santísima Trinidad Bolívar y Palacios Ponte y Blanco. I can imagine the introductions: "Yes, my formal name is a little long to remember. Just call me El Libertador."

Although Bolívar was born in what is today Venezuela, Colombians claimed El Libertador as their own. The nickname was given to him by Colombian troops, and his first successful independence campaign was in Colombia (then known as New Granada). Later, he successfully fought various independence campaigns for Venezuela, Panama, Ecuador, and parts of Peru, which he joined together with

New Granada to form Gran Colombia. Unfortunately, at the time of Bolívar's death in Santa Marta, Colombia in 1830, his vision for a united regional state of South America was already falling apart as countries separated from Gran Colombia to become independent states.

Yet that does not mean Bolívar or his vision is forgotten. Venezuela's late president, Hugo Chávez, declared his country a follower of Bolivarianism, and Bolivia is one of the few countries in the world to be named for a single person. It seems as if every city in Colombia and Venezuela has Plaza Bolívar, sometimes accompanied by a statue of him, usually on horseback, leading the charge of independence. The Bolívar statue in the city of Andean city of Pereira is unique—not in depicting him larger than life as he leans forward on his horse—but unique in that Bolívar is riding naked (I hope he never did that it real life, because that has *got* to be uncomfortable). Many think there are more statues of Bolívar than any other person in the world, except maybe the Virgin Mary. You can find him riding around (usually clothed) and standing nobly in his uniform in Washington, D.C., Berlin, London, Paris, Cairo, and even Tehran. The guy gets around. And in Colombia, Bogotá was trying to lay claim to him more than any other city—if the size of their Plaza Bolívar was any indication.

Any student demonstration, government protest, or local PTA meeting that wants to make a splash meets in the Plaza de Bolívar. The plaza also transforms itself every season for different holidays. Christmas season in this Catholic country lasts months into winter, and the plaza still felt like Christmas during the end of January.

A larger-than-life nativity scene sat in front of the cathedral, and the tall, carved figures of Mary, Joseph, and the Magi overlooked the plaza. From the steps of the cathedral, we also got a good view of a huge outdoor ice rink that had been set up. Despite the skaters needing to wear fairly ridiculous-looking old bike helmets, the line to ice skate stretched across the whole plaza and off into the street, past vendors, ladies selling corn for pigeons, guards, businessmen, and the strange sight of two alpacas wearing some old Converse All-Stars on their back feet. Needless to say, we decided to wait and do our outdoor mountain activities some other time.

Besides the seasonal entertainment, the other main attraction of the plaza was the expansive flocks of pigeons everywhere: on the roofs of the buildings, pecking away at corn or breadcrumbs on the pavement, hopping up stone steps, and stuttering a couple of feet through the air after being chased by small children. They flew from one side of the plaza to the other, forming a flapping cloud that was loud enough to hear above the traffic noise and the hustle and bustle of Colombia's largest city.

The final distinctive feature of the plaza was the large number of men who guarded the government buildings, standing on street corners and scanning the crowds from atop stone steps. Dressed in olive fatigues, many of the young guards (they all seemed to be in their early twenties) stood with uncomfortably large guns in hand, causing me to worry that tanks might suddenly come barging down the street. The men wore green cargo pants and utility belts with olive-colored pouches. Their simple canvas caps and high-strapped laced leather boots left me with the impression that they were battle-ready soldiers.

However, the patch sewn on the front of their shirts labeled these young men as the *policía nacional*, rather than in the military. They stood guarding the plaza and government buildings, some holding radios and keys, others walking around with their hands in the shirts, doing their best impressions of Napoleon Bonaparte. Another police officer was flipping through a giant book. (Maybe he was reading up on laws? Studying on the job? Hiding the Colombian version of *Playboy?*)

The high numbers of police in the streets—along with the slums of Bogotá butting up against the surrounding mountains and the homeless and beggars roaming even the most affluent areas—were reminders that Colombia was still in the midst of a crippling civil conflict. Half the population lived on less than two dollars a day.

But in many ways, Bogotá and Colombia were starting to thrive once again. The city was putting on a face for the public to prove to the world that Bogotá, and therefore Colombia, was back in business. Who knows? Maybe Hollywood will soon make a sequel to *Mr. and Mrs. Smith* with our gorgeous couple returning to Bogotá for their twentieth wedding anniversary, this time dancing salsa to flashes of fireworks instead of rocket explosions and grenades.

Bogotá was back and had much to offer.

Our orientation in Bogotá had given us a few good pointers to get us started, including some tricks of the trade, as well as an intro to some things about Colombian culture with the hope that we wouldn't get ourselves into too much trouble too soon. We got used to kissing people on the cheek in greeting or farewell. We learned to translate Colombian body language, such as the rapid squint or double wink from both eyes that made it look like a person was trying to escape a dust storm or stare directly into the sun, but instead meant "I don't understand." We began using this gesture a lot.

We learned not to take offense when Colombian men called lighter-skinned women in our group *monas*. Our first reaction was to shout back at them, since mona means "monkey" in English, but it was another way to say gringa, especially in reference to blondes (luckily I have dark hair, so I usually avoided the phrase). Being called a monkey was frequently followed up by more endearing terms such as being called "my queen" or (more strangely) "my life" from men we had simply passed by on the street.

"Mona!" a young guy with enough gel in his hair to stiffen a circus tent would call out. We'd ignore him.

He'd follow up with "Mi reina, mi vida" and put his hand over his heart. We'd usually respond with the politest "buenos días" we could manage, often accompanied by a curt nod. This would cool off most of them, though occasionally we would have fun getting into a flirtatious back and forth battle of wits (my rusty Spanish usually meant I lost the battle every time). If we were feeling extra sassy, we'd respond to his questions about us ("Are you married? Do you have a boyfriend? Are you American?") with a sly "squint squint." "I don't know," we'd say with our eyes, attempting to give him a Colombian shrug-off.

One of my new favorite phrases was "que pena," which was as versatile an expression as I've ever encountered in either English or in Spanish. You could use it to express your sympathies, in the sense of being sorry that someone's grandmother just got run over by a Bogotá moto. You could use it sarcastically, in the sense of "too bad you didn't realize the exchange rate meant you just spent $8 on a latte." You could use it to try to apologize for something you're embarrassed about in the sense of "Que pena, I think I just said *estoy casada* (I am married) instead of *estoy cansada* (I am tired)." You could use it as an expression of surprise and dismay, as in "Oh shit... I'm going to be in charge of 160 middle school students in a week." (*Que pena* can also become quite vulgar and, come to think of it, might rival the versatility of the f-word.).

Other important things to look out for included such practical treasures as the fact that the word for "batteries" (*pilas*) also meant to get a move on (both in the sense of hurrying up and in making sure you were not going to get run over by a rampaging horse cart) and that it was not a good idea to put toilet paper in the toilet.

This last tidbit was a widespread rule in most of Latin America since not all sewer systems and pipes can handle it when you put extra stuff in there. And as a general rule, I have found it is usually a good idea to avoid causing a toilet to overflow. Hotels and hostels post friendly (and some not so friendly) signs near the toilet to remind you that your used paper had its proper place: in the wastebasket. One hostel warned me to remember where it went or else I'd "flood the place in poo water."

Welcome to Colombia.

CHAPTER TWO

Saying Buenas to Santa Ana

After a month of enjoying the continual fall-like temperatures of Bogotá, along with teacher training, language practice, and learning classroom management tips and techniques, it was time to leave the damp chill and swanky coffee shops of the Andes, and head to the place where I would be living and teaching the rest of the year.

As soon as I stepped off the plane in the sweltering Caribbean coast, it was obvious the region of Colombia I was to call home bore little resemblance to the high mountains and sprawling cities of Colombia's interior.

Bogotá and the other major cities in the interior are part of what Colombians call the *tierra templada* (or temperate land), areas that never seemed to get too hot or too cold. In fact, 75% of the population of Colombia lives in the cities of Bogotá, Medellín, Cali, and other areas in the tierra templada. Head down the mountains and you reach Colombia's sweeping coastlines and less mild temperatures. Both the Caribbean and Pacific coasts are part of *tierra caliente*, or hot land. In fact anywhere below around 2,500 feet is considered part of this hot land, especially by Bogotanos who get tired of cool rainy weather, so the tierra caliente is also sometimes termed as "Summer Land." It is the place where wealthier Colombians take vacations to whenever they head out of the mountains in search of warm weather. What they find are some amazing beaches—and full-on stifling heat.

That heat made even loading our luggage into the back of some pickup trucks an arduous task, but soon we were away from the airport, passing through the city of Cartagena, and heading south.

Because our group was traveling together, we had the luxury of going by truck instead of the combination of bus, ferry, and motorcycle taxi, the usual manner of traveling from Cartagena to my new home in Santa Ana. However, we were one seat short with our eight volunteers, so I spent the ride to my new home doing a half pull-up, gripping the truck's handle with my right hand, and trying not to squish my colleagues too badly.

Santa Ana was one of three small towns located on Isla Barú, a long peninsula that stretches southwest into the Caribbean Sea, just south of the bustling port city of Cartagena. When looking at a map of Colombia, you can just discern Isla Barú (as long as the dot denoting Cartagena isn't too big), a strange protuberance into the sea that you might easily dismiss as an accidental slip of the pen by the mapmaker. It has been cut off from the mainland since 1582 when the Spanish dug the Dique Canal to connect the mighty Magdalena River (which is seventy-one miles away) with Cartagena Bay, officially making Barú an island and necessitating a short ferry trip between the mainland town of Pasacaballos and the island.

We waited at the dirt loading area by the canal and watched the ferry slowly near the landing site (in the heat I wasn't feeling generous enough to call it a dock). Our drivers backed onto the flat-bottomed boat, the bed of the truck hanging precariously over the water. There was a white metal handrail on each side and short metal beams to prevent cars from going over the side at the back, although it didn't look like it added much of a safety measure. One limp-looking life vest hung on a bar on one side, and I peered nervously out of the cab of the truck as we started to move.

The ramp we had driven on lifted up, slid in a little, and the ferry backed up. I looked around for the source of the power and located a long, thin wooden motorboat attached to the ferry on the starboard side. The motorboat's small outboard motor kicked in and powered the whole ferry as we slowly went in reverse, turned around, and then headed across the canal. Perhaps it was slow going, but with a couple cars and a big truck on the ferry, I didn't think trying to break any speed records would have been a good way to cross the slow-moving canal.

About ten minutes later we had crossed without any issues and bumped into a row of old tires that served as a dock. Once the ramp lowered and slid out onto muddy ground, we drove off, heading down a skinny, rocky road with dry fields to our right and leafy trees leaning over a barbwire fence to our left. We had officially arrived on Isla Barú.

On the upside, I would be able to boast about living on a Caribbean Island for a year (palm trees, a world-class white sand beach, and tropical breezes included). The downside of living on Isla Barú was that the island was impoverished: the remoteness of the area and the fickleness of tourism-based incomes meant few residents had much extra money to spend or the means to advance their situation.

The community of Santa Ana, which consisted of a little over 4,000 people, was 95% black (or *Afrocolombiano*), descendants of slaves brought into the area by the Spanish in the 16th and 17th centuries.

Over 50% of residents had only a primary education or less. The town was poor, no other way around it.

Santa Ana was a community where a basic knowledge of English could help a family with short-term goals like earning more money at the beach or getting a job in Cartagena or at the mega all-inclusive (read: exclusive) resort on the nearby tourist beach of Playa Blanca. Our hope was that English could help students realize long-term goals of attending university or technical schools, starting businesses, or becoming professionals. That's why we thought we were there at least.

My fellow volunteers who were sitting in actual seats stuck their heads out of the window of our truck, watching our luggage get dusted with the dry earth around us as we drove past part of town on the main dirt road running through the island.

From my cramped position in the truck, I looked out on Santa Ana.

Palm and jacaranda trees blew in the hot breeze. A few green bushes clung to the khaki dirt alongside the road. The streets were dominated by small concrete houses and dozens of small shops. Honking donkeys and lowing cattle moved through one of the streets we passed, a thoroughfare which somehow looked rutted with slimy mud and covered in dust at the same exact time. A few barefooted children chased us for a short distance, and some young men sitting on their motorcycles openly stared and watched us as we passed. We moved over to the other side of the street to avoid running over a small, elderly man on a donkey, his feet crossed in front of him as he prodded the burro lightly with a well-practiced movement.

We reached the edge of town and arrived at the gate of Instituto Ecológico de Barbacoas, the charter school in town where we would all live for the year and where four volunteers would teach. A white SUV that had boarded the flat-bottomed ferry with us on the mainland rumbled past on the road, its tinted windows making it unclear whether the vehicle's occupants had looked outside at the town they passed.

I would be living in the "Villa" at the school, a two-story concrete building that had been converted from a convent to a hospital and then to its current twelve-room dormitory. I bunked on the second floor with my seven fellow teachers, while a rotating group of Colombian doctors and dentists who were finishing their residencies at the small clinic in town lived below us.

I finished lugging my suitcase into the first room on the left and negotiated with my roommate, Shannon, about who got which bunk. Wiping sweat from our faces, we checked out our closets and attached bathroom.

It was already evening with the sun setting behind a few trees in the open field across the way and we breathed in the hot muggy air, much less polluted than Bogotá smog. It smelled of dry earth, plants, the ocean, garbage heaps, and a million other things.

I didn't feel much like unpacking that night and stood on an outside veranda that created a hallway of sorts with all of our rooms on one side and the open-air view of town on the other. I leaned against the railing, watched a few people walking on the dusty tracts to their homes, and wondered if I was looking out at any of my soon-to-be students. The sky was a pale orange, and the evening insects were warming up for their nightly concert. A breeze traveled across the twilight, caught a pile of leaves, and tossed them a few feet against the trunk of a tree.

My evening solace was interrupted when I felt a pinprick on my leg, and I looked down to see that I was surrounded by mosquitoes. I quickly darted into my room and shut the wooden door. After stringing up a mosquito net above my mattress, I finally settled into my new bed as a bit of a breeze brushed softly against my net from our open (but screened) window.

I fell asleep while listening to the sounds of the insects outside, trying not to scratch my mosquito bites, and still sweating a bit.

Sunday morning was hot.

I woke up before dawn to the sounds of loud roosters crowing and the abrasive creak-like braying of donkeys. Though the local burros were in the field across the way, it seemed like they were sitting right under our windows, sounding like the squeaking, scraping, and screeching of 100-year-old machinery. I longed to shout, "Shut up!" at my hoofed neighbors and throw a well-aimed can of WD-40 at them, but instead tried to shift my pillow, which didn't really stop any of the noises from filtering in. And in case you were misinformed, roosters don't greet the dawn with their crowing, but start up whenever the heck they please.

I went downstairs just as the first light was glinting off the windows to find our entire group gathering in our downstairs kitchen.

Adam, the only man in our group, was attempting to make coffee, his light brown hair sticking up in the back. TL—tall with short red hair and the unmistakable look of someone who was used to caffeine in the morning and hadn't yet gotten it—greeted me, but then turned her attention to helping Adam. They were attempting to strain some coffee with a sock because there were no coffee filters around.

Roommates Rachel and Kassira started a search for some pans to scramble eggs while Kayla and Alyssa, who were also roommates, unwrapped some thin white sandwich bread. Shannon and I grabbed some plates and soon breakfast was on the table.

We were a mixture of different looks, from Alyssa's long brown hair to Kayla's bright blonde tresses to Kassira, who was slim and dark-skinned. We were from various parts of the United States (the Northeast, South, Midwest, and West) and none of us had even been to Colombia before. But soon all of us would be teaching at one of the two schools in town, although none of us were really sure what we were getting ourselves into.

After breakfast, our group met with one of the Barbacoas teachers, Eric, an American from the U.S. who had been a volunteer teacher the year before and now had a paying position at Barbacoas.

"Okay," Eric said, crinkling his tanned nose, "so we're going to give you an introduction to town. On the surface it looks a little run down, but get to know the people and you'll love it."

We headed out of the school, passing open-air classrooms as we negotiated the hard cobblestone path and exited the gate to the main dirt street in town. We turned left towards the little of the town we had seen, and soon Eric stepped over a broken gate and walked up to a small concrete house painted a bright yellow. In lieu of knocking—there was no door—he stuck his head into the small front room.

"Buenas!" he called in greeting, and soon a thin woman appeared, a cloth in her hands. I should note that no one in Colombia says "hola." No one. The word doesn't seem to exist. "Buenas" is the versatile greeting of choice no matter what time of day.

"Buenas," she responded with a little laugh, staring at all of us. Her face was long and thin, wrinkled by age and sun, and her clothes hung a bit too loosely on her body. She smiled and gestured for us all to come inside and sit in the three wooden chairs in the front room. We felt a little awkward as we sat and stood around and Eric chatted with her.

I learned that finding out people's names wasn't a priority in Colombia, so we didn't catch hers (I later asked her and learned it was Eliza). Eliza's husband came in after a bit. He was old like Eliza, a bit weathered, shorter than his wife. His name was Elfriem and his hands were scarred from years of fishing.

"Bienvenidos," Elfriem greeted us, gesturing us through the house to the backyard.

Emerging from the slightly cooler kitchen, we stepped into the sun again. Some plastic toys were strewn across the tiny lot that was their backyard and the day's laundry hung on their fence, which was made out of wire and wood. Elfriem moved over to where layers of turquoise fishnet were draped over a stump and caressed the net's webbing with his gnarled hands.

"Before," he said in Spanish, "I had only a fishing pole and caught maybe ten fish a day. Now I can catch forty or fifty."

Elfriem was one of the many men in town who supported his family by catching fish, oysters, and shrimp in the sheltered bays and open Caribbean Sea surrounding the island. With the net, the family was able to do more than simply get enough food on the table, and had a disposable income from the fish they sold.

Eliza, still giving us a wide smile, returned to boiling chicken on an outdoor wood-burning stove, and we said our goodbyes.

We left and walked around large pits of mud and streams of unnervingly bright green sludge-like water. Turning down a few more streets, we passed dozens of small homes, many with bright-colored paint chipping off the walls. An occasional car rumbled past, but the traffic mostly consisted of motorcycles (*motos*), which resembled dirt bikes more than any polished Harley. The motos bumped on the uneven streets and weaved around the worst of the mud holes and the many pedestrians.

Music from a genre I did not recognize (if my ears did not deceive me, it seemed to involve accordions) blasted from homes and a few shops. A couple of older men, with steel gray hair curled tight against their heads, sat on a dusty patio playing something that looked like dominoes. A group of men were getting their hair trimmed while sitting on a concrete ledge beside the town's Catholic church in front of young men with small metal scissors.

This seemed to constitute entertainment in Santa Ana on a Sunday morning.

Curious kids who were our future students came up to us, some shyly hiding behind their older brothers or sisters, others walking right up, touching our hands, and asking to play with our cameras. They were dressed mostly in shorts and flip-flops and their shy smiles soon turned into toothy grins as they sucked on lollipops, shifted for spots in the shade, and giggled at their image on our cameras' LCD screens.

We got a few strange looks from shopkeepers as they leaned on their counters and wide open stares from some teenagers who were walking by. Since nearly the entire town traced their heritage back to Africa, we stood out even more than we would have elsewhere in a Latin American country.

We looped back in the heat that had risen significantly as the sun continued to shine and had a phenomenal lunch at Barú Grande, the only restaurant in town. We sat at plastic tables for about an hour while they cooked up our meal, the wait helped by some bagged green plantain chips. The lunch was well worth the wait: salad, succulently seasoned chicken, rice cooked with coconut, and delicious French fries served with a refreshing mixed fruit juice.

At only 5,000 pesos ($2.75) for the meal and juice, I could see how many of the Barbacoas teachers were in the habit of coming there for most dinners. But we had a decently big kitchen at the Villa and got a delivery of fresh vegetables, fruits, all the local carbohydrate-loaded staples (rice, beans, lentils, spaghetti, corn flour, bread, potatoes, plantains), as well as butter, salt, and milk, the latter of which came in liter bags that didn't have to be refrigerated until they were opened. We even got some luxury items brought over from Cartagena such as tortillas, jam, and apples. However, the luxury items did not include coffee, unless you count instant coffee (which *should not* be counted as coffee in my opinion). It seemed finding a regular cup of *café* in Colombia would be harder than I had thought.

Although I wasn't earning money from my volunteer gig, at least I got paid in groceries. Because of this, I planned to cook a lot even though Barú Grande's meals were delicious.

Still, I didn't know the recipe for coconut rice yet, so I scraped my plate clean and enjoyed not having to do the dishes.

It was only a ten-minute walk from Barbacoas to the K-11 public school where I would be teaching with three other volunteers. Institución Educativa de Santa Ana (IESA) was located on a side street right off the main road that passed by town, so one warm morning, four of us left the Barbacoas bubble to check out our new workplace. Alyssa would be teaching kindergarten through second grade, Kayla was doing third through fifth, I would be teaching middle school, and Kassira was assigned one of the eighth grade classes plus ninth through eleventh.

We entered through a dark green metal gate that had the name of the school and IESA's seal painted on it. The seal was blue with a white circular border and stated the name of the school with "Barú Cartagena" written below it. Inside the seal was a golden orb of a sun, a palm tree, and a wave that in the painting looked like it was going to knock over the tree after it crested. I assume it was supposed to reflect the natural beauty of the area, but I stared warily at the giant wave, realizing I did not know if Colombian flooding could become tsunami-worthy (I learned later that flooding *could* be a serious problem though tsunamis rarely occur in the Caribbean). The seal was rounded off by the school motto: *ciencia, conocimiento y honor* (science, knowledge and honor).

We stepped through the door in the solid metal gate and looked around. The center of the school was a wide-open dirt field, surrounded on all sides by buildings, a concrete sports field, a covered multipurpose area that was roofed but open on three sides, and a few nice shade trees.

We peeked through the windows at a computer lab of sorts and the library (air conditioned!) where books were kept under glass shelves to the dust out. Explorations of the rest of this long and thin building revealed a tiny cafeteria and kitchen, an even tinier office (presumably the principal's), and a teacher's lounge which looked dark and cramped but brought the total number of rooms with air conditioning where I lived and worked up to two.

The five main buildings lay on all sides in the rectangular complex, painted bright red and yellow, though earlier ivory-white coats of paint were visible all over, creating map-like patterns on the walls. Without maps in the classrooms, I imagined taking my students outside to the wall to the left of the principal's office where one peeling section looked strangely like Australia.

The metal and wood desks inside the classrooms were as chipped as the walls. They were worn, covered in carved graffiti, and many were missing metal bars. The classrooms were all equipped with nice-looking whiteboards covering the entire front of the classroom, and I made a mental note to make sure to buy a variety of dry erase markers the next time I went to the city. With the exception of the whiteboards, the classrooms were depressingly bare, with concrete floors, empty walls, and fans and lights overhead. No shelves, alphabet letters, or pictures.

I stood in the doorway of one classroom near the library, leaning against the dusty concrete wall. I flipped the lights and fans on, and the fluorescent lights glowed feebly, which did nothing to add a feeling of friendliness to the room. The windows of this particular classroom were tiny, made up of thick white tiles, blocked most of the breeze, and were just big enough to fit your hand through. The room looked like a cross between a jail cell and an abandoned storehouse.

I foresaw a couple of problems with teaching within these walls, but I tried to push those dark thoughts to the back of my mind.

We walked back to the Villa, past the concrete homes, small shops, and *Santaneros* lounging around in whatever shade they could find. I started to plan how I would start my first day of teaching. The trouble was, the courses we had in Bogotá seemed a long way away, and my confidence waned more and more with every step I took.

We passed through the gate of Barbacoas, past their open-air classrooms, and headed back to the Villa, enjoying the shade the Barbacoas campus offered.

It might have been the heat, but the walk and getting to know my new home was draining, both physically and mentally. The Colombia we had gotten to know for the first three weeks in Bogotá was a distant memory from the realities of Santa Ana. I felt overwhelmed and hated myself for already appreciating the relative peace and quiet of the Villa. The excitement of being in a new place wasn't exactly wearing off, but it was now being overshadowed by the overwhelming task of being in charge of the future of 160 middle schoolers.

I also felt like I was never going to be cool again as I walked up to the Villa, feeling dehydrated from our walk. Though the only air conditioning came from open doors and screened windows, the concrete interior of the building still felt cool as I entered my new home. I headed directly into the kitchen where our giant jugs of filtered water sat. (Most locals boiled the water to purify it, but with fifteen people in the Villa, that was fairly unpractical, especially since it would take the whole day to cool. So we had the luxury of a water filter up at the Barbacoas office, though this did mean we had to lug the containers around once in a while. If you have never hauled a couple of gallons of water around in tropical heat, count yourself lucky.)

Back upstairs, I cranked my fan to the highest setting, making sure it was pointed up towards me, and settled against the wall on my bed with my feet hanging over the bunk. With the fan and a little breeze from the outside, it was definitely much cooler in our room than even downstairs. I looked at the thermometer on my alarm clock. Eighty-seven degrees. If that was the temperature that felt cool in my room, I didn't want to know what it was outside.

I unscrewed the cap of my water bottle and took a long drink, then stared idly at my bottle. I counted numerous flecks of dirt, three ants (none moving, thankfully) and one unidentifiable insect (also floating belly-up). I watched the drowned bug bobbing up and down and wondered how long it would be before I got sick. Feeling tired from the hot walk and probably still dehydrated, I stretched out onto my cool sheets.

Did Colombians take siestas? I wasn't sure, but in that afternoon heat, it seemed like the only thing to do.

I was just about to close my eyes when the grating squeak of our neighborhood donkeys started up again. I rolled over when what sounded like a whole flock of roosters provided backup for the donkey chorus. Squeezing my eyes shut as if somehow that could shut out the noise, I resolved to go back to Barú Grande as often as possible and eat as much chicken as I could.

CHAPTER THREE

At Institución Educativa de Santa Ana

January 31st: our first scheduled day of school at IESA.

My apprehension of the year ahead was overtaken by how excited I was about my first day. I got up at o'dark thirty (5:25 a.m.) and headed off to school at 5:50. It was barely dawn, with a pink glow visible on the horizon and a thin crescent moon hanging in the sky. I successfully avoided stepping on a frog at the bottom of the stairs, didn't startle any of the donkeys that grazed by the side of the road, and headed towards school. Although I wasn't sure quite what to expect from a Colombian public school, didn't know where any of my classes were, and had no clue what the day's plan was, I was ready to get started and walked through the quiet town with a spring in my step and a bagful of notebooks and pencils.

I gave the uniformed guard a cheerful "Buenas!" as I walked onto the school grounds. He gave me a strange look.

Thirty minutes later, I realized why. Ten minutes after school was supposed to have started, my only company was the guard, one of the janitorial ladies who was sweeping, and a scraggily rooster who had wandered in from the neighbors'. There were no teachers and no students.

Just when I thought I had gotten the day and time wrong, students started wandering in and a battered old van—looking like it may have just lost a fight with a bulldozer in the Amazon jungle—sputtered through the school gate and the school staff piled out of it.

Game on.

With students, staff, and a ridiculously early gringa teachers all accounted for, at around 7:15 (forty-five minutes late), the *rector* (principal) called the students together in front of the main building which housed the teacher's lounge and his office. "This is going to be a good year here," he shouted, at least that's as much I could translate with his megaphone fading in and out. "A better year. The teachers are ready and you are all going to work hard and study!" I noticed some teachers zoning out, and the chatter from the students grew as the rector talked on.

I would be co-teaching all my classes with the Colombian teacher in charge of sixth, seventh, and eighth grade English: a man from Cartagena named Pedro. After the rector finally dismissed the students, we met with Pedro's homeroom class. There were two classes in each grade who had all their subjects together and stayed in the same small concrete room the whole morning. Our homeroom was simply named 6-2, the second group of sixth grade. Pedro started off the class by telling the students his rules ("Diciplino! Respecto! Participación!"), spent fifteen minutes calling roll, then introduced me as a "teacher to help improve your English."

"My name is Bryanna," I said in English, finally introducing myself. Holding up a world map I unfolded from my bag, I pointed to the northwest corner of the United States. "I am from the United States and I am excited to be here in Santa Ana and Colombia teaching English for one year." I was about to repeat this in Spanish and explain to them that I would only speak English in the classroom when an air horn suddenly sounded from nearby, making me jump. I lowered the map as the sixth graders streamed outside without a second look at Pedro or me.

Apparently the air horn served as the school bell and apparently it was our daily *descanso*: a thirty-minute break. And apparently getting students to pay attention to me whenever I spoke more than one sentence was going to be an issue.

Back to class after the descanso, Pedro took the next forty minutes to explain to the class their schedule for the year. The pink poster board with the schedule was decorated with Styrofoam cutouts of Spongebob Squarepants (a strange choice, to be sure) and listed the subjects the sixth graders would be taking: biology, Spanish, math, ethics, art, P.E., English, and something called Afro (or Afro-Colombian culture).

While Pedro lectured the class anew on his rules and the upcoming year, I helped finish gluing the poster to the concrete wall. Turning around, I found a tall, dark girl with wide pale eyes behind me.

She was taking deep sniffs from the glue bottle.

"Aya! Por favor, no usa este... para..." In my surprise I couldn't remember the words for glue or smell but my facial expression and frantic pointing must have told the girl that I didn't approve. She slowly set the glue bottle down and I grabbed it from her, putting it in my back pocket.

Pedro, not noticing, continued his lecture as the girl sat down. When she shuffled out of the room when class ended, Pedro dismissed her with a wave of his hand.

"Esta chica es perezosa," he said, warning me about her, and headed out of room after the chatting students. Lazy.

"What is her name?" I asked Pedro, but he didn't respond. I wasn't sure if he simply did not hear me, did not understand what I said in English, or if he didn't know her name.

Since she was fourteen and still in sixth grade, she obviously had to repeat a couple of grades, and the fact she that was sniffing glue certainly wasn't going to make it easier for her to pass this year either. Still, I was unhappy with Pedro's easy dismissal of her. I didn't know anything about her and couldn't get her pale wide eyes out of my mind, so before I left for the day, I approached the teacher who taught high school English at the school, a woman named Arelis. Tall, with a confident jutting chin, she greeted me with a smile.

"Sabes el nombre de esta chica ahí?" I asked her, pointing to the girl as she shuffled across the dirt courtyard.

Arelis nodded with a look of concern on her face. "Her name is Arlin," she responded in English.

"Thanks," I said, making a mental note as I watched her walk through the gate off into wherever she lived in town.

I was determined to give every person at that school an equal chance to succeed until they proved to me otherwise. At the very least, every student deserved a name instead of just a label.

Beyond that, I wasn't too sure how I was going to handle the students I was now charged with teaching.

The first week of school continued with orientation activities, which included a presentation of the student manual of rules, more lectures on the school's mission and policies, and watching an episode of *Roots* dubbed in Spanish and what I think was an Algerian film (which had Spanish subtitles). I was getting a little antsy to start class.

But following yet another meeting with homeroom on Friday, before I even started teaching, I had my first parent-teacher conference. It was parent day at school and I enjoyed greeting parents and introducing myself. Having the parents around school that day also proved convenient for the day's discipline issues.

I walked into 6-2 to find Arlin violently rocking a student's desk back and forth, trying to oust another sixth grader out of her seat. I got both of them to calm down and attempted to hear both students' explanations, but I was interrupted when Pedro grabbed Arlin's arm and pulled her out of the classroom. He headed towards the teacher's lounge, abandoning our class. Hesitating, I followed them to our parent-teacher conference with Arlin and her grandmother.

Arlin's grandmother—a thin woman who had strong hands and was wearing a skimpy tank top, a skirt, and flip-flops—simply agreed with Pedro's dismissal of any hope for Arlin to improve her behavior.

"At home she never listens, she does not have any respect," the abuela stated matter-of-factly, as Arlin sat there, staring at the table.

The other adults left, but I stayed behind to try to talk with Arlin. I smiled at her as I explained I did not know what problems she had in other years but I wanted her to have success in school this year. After looking cautiously at my smile, she returned it.

"I like it better when you smile," I said, and Arlin looked surprised.

Sometimes a smile goes a lot further than any hour-long English class could, which was good because with a week of school gone, I still hadn't gotten an hour of teaching in.

While I was beginning to wonder if anyone actually taught at the school, the next Monday proved that Colombian schools did hold class once in a while. This, however, did not mean I understood the schedule that day.

We had a little bit of a late start—my eighth grade had to raid nearby classrooms for desks—but Pedro and I did go over the agenda and I got to introduce myself fully this time in both English and Spanish, feeling the excitement of actually having my first real class.

I started to introduce an English dialogue that students could practice when the social studies teacher Luis walked into the classroom. Seeing no reaction from Pedro, I asked Luis if he had class.

"Si, ahora," Luis said.

Apparently English period was over, and as I walked out, I consulted the tiny scrap of paper where Pedro had written out the schedule for me. Checking my watch, I walked to the teachers' lounge behind Pedro, confused. The rest of the day was the same baffling blur and I was never sure when I was supposed to be where.

The scheduled 12:30 bell (a.k.a. the air horn) sounded at 11:20 as I walked around the rows of one of our two classes of seventh grade. I looked to Pedro for help, but he was slowly getting up from a desk in the back and not paying attention.

"Quédense aquí para un momentico," I said, telling my class to hold on while I went to check to see what was going on. I stepped outside in the bright sunlight and saw students milling around and streaming out of the entrance gate.

I turned to see Pedro meander out of the classroom. Unsupervised, my seventh graders strolled out behind him to join their schoolmates headed home. I had a quick internal debate: do I try to set a precedent and attempt to herd my students back into class to let them know I am serious about being in charge? Or do I let them leave, realizing that there were things in the Colombian school schedule I might not be able to change in one day? I paused, then decided it wasn't worth the fight, so I wished my students a good afternoon as I headed back inside to grab my materials and try to figure out what was going on with the schedule.

I asked a few staff members what was going on and quickly learned that the school guards, Ubadel and David, were the source for all insider schedule questions, not the administration or the other teachers.

The reason for the day's shortened schedule?

"Hay un problema con los baños," Ubadel told me. "Están llenos..." he trailed off, shrugging.

The bathrooms were "full" and so the plumbing was unusable... for two weeks.

Since the administration realized that students might not be able to pay attention if they had to "go" and no bathrooms were available, the first two weeks of actual classes were on an officially sanctioned Bathroom Schedule. Classes finished as early as 9:30.

The broken facilities may have been caused by an engineering flaw. Or maybe the pipes got clogged from students, not used to flush toilets, breaking the cardinal rule of Colombian living and forgetting the proper place for toilet paper. And these bathrooms were built just a year earlier and were the pride of the administration—an entire half hour during orientation week was devoted to talking about them and the rules that were related to them. While I am not used to school pride revolving around restrooms, having sinks and flush toilets in Santa Ana was fairly remarkable, as well as hygienic.

However, the administration decided that to keep the bathrooms as pristine as possible, the students should use them as little as possible. So the facilities were locked before school, during classes, and after school, and only opened during the thirty-minute descanso. During the break between periods, the bathrooms were full of teenagers doing their thing (i.e. looking at their hair and gossiping) and then the bathrooms got shut up tight again at the end of the break.

As a teacher, at least I was able to search for the cleaning staff to see who had the key ("Mabel, do you have the key...no? Rosa? Do you know where she is? No? Okay, I'll just pee my pants then, thanks").

The one positive thing was that it made my classroom bathroom policy easy: you can't leave class to go pee if the toilets are locked.

Teaching was already becoming a bit of an adventure.

My alarm buzzed, interrupting my dreams and the morning noises of insects, frogs, chirping birds, donkeys, and roosters. I hit the alarm clock twice and finally got up at 5:40, a gray-pink glow just starting to infiltrate the dark of my room. I set my alarm aside (it also told the temperature, that day letting me know it was 82 degrees already), and climbed down from my bunk, trying not to wake my roommate, Shannon, who taught primary grades at Barbacoas and thus had a later schedule than me.

It was a week or so into real classes and I hadn't exactly pinned down how to go about teaching, but I was starting to get into a daily routine.

I got dressed in the semi-darkness. Since all IESA teachers were supposed to wear a specific color depending on the day of the week, I rubbed my eyes and tried to think what day it was. Wednesday. I chose one of my two red shirts to wear.

I headed downstairs for breakfast at 5:50 or so, and greeted fellow volunteer TL who came down to boil water for her coffee, then went back upstairs ten minutes later. A red sun was just breaking over the horizon.

By 6:15, I headed downstairs and out the door with Kassira, my upper-grade colleague at the public school, crossing the bumpy cobblestones of the Barbacoas paths.

"Hi, Palo," I said to a skinny black and brown dog, who I then had to berate for trying to nip at the backs of my calves as we headed towards the front gate.

"Buenas, Marcos," Kassira and I said to the guard, almost in unison.

"Buenos días," he responded with his usual wide smile. "Cómo están?"

"Bien," one of us replied. "Y tú?"

"Bien, gracias a dios," Marcos replied with another grin, and swung open the wooden gate for us.

Past the gate, we turned left and headed down the dirt road towards the rest of the town and the school. By looking left and right we could check the traffic report for the day. Three motorcycles, one car, maybe fifteen pedestrians like us, a cow by the side of the road, five dogs in sight, and two donkeys plodding along in our direction. We switched to the other side of the road to let them pass.

We walked past a shop and a few houses on the wide dirt road. The sun was still mostly blocked by the rest of the town to our right. We passed a few Barbacoas students in their dark blue pants or light blue tartan pinafores and greeted them with a cheery "good morning." Like always, their sometimes-shy responses never failed to make us smile, especially when the smallest of the students squeaked a happy "morning!" back.

We cut the corner of the road by passing through a small vacant lot. In February, it was just an expanse of dusty and rutted earth, but in a few months it would be covered in dense green shrubs. Sometimes we tiptoed through the vacant lot, treading lightly around five or six tan cows chewing methodically on their morning cud and watching us with giant brown eyes.

We turned, walked barely a half minute on a concrete sidewalk, and soon were at the gated entrance of Institución Educativa de Santa Ana. Across the street a panadería had just opened, and the owner of the bakery, Javier, swept the concrete patio. A woman was selling fried corn dough and cheese from a table next door as students slowly headed towards school.

We greeted the guards, who were dressed as always in brownish blue uniforms, and made a beeline for the teachers' lounge—and its air conditioning. After five or ten minutes, other teachers arrived. They promptly sat down and pulled out plastic containers of cooked potatoes, unwrapped foil to reveal legs of chicken, and poured themselves steaming drinks of sweetened *tinto,* the black coffee (of sorts) that the janitorial ladies at IESA had set out.

I walked out of the cool teachers' lounge and into the bright courtyard. I was grateful for the large jacaranda tree for providing the dry ground with some shade.

Carlos, the chemistry teacher, was holding the megaphone in his hand.

"José David! Jerlane! Acércase! En formación!" he called across the dirt courtyard to students who stood around the bathroom, telling them to come line up. They looked up and mostly ignored him. It was still 6:40 and they knew they had a least another five minutes to munch on their morning rolls before they had to start getting serious about lining up.

Every Monday, Wednesday, and Friday we had *comunidad*, a gathering of the student body and teachers for morning announcements. Every day it was a fight on the megaphone to get the students lined up in front of the rector's office. From right to left, sixth through eleventh grade stood in what were supposed to be perfectly straight lines. Each class section had one line for the boys and one line for the girls and they were supposed to line up shortest to tallest, though this always took a little extra jostling.

I turned my attention to a group of three seventh-grade boys, all over sixteen, lounging by a classroom wall.

"Good morning, how are you? En formación por favor." I touched them each lightly on the sleeve, trying to herd them over to where I knew they would eventually wander over to in the back of their line to zone out or talk while the announcements went on.

I slapped a mosquito that was trying to bite me through my jeans and felt aggravated as the day's first line of sweat traced a line down my back.

I made small talk with some girls who were actually in line, then noticed Arlin sitting on a broken desk outside the nearest classroom. Heaving a sigh, I headed over to her.

"Good morning, Arlin. How are you? Sabes que no puedes sentarte." I tried to say it with a smile, reminding her for the second time that week that she couldn't sit down during comunidad. After I repeated the request and gave her a light touch on her shoulder, she shuffled off to the very back of her line of sixth grade girls.

Once comunidad started, we would receive morning announcements about upcoming events and assemblies, reminders about holidays or testing, and the *coordinador* (the vice principal, a tall thin man named Abram) would let us know if there were any scheduled changes for the day. Sometimes, one of the teachers would lead the students in prayer.

Some days one of the teachers or the coordinador would be inspired to lecture the students on a topic of special interest to them— most commonly about the appearance of their uniforms (make them cleaner!), haircuts (make it shorter!), or studying for exams (make yourself actually do it!). Appearance was emphasized: if students didn't have their uniform, they were not admitted into the school grounds, and a good amount of hand scrubbing kept the shirts and pants looking clean, though a little worn. The mostly hand-me-down uniforms consisted of burgundy pants for the boys and burgundy skorts (shorts with a fabric panel in the front making them resemble skirts) for the girls. Both were worn with off-white polo shirts and black shoes.

However, no matter who was in charge, how late comunidad had gone into first period, or if it was especially buggy or hot, the teachers would *always* lead a usually unenthusiastic singing of our school song. Imagine lines of middle and high schoolers mumbling the words in Spanish:

CHORUS
Forward we will lead
This noble society
With study and with work
Our town will triumph.

Institución Educativa de Santa Ana
With love fight for prosperity
Of a humble town that looks for in your classrooms
The great rise of your community
Of a humble town that looks for in your classrooms
The great rise of your community.

Institución Educativa de Santa Ana
Between the breeze and majesty of a beautiful sea
Raise the distinguished light that illuminates
A way of hope and peace.
Raise the distinguished light that illuminates
A way of hope and peace.

CHORUS x 2

Institución Educativa de Santa Ana
Your administrators and teachers always come
Sowing gifts of science and culture
In order to harvest progress and liberty
Sowing gifts of science and culture
In order to harvest progress and liberty.

Institución Educativa de Santa Ana
Your children will remember their whole lives
Your sweet voice, strength of mind and patience
Your great virtue to serve and educate.
Your sweet voice, strength of mind and patience
Your great virtue to serve and educate.

CHORUS x 2 *(Chorus twice through... again)*

The song is full of ambition, very optimistic, and perhaps a bit pompous-sounding in places. But in all truth, an optimistic but hopefully not unreachable vision of what a school, our school, could be for its students and community.

The song was also very long.

Some days we sang along to a recording of electronic drums and trumpets, but on the days without it, the tired students would drag the song along until it felt a bit like a funeral march. The already-long four minutes when it was with music turned into at least five or six on the days without it.

Perhaps its words did not reflect the current reality of the school. For instance, I knew for a fact that the teachers didn't come to work every day ready to sow seeds of science and culture, and the voices of the teachers and administrators sometimes but rarely sounded "sweet."

Still, it was a song that was all our own and it connected the school to the community. Hopefully, it was actually a source for inspiration on some days. And maybe some day it could even be the truth—although I was still struggling through how to best "sow seeds of science and culture" to my students, I actually believed that "with study and work/our town can triumph" and that education could create a better future. That's why I was teaching in Colombia in the first place.

I was getting to know my students as well as my fellow teachers. And my colleagues were turning out to be an interesting and diverse lot.

Some were always working on lesson plans or grading while others sat in the library and gossiped well into their scheduled class time. Some stopped to talk to students as they arrived at school, some headed into the teachers' lounge as soon as they arrived, pulled out their breakfast, and wouldn't emerge until well into first period. If they had wanted, the seventeen secondary school teachers at IESA could have made big bucks as characters on any sitcom in Latin America.

Arelis, the English teacher of grades nine through eleven—tall, strong-jawed, with chocolate black skin—was definitely the matriarch of our IESA family.

"Good morning, Bryanna. How was your weekend?" she'd always greet me at the start of each week. During comunidad, Arelis would usually be up front, giving misbehaving students a stern look. "Dilson," she'd call over to one of my sixth grade boys, "presta atención."

Then there was Marilin, who always seemed more preoccupied with selling beauty products (a Colombian version of Avon) than preparing for her math classes. Carlos was the fair-skinned chemistry teacher, always ready with a friendly smile and handshake. Gustavo had a perfect example of a Latin mustache, which he always kept just as organized as his philosophy classes. Luis, with his tiny hands that were at odds with his wide and stout stature, liked to walk around comunidad with a stick, prodding students back into their lines. Germán, the art teacher, would talk to me anytime about music, especially jazz. And there was Norman, with his creepy stare and loud, gravelly voice.

The religion teacher, Ileana, could have had a comedy show all her own. She possessed the largest beer belly I had ever seen... on man or woman. It was the kind of stomach that made you want to ask her when her quadruplets were due, yet its size never wavered in the eleven months I was there. A bit of a pot-bellied pretend pregnancy stomach was common on many Colombian ladies, but Ileana's was simply ridiculous.

The P.E. teacher, Tajan, had a face that looked like a caricature. If he ever becomes famous enough to warrant an editorial cartoon about him, the cartoonist wouldn't need to change anything about his features. Tajan's face was long, with large ears that stuck out. He had small, long eyes, and his skin seemed to bunch up in new and interesting ways whenever he talked animatedly, which was how he talked most of the time. Tajan's most distinguishing feature was his mustache, which he kept long and thin. It was a scraggly mess and I was always surprised it didn't have large chunks of chicken or fish stuck in it.

The teachers came from all around the country. Some were young and unmarried, others middle-aged with families. Racially, the teachers reflected Colombia's diversity: black, white, *mestizo*, and every mix of the three. But they had one thing in common: they all lived in Cartagena and commuted to school every day in a rickety old van (which tended to break down and make them late for school). And as soon as the last bell rang, they were back in the van for their hour and a half ride to the city. Santa Ana was not their home and also wasn't where most of them wanted to teach. Teachers were assigned schools at the federal level based off their own performance at university. IESA was what we in the U.S. would call a failing school, and teachers who had done poorly on their certifications were assigned to Santa Ana.

I was sitting with my co-teacher, Pedro, in the relatively cool air-conditioned library during one of the periods we had off, and I asked him why he had decided to go into teaching.

"I entered university to study to be doctor," he said, "but I did not get a high mark. I decide to study linguistics. And to get a job to be a teacher."

He rubbed his broad forehead and close-cropped hair. "And now I stay here," he said, not looking too excited about it.

Pedro was a friendly guy who would always greet me with a grin and a handshake. He had dark tan skin and a protruding stomach, was from Cartagena, and was rarely seen in anything but striped polo shirts. His English was heavily accented and his vocabulary was limited, so we always chatted in Spanish (like I did with my students and the other Colombian teachers). He could rattle off the rules on the present progressive tense and wax on about pedagogical methodologies, but his conversational English was mostly reduced to asking me how my weekend was and telling me what he liked to eat.

This didn't bother me much; after all, part of the reason why I was there was to be the English "expert" (to use the term loosely, of course). Instead, what I soon found myself in contention with was Pedro's attitude towards teaching: namely that he didn't want to be a teacher. I may have had less training, but I felt that wanting to be in a classroom did give me a bit of a step up on him (despite not knowing quite how to pronounce pedagogical in either of our languages).

So by my second week I had made a decision: my priority had changed. I would no longer just be the best English teacher I could be and try to immerse my students in a new language: although I was only supposed to only speak in English in the classroom, I would now also speak in Spanish to try to connect with my students and help them in any way I could.

I may have chosen to teach in Colombia for a myriad of romanticized reasons, but I had first and foremost come to teach. And I would try my hardest to be the best teacher I could be.

CHAPTER FOUR

HELL'S KITCHEN (WHERE THE FOOD IS GREAT, AND THE HEAT IS GREATER)

March officially marked the beginning of spring, but while I was technically sitting in the Northern Hemisphere, with the heat and unchanged weather, I couldn't yet find any way to mark the change of seasons.

I sat down once and tried to convince a Santanero that it was officially winter.

"I know it's not cold, but since we are north of the equator it's winter until March 22nd," I stated, thinking my argument consisted of unbreakable logic (though perhaps delivered in less-than-perfect Spanish).

"No es invierno ya," Alejandro responded, half laughing as he tried to fan himself with his blue Barbacoas guard shirt. It was not winter now, crazy *norteamericana*.

I thought I understood the confusion. "It doesn't feel like winter, I know. The seasons are different in Colombia of course, but it is still technically winter now."

Alejandro shook his head again, looking perplexed. "Winter comes in April for a month or two, then we will have the long winter in October, November, maybe December."

This made no sense. Two winters? A short and a long?

"So when does summer begin?" I asked.

"After winter ends," he responded, his brow furrowing due to my lack of understanding. "Cuando termina la lluvia" (Whenever the rains stop).

Of course.

The tropics are generally a land of two seasons: wet and dry. While this may have been true for Bogotá and other interior areas of Colombia, Santa Ana seemed to be a land of humidity and heat. I was beginning to understand the simple term of tierra caliente. While Colombians may only consider it summer when it's between rainy seasons, for all intents and purposes, it always seemed like summer on the Caribbean coast.

The first time I walked back from school I had to close my eyes to combat the bright glare from the sun. With my eyes closed, I envisioned myself in the vastness of the Sahara desert. Sweat dripped off my forehead and I changed my mind: I was now in a Helsinki sauna. I opened my eyes, which instantly burned from the combination of the bright sun and my sweat, and I decided that I must have been in Death Valley—not the part with the nice air-conditioned visitor center, but the part with the world's hottest temperature (a whopping 134 degrees Fahrenheit, almost 57 degrees Celsius). Wiping the sweat from my eyes while trying to wave to one of my students, the heat that I would have to deal with for the rest of the year finally hit me in full.

Okay, it never reached 134 degrees, but the point I am trying to make is that Santa Ana was hot. The last time the temperature was *not* hot was probably around 1.8 million years ago at the end of the last

Ice Age. It has pretty much always been hot, and considering current global warming trends, it will probably be hot for a long time to come. The days were consistently in the '90s (an average of about 95 degrees that occasionally rose into triple digits), and while this was a far cry from actual record-breaking heat, the combination of heat, sun, and humidity created conditions that were wonderful for the inside of a tropical butterfly house, but less wonderful for human life.

No matter where I went or what I did, I rarely had a moment when I was not wishing for a little more winter in my life. I was usually already a bit sticky from the humidity by the time I rolled out of bed in the morning. The kitchen was stifling by the time I washed my breakfast dishes, and the sun was already high in the sky as I walked to school. By the end of comunidad's morning announcements, the school anthem, and prayers (please, God, make it only in the '80s today), sweat would be dripping down my back, and I would head off to my first class. By the time school ended, sweat had usually started to seep through my pant legs even if the fans in the classroom were working.

I would leave school around noon, walking back in that bright and horribly strong sun that reflected off the beige dirt road, and my skin would scream in protest. After a few weeks, I took a cue from the locals and bought an umbrella to use as a parasol. In Santa Ana, the word for umbrella was usually translated as *sombrilla* or "the thing that gives you *sombra* (shade)" rather than the more common *paraguas,* "the thing you use to stop the water" (*para* = stop, a*gua* = water). That would come later, but for most of the year, my sombrilla saved me a few degrees of heat (it was noticeably cooler in my portable shade) and saved my skin from having an unpleasant relationship with high noon UV for eleven months. I usually associated parasols with dainty Jane Austen-type characters who were too delicate to be out in the sun, but I figured all my dark-skinned neighbors were doing it, so I popped my parasol out every time I headed home.

The nights were cooler, but I never saw the temperature go below 75 degrees. Whenever it dipped under 80 degrees, it was cause for celebration—time to write home with the news, dig my jacket out of the closet, and try to quell the impulse to sing Christmas carols.

The high humidity was the worst thing about the heat. There were times I walked out of the air-conditioned library at school and felt like I had entered a greenhouse or a butterfly house at a zoo. My glasses even fogged up after walking outside once or twice (which couldn't have been a good sign). Let's just say that whenever my food was labeled "keep in a cool, dry place," it was impossible to follow the directions.

Could I really blame tropical cultures for living at a slower pace? In temperate regions, cultures had to learn how to fight against nature to survive (i.e. planning for winter); in the tropics, cultures seemed to have decided it was easier to just embrace nature as much as possible.

In Colombia, the *costeños* (people who live on Colombia's coasts) had a bad reputation for being a bit lazy compared to their hardworking cousins in the interior who live in the tierra templada's spring-like climates. In my experience, there was nothing about the people on the coast that convinced me laziness was somehow inherent. (I admit, though, a few students and teachers seemed to have made it their life goal to prove interior Colombians right about costeños.)

However the stereotype that costeños were more laid-back and went through life at a more relaxed pace was certainly true, and costeños in turn liked to characterize interior Colombians as boring and stuck-up. Costeños also have a reputation for partying; one brand of Colombian beer is simply called Costeña. Of course a costeño party takes place after the sun goes down and the heat abates—even for the most dedicated drinkers and dancers, the midday heat was not something to be trifled with.

I was a complete wimp in the heat myself, but it always made me feel better whenever I'd strike up a conversation with a Santanero and they'd be the one to bring up how it felt especially hot that day.

"Today is... how do you say... hace calor... hot, yes?" my favorite IESA guard, Ubadel, would say, wiping his face with a large blue handkerchief. Ubadel was dark and stocky, with a long mouth that he'd turn into a big grin whenever he greeted me in the morning.

Learning English and always ready to practice, "hot" was one word Ubadel used in conversations every day.

There were few places I enjoyed spending my time during the heat of the day, but my least favorite was the Villa's kitchen.

Tucked into one corner of the Villa's big downstairs room, there was no chance for a cross-breeze and it was sweltering even with the windows always open. Cooking involved standing over the open gas flame on the stove, sweat dripping down my face and back.

We did have a nice sink, a refrigerator, a decent supply of pots and plates, and an oven (also gas, but despite the heat, sometimes the need for chocolate chip cookies outweighed the discomfort from the extra flames). The fridge would get pretty packed, especially after weekend runs to the supermarkets in Cartagena and considering that all eight volunteers were using it. Often, I would feel around for a container of leftovers I knew I had left in the back and end up accidentally putting my hand into an open plate of watermelon, or worse, a package of costeño cheese.

Costeño cheese (also known as *queso fresco*) is soft and spongy and literally squeaks when you bite into it. As far as I can tell, it was called "fresh cheese" because after about five hours of opening the package, it turns both hard and slimy and oozes a sour-smelling yellow water that would leak all over, just waiting for some poor soul to put their hand in. If any amount of time had passed since it was opened, it not only ceased to be fresh, but it was difficult to continue to refer to it as cheese.

Costeño queso fresco would never melt, no matter how long you left it out in the Santa Ana heat, but bought fresh off the street, it was fairly enjoyable. When it was in our fridge, it was the enemy.

Of course sometimes all we were able to make for dinner was a cheese sandwich (with non-melted cheese) because our kitchen got crowded: with eight volunteers and anywhere from three to seven Colombian medical students all in the same kitchen (the *medicos* at least shared a second fridge), there was rarely time to cook anything more complicated than a sandwich. We had thirteen people and only two working gas burners, so it was usually best to whip up something quick and escape the kitchen as soon as you could.

As soon as my food was on my plate, I usually headed up to my room to eat in front of my fan and watch a TV show on my computer or read. If you sat in the kitchen or outside, you were inviting all manner of bugs to share your dinner with you (and also inviting many bugs to have you for dinner).

The tropics are known for a lot of things: hot muggy weather, jungles, diseases, people with good rhythm, and a disproportionate amount of military coups and guerrilla fighters.

The tropics also have a disproportionate amount of insect life. It's as if the world's arthropods all belong to the same travel agent and receive the same advertisements for timeshares in tropical paradises.

"Warm climate year-round! Plenty of water to have fun and reproduce in! Millions of tasty humans to feast on! The tropics invite you to come and stay. And bring your thousand children!"

I would wake up many mornings to cockroaches laying belly-up on my floor (I could have sworn cockroaches could survive anything from Raid spray to explosions to the Apocalypse, but apparently the Santa Ana heat was too much for them), but the main annoyance was mosquitoes. In Santa Ana they did not carry any disease (in contrast to other parts of Colombia, namely the Amazon), but it was easy to forget that blessing when you left the teacher's lounge with your feet itching like crazy. I would walk downstairs to get some more water in the kitchen doing a Colombian version of Riverdance to try and dissuade the ravenous bugs from landing on my feet. Sorry fashion police, but I admit to pulling a "Seattle" a couple times and paired socks and sandals.

Also flying around was a species of beetle that looked like a large hummingbird or a B-29—I was never quite sure which. When they buzzed past me like a fighter jet, I could never decide whether to duck out of the line of fire or trust its insect radar to not crash into me. Besides the fact that I would have been left with gooey gray beetle innards all over me, I was a little concerned the beetles would give me a concussion if they ever decided to become kamikaze pilots. I wasn't sure if they bit, stung, or just buzzed around menacingly.

If I leave you alone, you'll leave me alone, right? I silently transmitted to them, hoping they had also studied theories of mutual assured destruction.

Colombia also came with quite a variety of ants. The leaf-cutter ants, who trooped their way through the jungle floors, were perhaps the most famous in the country, though almost as well-known were the ants known as *hormigas culonas*, which can be best translated as "big-ass ants." They are also edible and would make for a good episode of *Man vs. Food*: the wings, legs, pincers, and heads had to be first pulled off, then the remaining body was slowly fried before they were ready to be eaten. Apparently they taste a little like bacon-flavored popcorn.

While our ants in the Villa were not edible, they were attracted to everything in our kitchen that was.

The smallest ants were so tiny they were barely discernibly. If every frat house had ants like we had, doing dishes would never be a problem—you learned quickly never to leave anything out. They were most attracted to water or meat juices (the ants that is, not the frat houses), but leaving pretty much any food or liquid on the counter brought those guys swarming onto it.

Our ants may not have been destroyers of everything in their path, like those in *Indiana Jones* or "Leiningen Versus the Ants," but they did get around. Luckily we had a fridge that closed tightly and we invested in Ziploc bags and Tupperware (or at least their Colombian equivalents). If it wasn't for that, we might have the experience of grabbing a box of Cocoa Crisps and feeling little ant feet all over our hands. Then we would set the box down in surprise and seventy-five ants fall onto the counter. Tap the box on the counter a couple more times, and the number of ants is closer to 200. This isn't hypothetical.

The kitchen seemed to be ground zero for all things creepy, crawly, and problematic. We kept it fairly neat and tidy, and the school cleaned it once a week, but that didn't stop all manner of creatures from taking up residence on the tile floors or inside the metal cabinets. There was a tiny hole in the back of a cupboard which led to what we could only assume were labyrinths of mice highways (a few times we saw a furry creature wiggling its way out of sight). Lizards and toads also strutted around our downstairs room nonchalantly.

However, the biggest health concern in our kitchen didn't come from all the animal life running around.

One typical morning before another early school day, I went to open the fridge and felt my sock get wet as a smell like raw sewage hit my nostrils. Unfortunately, these two sensations were not unrelated. I looked down, hoping that the puddle on the floor had come from something less benign than what it smelled like—perhaps from a melting freezer or a puddle of mouse pee—but the source of the milky-brown color soon became apparent. Trying not to gag, I leaned in over the drain in the center of the kitchen floor. Seeping out of the drain was what was unmistakably wastewater, which filled the kitchen with its smell and, shall we say, other problematic substances.

With the help of mops, one of the Barbacoas workers named Bleidis, and the ability to work while holding my breath, I was able to get most of the kitchen dry before the end of the day.

But not even sewage could scare away the creatures in our kitchen.

A large fuzzy spider creeping around our cabinets was not bothered by me, but when Bleidis saw it, she turned it into a pile of gray goo with a sharp slap of her sandal.

"Peligroso?" I asked. Dangerous?

"Si, la pica se mata," she responded. The bite would kill you.

I was hoping this was just rumor—we hadn't heard that from anyone else, so I am pretty sure we would have been okay, but still, I didn't relish a spider bite. Especially not in my own kitchen, so I stopped following the "be kind to spiders" rule.

However, despite the heat and bugs, life in the Villa was, all things considering, fairly luxurious. Two to a room and bathroom. Running water for sinks, toilets, and showers. Electricity. Wireless internet just a four-minute walk away in the open-air teachers' lounge.

But having all these luxuries available could change abruptly.

It was a typical night in the Villa. I had already eaten and cleared out of the kitchen and I was on my computer in front of the fan. Music from across the way blared through my open window and I could hear shouting and laughter from the homes lit up along the road.

Then the lights went out, the music stopped, the breeze from my fan withered and died, and only the glow of my laptop was visible in any direction. A great shout and groan emitted from the dark town outside, and I sighed with them as beads of sweat formed on my forehead from the lack of breeze.

Electrical outages were common; sometimes the whole island's power got cut, other times it was just Santa Ana, and a few frustrating times only Barbacoas' power was out for a weekend until Monday morning's repair crew came to fix it.

Usually the power would be out for just an afternoon or a night, and the almost weekly disruption was annoying and made all of the rooms at least twenty degrees hotter than I would have liked, but it was just a part of life on the island. The two, three, four-day stretches without electricity? Those did me in.

During outages, the classroom fans stood still at school and temperatures topped 90 degrees inside our sweltering classrooms. And of course when class finished, there was no air conditioning to run to, no computers to work on, and no way to print tests or worksheets. Back inside the dark classrooms, I struggled as badly as my students to focus in the heat—when all I could think about was taking a cold shower back at the Villa.

But electricity wasn't the luxury I missed the most. I was more likely to groan in resentment after hopping in the shower (in my usually state of sweat), turning on the nozzle, and watching five pitiful drops float pathetically to the floor.

At least every other week, we'd have these unfortunate moments when we'd turn on the kitchen or bathroom faucet and stare down at the unresponsive sink. Dishes piling up, unwashed hair and bodies— the Villa was at its worst whenever the water stopped working. We would dip an old plastic container into the murky barrel of rainwater outside (if some happened to have collected in it), climb the stairs, and take a bucket shower to ease the stench and try and appear presentable for class, but it was never the same as rinsing cool bug-free water all over ourselves and actually getting clean.

It was always a joyful moment when the water would finally start flowing again.

And we missed the electricity as well; when the power did go back on, the town would produce a great cheer, with Santaneros whooping and clapping as they returned to their TVs, cranked their fans, and turned up their music. The cheer would come into my room just as the soothing noise of my fan started back up, signaling a cool breeze was finally just a few moments away.

It was a good moment, and a reminder of days when water, electricity, and internet all went out at the same time (a triple threat) and there was little to do but go down to the sweltering kitchen and try to eat everything in the refrigerator before it went bad.

"Mondongo today!" I called (a little wickedly) over to Alyssa as she walked into the shade of the Barbacoas cafeteria. I could have sworn every organ in her body stopped. Not in shock, but in the sort of way you would brace yourself if you were about to get hit by a baseball or a rampaging Soviet tank.

While we were learning to whip up a few Colombian dishes in our kitchen, *mondongo* was one of a few Colombian delicacies that we refused on sight (and smell) to partake in. This well-loved Colombian soup was a tough sell for U.S. Americans who were used to all-white breast meat and couldn't handle meats scarier than bologna (fast food notwithstanding). Mondongo is tripe soup. Or, to describe it in more detail: broth with chunks of cow stomach floating around. Chewy and smelly, it was hard to disguise, and Alyssa's reaction exhibited our usual response to this specialty of Colombian cuisine. On days where the cafeteria served mondongo, I longed for the taste of chicken noodle, minestrone, or at least some changua.

On the days when mondongo was not on the menu, the Barbacoas cafeteria usually served decent food, which was good since we ate there every weekday for lunch. Four ladies in light blue aprons worked there every day—spending hours over steaming pots—cutting, peeling, and mixing to feed the over 500 students at Barbacoas. Considering they cooked with charcoal stoves, basic ingredients, and fed so many students, teachers, and staff, those ladies worked miracles.

At around 12:30, all the Barbacoas teachers would walk up to the cafeteria counter, where stacks of sturdy plastic plates (with little dividers so the different side dishes wouldn't touch) were filled up. We would stand a little to the side until the ladies handed us our plates, filled with whatever was on the menu for lunch that day. After grabbing a metal fork or spoon and a plastic mug of juice, we would go head to one of the polished wooden picnic tables.

I'd look for other volunteer teachers or some of the Barbacoas teachers, who I was getting to know, to sit with. Norcy, who taught English and was always a little serious, would gesture me over if I came her way. I might also end up sitting with some shy students, who would greet me with a quiet "good morning," or I would be joined by Sergio, the P.E. teacher, who was always a lesson in *machismo* whenever he talked (read: flirted) with female teachers.

By far the teachers I was closest to were the Barrios Florez sisters, Lilybeth and Marelis. Lilybeth was always ready with a smile full of braces, and Marelis, who taught English, was always good for a conversation about something new about Colombia or the amount of paperwork she had to do. Thin with milk chocolate skin, her English was excellent and we'd talk about strange U.S. American customs, difficult classes, and upcoming holidays that would likely cancel my classes at IESA yet again.

The topic of conversation would also inevitably go back to whatever dish we were served that day.

The menu changed daily, but always included white rice, some protein, and vegetables. Some days we would get pinto beans, other days the protein would be lentils cooked with vegetables, a chicken stew of sorts, a salty cut of beef, or noodles with chicken or ground beef. They always had *arroz con pollo* on Fridays, which was a little greasy and not incredibly filling, but the salty rice and chicken never failed to hit the spot.

The Colombian definition of vegetable did not always go hand-in-hand with mine, however, and I'm not talking about the eternal "Is a tomato a vegetable or fruit?" debate. Most side dishes that were termed the vegetable serving made me want to go look up the definition of *verdura* in Spanish. Exhibit #1: fried ripe plantains. These were starchy bananas that would come sitting in a shiny pool of oil, limp and soggy, and it was hard to see how they were adding any nutritional value to my lunch. (As much as I detested ripe plantains, I had a hard time stopping myself from eating unripe green plantains when they were fried up and served chip-like with a pinch of salt. The twice-fried thick patties of plantains known as *patacones* were easy to make and soon became my favorite Colombian food, though they were no more of a vegetable than potato chips.)

Each meal at Barbacoas was also accompanied by a juice, a fruit concoction usually about one part fruit and three parts sugar—so of course it almost always hit the spot. Bleidis, who each day would be dressed neatly in a white apron and was ready with a smile, would ladle a mug-full of juice out of a giant plastic tub. Mango and passion fruit were regulars, as was a fruit called *tomate de árbol*, which was not actually a "tree tomato" but an oval orange fruit that was bitter until mixed with cups of sugar and ice.

However, I never acquired a taste for the cafeteria's *panela* juice. Made from a hard, molasses-like brick that had been mixed with water and a little lime, its flavor resembled sugar water with a strange bite. On its best days, panela was akin to refreshing iced tea, but Bleidis soon learned to skip over me on panela day and not to take offense when I was in the mood for mango juice and found myself bitterly disappointed yet again.

Barbacoas' cafeteria could have that effect on your day. After a hard morning of teaching, where nothing seemed to go right, well-seasoned beef with salad could make it all better. Of course, even the greatness of a fantastic teaching day dimmed a little when it was followed by the Barbacoas Starch Special.

In Colombian cuisine there seemed to be two main components: starch and oil. Hundreds of years of culinary experimentation have created thousands of varieties out of these two basic food groups. And by far the most-common starch is rice, which was served every day at the cafeteria. Colombian rice is not like Mexican rice, which is cooked with spices—Colombians as a rule don't like anything spicier than cilantro and the rice is normal white rice, cooked with a little oil. Every day the sticky white grains sat on my plate, glistening with oil and making all my lunches taste a little too similar.

Out of the more than 300 meals I had at the cafeteria, only one, yes *one*, did not include rice (someone had obviously made a serious inventory mistake).

Colombians also eat a wide variety of different roots and tubers including potatoes, the ubiquitous starchy plantain bananas, white *yuca* (cassava) root, and *ñame* (the nasal pronunciation in the latter evokes the toddler in everyone—try saying this without smiling: "Ño, ñanna, I don't want another ñame").

But carbohydrates were not solely from foods Colombians could grow underground. The Starch Special, which was served at least every other week, was a generous helping of oily rice that was served with a main course of oily pasta and a side dish of deep-fried plantains. My arteries and taste buds would simultaneously wail in protest. I'm surprised our cooks didn't mix in some potatoes with the pasta and throw in a bread roll on the side.

As much as I hated the Barbacoas Starch Special, all those tubers and roots were expertly combined into a soup called *sancocho*, which was a lot more edible than mondongo. Sancocho has a broth base with vegetables and cilantro, and was always tasty. It had large (cut-them-into-ten-pieces large) chunks of beef on the bone, plantains, yuca, potatoes, corn (on the cob), and, ñyes, ñame. Sancocho was always served with a wedge of lime—and with rice on the side (I was starting to think including it was a Colombian law).

And though eating sancocho from a plastic plate provided a bit of a challenge, the soup always hit the spot. Anti-Atkins dieters dig in.

To escape this small-town carbohydrate paradise, travel north from Santa Ana an hour and a half, and you'll find a city where you can feast your way through any variety of food you want. Order pizza, grilled sandwiches, and even (gasp!) meals that don't come with rice.

Cartagena de Indias.

CHAPTER FIVE

CARTAGENA DE INDIAS

As underdeveloped and struggling as Santa Ana was, the city of Cartagena de Indias had everything Colombia was trying to promote itself to tourists with (okay, maybe they didn't overtly try to promote prostitution but if secret service agents are any indication, apparently that was a big draw too).

Consider the rather rhapsodic descriptions of Cartagena that English-language guidebooks promoted the city with:

"A colonial city with a beauty and romance unrivaled anywhere in Colombia."

One of "the continent's most enthralling and righteously preserved colonial destinations."

"One of the greatest cultural treasures in the Americas."

And as hard as it was for me to first grasp the idea, Cartagena *was* a major tourist destination. The city is Colombia's top tourist attraction—and not just for intrepid backpackers or volunteer teachers. There were 200 landfalls for cruise ships in 2011, hundreds of thousands of passengers wandering this "cultural treasure" every year.

Most of the ideas about the romantic and historic side of the city stemmed from the small portion of the historic Centro, a part of town also called "the walled city," referring to the well-preserved remains of a stone wall (*Las Muralles*) built to repel pirate attacks in the 17th and 18th centuries. Las Muralles were not just some old rocks; you could walk on top of almost all of it, your feet treading on four-hundred-year-old stonework. It was a bit hot in the direct sun, but otherwise it was a pleasant morning or evening stroll from one end of the historic Centro to another—on one side the crashing Caribbean Sea, on the other the bright colors of the colonial city.

Cartagena was founded in 1533, but its mostly wooden structures burned down in 1552 and were rebuilt with stone, and today the old city consists of the districts of Gestemaní and the Centro. This city on the Caribbean prospered during the 1600s and 1700s as a port of call for everyone from pirates to slave traders, and the historic Centro's stone buildings have lasted through the good times and bad.

On one of my first overnight trips to Cartagena, I rolled out of the hostel bed, actually feeling cool, and I walked out the front door into the morning light that shone on the Caribbean. I strolled down the boulevard and turned into the Centro's maze.

I wandered past shops with their steel grates pulled down and by homes where families sat in shorts watching TV. Two elderly men in worn trousers and thin tank tops leaned on worn wooden grates, chatting about an upcoming soccer match.

I was lucky I that had no destination in mind considering I was soon completely lost. The Centro's iconic narrow and twisting streets might be great for postcards, but they were not great for taking direct routes to where you needed to go. (The streets were also great for other reasons; for example, you almost never had to watch out for traffic since the streets were narrow and motorcycles were banned, which was a superior improvement over Bogotá.) I was glad I didn't have anywhere to be in the Centro because I could never figure out how the streets were laid out.

I would think I was just one street over from a familiar landmark and suddenly the street would end and I would find myself at the historic wall and the ocean. I would reenter the maze, attempt to get to an ice cream shop or hostel in the middle of the Centro and would somehow exit the entire neighborhood, arriving ten minutes later at the busy street that borders the Centro from the other side. I was never sure how this happened.

The main problem was that when I looked up and down a block, the streets *appeared* to be laid out in a straight grid when they actually turned and veered off into different directions with new streets appearing out of nowhere. The surrounding roads, wall, and the Caribbean certainly did not run in neat little lines either.

However, the Centro wasn't all that big and the mistakes I made were always the same: either I ran into the wall, Calle Venezuela (the street dividing the Centro with the district of Gestemaní), or the wall *and* the water. Worse comes to worse, I could just follow one of these landmarks before venturing back into the careening streets. Eventually I'd get to where I was trying to go, or least find somewhere else interesting to spend my time. I have no shame getting lost—I am the kind of person who checks with the bus driver and at least three other passengers that I am headed the right way—but even *Carta-generos* have a hard time making a direct path for anything in the Centro. Even after a dozen visits to the city, I would find myself on some side street which was completely unfamiliar and simply enjoy the new sights until I found the wall, the water, or busy border streets of the Centro.

I walked past tiny shops, and peered around carved doors, opened to reveal surprisingly spacious courtyards, complete with columns, potted plants, and intricate tile floors. Two or three-story homes and apartments had bougainvillea vines wrapped around window boxes on the ubiquitous balconies. Adding to the color of the flowers, all the buildings were painted bright oranges, reds, and yellows. One house was cheery gold with a polished brown railing, the next was peachy pink with bright blue windows. Quiet neighborhood side streets soon merged with shops and cafes, and by the time I was on the western side of the Centro, I was surrounded by towering stone churches, cool and green plazas (including Cartagena's own Plaza Bolívar), and a smattering of hotels and museums. Vendors—under umbrellas with logos for rum, cell phone companies, and English soccer clubs—sold cut-up mangos, coconut water, or a variety of fried street food. Others had metal hand-presses for fresh-squeezed orange juice and limeade.

The Centro was named a UNESCO World Heritage Site in 1984 and all of its clichés about being romantic and full of colonial charm (whatever that even meant) seemed to be true.

I sweated in the humidity, but the morning breeze was cool and the sun was still low in the sky, being blocked by the two and three-story buildings that rose high above the narrow streets. I looked around for a place to grab breakfast. There were a few bread and juice shops I remembered from the day before, but of course I couldn't remember which street they were on.

I soon noticed a man standing behind a scratched steel cart that was wafting steam into the warm air.

"Buenos días," I greeted him, noticing the array of fried goods laid out on shelves in the front of the cart.

"Buenas," he said shortly, quickly giving me a second look, probably noticing I wasn't one of his regular patrons.

"Qué comida tiene?" I asked, not sure exactly what the different fried corn dough items were.

"Arepa con huevo," he said, pointing to one that was flat and disc-like. "Empanada de pollo, de queso, y de carne," he said about three triangular-shaped ones. Finally he pointed to a ball-like one which he named as a "Papita."

"Y eso? Qué es?" I asked, pointing to the steel vat steaming in his cart.

"Avena" was his brusque reply. Oatmeal.

I decided to splurge and commit artery suicide by trying the *arepa con huevo*, the *papita*, and the *avena*. The man grudgingly put the first two into a paper bag for me and ladled the avena, which was more liquid than solid, into a plastic cup.

Then I crossed the plaza and stopped and watched a small group of men as they stood around and sipped a hot liquid in what looked like thimble-sized plastic cups.

Going closer, I smelled coffee and realized it was *tinto,* a strong coffee, sweetened with loads of sugar; a popular drink with the IESA teachers before they dragged themselves off to class. While tinto may be made from some of the worst beans in Colombia and had at least a 2:1 ratio of sugar to liquid, it was a step up from instant coffee, which was inexplicably the usual choice for most Colombians.

I walked up to a man carting around a handled metal carrying case with two stacks of different sized plastic cups and six plastic thermoses.

"Un tinto, por favor," I said, and was disappointed that he did not look impressed that I knew what he was selling. Unsure of the going price, I handed him a 1,000 peso bill in exchange for tiny cup of coffee. I received my change and learned that the large size cost 500 pesos (25 cents). (If you really just want a few sips to wake you up, a shot glass sized cup would only put you back 200 pesos.)

Balancing the cup of tinto in one hand and my cup of avena and bag of greasy breakfast in the other, I managed to make it to the edge of the Centro and walked a bit along the wall until I found a place I could walk up and sit. I leaned against four-hundred-year-old stonework, looked out at the sea, and opened my breakfast, the paper bag nearly translucent with grease but wafting a delicious smell that made my stomach growl. I dug in.

The arepa con huevo leaked oil everywhere, but it was delicious. The almost fluorescent orange disc contained a fully-cooked fried egg deep-fried in its cornmeal shell. It paired nicely with the papita, which was basically mashed potatoes with a bit of ground beef inside; it had also been battered in cornmeal dough and deep-fried. As for the tinto, it may not have been a fresh-brewed Italian roast, but it was hot and sweet and complemented my breakfast well.

I was less excited by the avena, which tasted like a little oatmeal had been liquefied, diluted, and mixed with about a cup of sugar. I decided to stick to the basics: no matter where you are in the world, it is hard to go wrong with deep-fried street food.

As I munched on my breakfast and tried not get oil stains everywhere, I watched early morning fishermen getting splashed by waves and the traffic on the street below me. I leaned back, feeling a little guilty about my breakfast, and wiped my fingers on the paper bag, which now resembled waxed paper. Finishing the last of my tinto, I looked out across the city, following the route of the wall until my eye caught a giant Colombian flag flying above a stone fortress.

In addition to great street food, its ability to get tourists lost, and a romanticism that guidebooks drooled over, Cartagena also had a castle: Castillo de San Felipe de Barajas.

On the last Sunday of the month (when the entrance fee was waived), I headed out to the castle with my fellow volunteers Alyssa and Kayla. We got off our bus after the castle appeared on our left, then circled its broad stone base for a bit, trying to figure out how you got in. This took a surprisingly long time, but I suppose castles that were built to repel pirate attacks don't usually have big welcome gates.

On our loop around the fortress, we passed a bronze statue of a man looking off at some distant part of the city with his saber raised triumphantly into the air. This was fairly usual for historic military sites and I spotted the entrance to the castle, so we were about to head up when I paused, turned, and took a second look at the statue. The man in bronze was sculpted with only one leg and one arm.

A little digging revealed it was a statue of the strangely named Don Blas de Lezo, who helped lead the successful defense of Cartagena against the British in 1741. And instead of the pirate attackers, *he* was the one who had a peg leg, having lost that appendage and an arm in previous battles. A closer look at the statue revealed the man also only had one eye. No wonder his nickname was changed from "Peg Leg" to *Mediohombre* (or Half-man) partway through his life.

Unfortunately for Señor Blas the Half-man, his nickname became an accurate representation of him after he lost his other leg in the 1741 battle and died from infection soon after. But luckily for him, his statue gave the no-legged, one-armed, one-eyed admiral at least a bronze peg leg to stand gallantly on (a decision that was more likely due to the laws of physics than a desire to be historically accurate).

We left poor Admiral Blas and headed up a wide stone walkway, climbing for about five minutes before we reached the top of the fortress, which was surrounded by stone bulwarks and a panoramic view of Cartagena.

The castillo was not a Disneyland/Neuschwanstein type castle. It was more a stone fortress. It was the strongest fort ever built by the Spanish in any of their colonies in the Caribbean or South America, and despite many attempts by pirates and warring nations to breach the defenses, the fortress never fell. The castillo/castle/fortress was originally a tiny affair started in 1657 on top of a 130-foot hill just outside the now historic Centro and was expanded to its current size in 1762. It was one of a series of forts the city built to fend off the many pirate attacks it suffered (after six major attacks during the 1600s, the Spanish finally decided to take action).

Rather than its wide stone walkways or thick walls, the castillo's main architectural feature is a maze of underground passageways. The architects built them so you could hear anyone creeping up on you (or running quickly towards you with a large sword and an eye patch) no matter where you both were in the tunnels. This was helpful for communication in case of an attack or just to pass the time on another boring night watch. Today, the cramped stone tunnels are musty with pitted walls and have dozens of small side rooms, which must have originally held armaments. I found circling around in the cool air actually more fun than it seemed, especially when the passageway was lit up and I could see its length and details. Of course, it may have been more exciting with sputtering torches, but the energy-efficient compact fluorescent bulbs made sure we could find our way around.

Back into the bright sunlight and modern Cartagena life, Kayla, Alyssa, and I looked out one more time over the city. The Caribbean shimmered in the sun, and to the west I could see the wall surrounding the tall churches and tightly-packed buildings of the Centro. Further southwest rose the tall, shining white skyscrapers of the ritzy Bocagrande district, which paired glass high-rises with three-hundred-year-old stonework, cannons, and battlements.

The guidebooks like to split Cartagena into three cities: the well-preserved historic bits, ritzy Bocagrande, and then the rest of "real" Cartagena.

Bocagrande was usually described as Cartagena's Miami Beach. It was a thin peninsula jutting just southwest of the Centro with beaches on both sides, filled with tourist shops, expensive hotels, tall luxury apartment buildings, and people with too much money. It was the place in Cartagena where you could find a McDonalds, a Hilton Hotel, and an Apple store. Cartagena's white high-rise buildings stood out against the blue sky, looking like a swanky downtown of a Florida or California city. Colombians had a fun way to describe high-class swankiness, which was a gleaming sign of Colombia's wealth disparity: *pupí* (yes, pronounced poopy), usually accompanied by raising one's little finger in the air while you say it.

I loved historic Cartagena. Pupí Cartagena, I was less a fan of. But the rest of Cartagena, home to more than a million people, was the real city.

Busy markets, tiny shops, and run-down neighborhoods (that weren't full of tall apartments or postcard streets) stretched out in every direction. Cartagena soon lost its feel of a large city as you went away from the downtown areas and into its other neighborhoods. These sections were crowded with small shops, honking buses, speeding motorcycles, vendors, the working poor, the homeless, and everything that every city in the world has.

But I do disagree with the guidebook's three-city interpretation, because a fourth city emerged at night. As the temperature dropped, out came more street vendors, more tables in front of restaurants, and more people. Bands played, the city lit up, and the clip-clop of horse carriages echoed through the streets as couples and families took tours of the city's historic streets. Swanky clubs tucked in old stone buildings would blast salsa, reggaeton, and Latin pop, while outside the Centro, cafés full of patrons drinking Aguila and Club Colombia beers would shout to be heard over the thumping beats of *vallenato*, *champeta*, and *cumbia*.

If there was ever a part of a city where it was safe to walk around late at night, it was the bustling Centro, which was full at every hour of the night with partygoers, vendors, and policemen. However, it was a different story just nearby in Getsemaní. While I generally felt safe walking around this historic neighborhood, my fellow teachers and I would be accosted by people offering us drugs, and prostitutes stood along the sidewalks. The night brought out both the best and worst of Cartagena.

Night or day, I obviously did a lot of wandering. But after strolling through the semi-shaded streets of the Centro in the afternoon heat, I needed replenishment and I would head to any number of tiny cafes for a tall fresh-made juice, blended with ice and milk. *Jugos naturales* (fresh juices) were as ubiquitous in Cartagena as stonework, taxis passing in the streets, and tourists in floppy hats.

There were more flavors of juice than I knew what to do with. I would have to stare at the different choices on the sign for a while before deciding on my flavor. As with all tropical countries, the variety of fresh fruit in stores, markets, and on the street brought bright colors and a lifetime's worth of Vitamin C to anyone passing through. *Mora* (raspberry) with milk was always good since it tasted a bit like a berry smoothie. It was hard to say no to mango or *maracuyá* (passion fruit), but Barbacoas' cafeteria had those, so I usually ordered something I couldn't get on the island. I was never a big fan of *cereza* (cherry) or papaya, but I had grown fond of *guanábana* (a creamy white fruit that translated to soursop in English, but I had never heard of in any language). And I only had to try the untranslatable *níspero* and *zapote* fruits once before I learned to avoid them—they tasted like someone had mixed whatever they could find in their kitchen, then mixed in sugar and chalk to round it off. But the shop's board had another offering that I stared at for a while and finally gave into.

I stepped up to the counter.

"Quisiera tener un jugo de Milo, por favor," I requested, and watched as the young woman in a lime green polo shirt blended it up for me.

A confession: Milo is not another exotic tropical fruit. Instead, it is a brand name of chocolate sold throughout the world. Though listed under juices, there was no denying that what I had just ordered was more like a Wendy's Frosty than a Jamba Juice smoothie.

Why not though? Whenever I was in Cartagena it felt like vacation and so I gave myself permission for the indulgence. I sipped on the "juice" and enjoyed my first milkshake in months.

After finishing the last of my Milo juice and swinging by a downtown grocery store to grab some things I couldn't get on the island, I debated how to start the first leg of my journey back to Santa Ana. The Cartagena-Santa Ana bus only ran two times a day, so I usually had to take the more frequent Cartagena-Pasacaballos bus to the town across the canal from Isla Barú. While coming from Santa Ana (or Pasacaballos) the bus would drop me off a mere block from the entrance to the Centro, the bus stop going the opposite direction was a good mile and a half walk away in the unforgiving coastal heat.

Taxis were certainly an option for me to get to the bus stop. The small, bright yellow European-style cars zipped around like bees— hailing one on Calle Venezuela would be easy. However, Cartagenero taxi drivers did not drive any calmer than the ones we had dodged in Bogotá and they had a strange obsession with their car doors. If you closed a taxi door with any more force than you would use to set down your own baby, your driver would emit a loud yell (as if you had slammed their fingers in the door) and give you a long lecture.

So instead of a taxi, I decided to take a bus. Not only were they cheaper, but since most buses in Cartagena drive with their doors open, the driver wouldn't complain about my failure to use the proper door-closing technique. While the bus driver might end up being even more of a risk-taking adrenaline junkie than a typical taxi driver in the city, at least the vehicle would be built like a tank, so I liked my survival chances.

It was easy to find a bus stop. A long line of buses always slowly maneuvered their way out of the Centro on the street next to Cartagena's iconic bronze statue of Catalina. Catalina was an indigenous woman who acted as an impromptu guide and diplomat to the first Spaniards (sort of a Colombian Sacajawea—if Sacajawea had been kidnapped and forced into being a translator). Unfortunately, Catalina was immortalized in the statue in the same way that some women in history tend to be remembered: bare-breasted.

I hopped on a bus near the statue and headed over to the Mercado, where I could catch the Pasacaballos bus.

Mercado simply means market (its proper name is Mercado de Bazurto, but I never heard it actually called that). This was not the Cartagena of Adidas stores and six-dollar cappuccinos. This was the Cartagena of Cartageneros.

It was one of those markets found in every country that sell anything you could ever desire. Vendors stood under the shade of their tarps or small huts, selling fresh fruits and vegetables, just-caught fish, giant bloody cuts of pork and beef, umbrellas, juice, plastic buckets, woven baskets, backscratchers, used clothing, and black market DVDs.

The market may have only covered an acre or two, but once you were in the middle of it, it seemed to go on for miles with tiny corridors circling between wooden stalls, under tarps, and through open buildings. The guidebooks warned you to watch your wallet, but I was always more worried about watching my feet. Puddles and deep mud had to be negotiated carefully and it was always better when I didn't step on rotting pineapple skin or half-scaled fish heads.

I exited the tight quarters of the inner market and walked between its edge and the road, where it was important to watch for careening bikers, motorcyclists, and buses. Large crowds of men and boys stood blocking the way, mesmerized by the dancing figure of a woman on a fuzzy television, which was a bit of soft porn pretending to be a music video.

On the southernmost edge of the Mercado is a side street where the old and clunky green buses that are headed to Pasacaballos leave every hour or so. Usually when I took one of the buses, it would sit for forty minutes to an hour before heading out. There was no set schedule and buses left whenever the bus's driver and conductor decided—usually when all the seats filled up. I would wait, leaning back against the seat, sweating, before a cooling breeze from the open windows meant we had finally gotten on our way.

This day its engine was already on—a sure sign that it was about to leave (and that it was also running successfully, which was surprising considering the condition it was in). Already quite hot and sticky, I tightened my grip on my grocery bags and jogged a bit to show the conductor I wanted to catch his bus.

I got on and there were no seats left, so I set down my plastic shopping bags next to a large sack of rice and held onto the handles on top of the seats. After only a minute, the bus rumbled and bumped out of the market, heading south from the city, the trash-lined shoreline we followed going in and out of view.

Passengers were not the only people getting on and off during the hour ride. A few young men hopped on a couple of times, trying to sell their wares to the passengers. The first one sold some vanilla wafers while the other gave a ten minute talk on the benefits of some magic powder that was in a small green box (good for whatever ails you, including lack of vitamins, back pain, and depleted sex drive). I declined his special offer ("today only!") and narrowly avoided smashing an older woman's foot as I fell backwards when the bus veered to avoid a bicyclist.

I couldn't see out the windows while standing but could easily tell when I was about ten minutes away from Pasacaballos from the smells that wafted into the bus. A natural gas plant, a sewage plant, and something that must have been a seafood factory passed by as we neared Pasacaballos. I tried not to breathe too deeply. The conductor finally wedged himself past all the passengers who were standing and got to my part of the bus, clicking his coins together. I paid him the 1,500 peso fare and he moved on to collect fares from the others who were sitting and standing behind me.

We passed through the rutted and dusty streets of the town of Pasacaballos, past brightly colored homes and shops advertising phone minutes and beer. I got off at the far side of town and stood in the searing heat for a moment, adjusting my grocery bags, but before I could make a move, a friendly local shouted over at me.

"Playa Blanca?" he asked, assuming I was headed to the popular (and touristy) white sand beach on Isla Barú.

I nodded in a non-committal way. "Más o menos. Santa Ana."

A look of surprise flickered across the weathered black face of the Pasacaballos resident and he gestured ahead with his hand. "Ferry para Barú está ahí."

The main beach on Isla Barú was a lovely strip of white sand and popular with tourists. Cartagena had some nice beaches with crashing waves and lots of sun and sand, but Playa Blanca was the type of picturesque Caribbean beach that tourists wanted to find themselves on during their tropical vacations. But unless they had their own car, most hopped boats from Cartagena instead, which made tourists a bit of a novelty in Pasacaballos.

I walked down the dirt road and headed to the dock, passing two fishermen who kindly pointed the way to the "Ferry para Playa Blanca." There seemed to be only one reason a gringo would be in Pasacaballos.

If I ever got amnesia, I'm pretty sure getting back to Isla Barú wouldn't be a problem, although I'd end up on the beach instead of in my classroom. I paused to consider this tempting option for a moment.

I passed the car ferry and headed to a beckoning boatswain who already had three passengers in his large canoe-like boat and was ready to shuttle them across the canal. We agreed on the normal 1,000 peso crossing fare and I sat on a wooden crossbeam for the ride. Some boats had tiny motors that would power us across the wide, slow-moving canal in just a few minutes, but this time my boatswain was a thin, sinewy man with a wood and plastic paddle. As he paddled against the current, we had plenty of time to enjoy the view and the plants floating in the canal. We also had a lot of time to sit in the direct sun.

We managed to cross successfully, so I said a quick prayer of thanks and jumped off onto Isla Barú soil. A couple of different young men came up to me, offering rides on their motorcycle taxis.

One driver recognized me. "Para Barbacoas," he said with a smile, as other drivers' faces fell a bit upon realizing they wouldn't get a 10,000 peso fare to the beach out of me.

I swung my leg over the leather seat of the moto and put on the helmet I'd been carrying around Cartagena just for this ride. With my head protection secured, one hand gripping my shopping bags, and the other holding onto the seat and small bar behind me, I told my driver, "Okay, estoy lista."

He changed gears and we bumped away past a line of trucks and cars that were waiting for the ferry back to the mainland on the short dirt tract that connected to the main road. The route was full of divots and bumps, rocks and ruts, and we barely broke twenty miles per hour. We soon hit the island's newly redone main road, which was smoother with compacted dirt that was almost concrete-like in its hardness. We sped up and passed a truck, then depending on what part of the road had the fewest bumps, the driver went back and forth between the left, right, and middle of the road. As always, I was happy to have a helmet as we jolted around, my plastic visor blocking most of the dust from passing vehicles.

It was about a twenty-minute ride into Santa Ana through landscape that wasn't too different from East Africa with its dusty, low-lining bushes. Two white cows blocked the middle of the road and we had to drive close to a barbed wire fence to pass them, then we successfully zipped past a donkey, her foal, and a pig brown with mud as they crossed the road. There were also a few people walking along the side of the road, and I waved to one I knew as we reached Santa Ana. We passed by most of the town quickly, following the main road that continued to Playa Blanca and the community of Barú, a town located on the very southwest tip of the island.

And we pulled up at the wide wooden gate of Barbacoas.

I swung my leg over the moto, feeling a little stiff from carrying the groceries, and pulled 3,000 pesos from my pocket.

"Gracias," I told my driver, who put the fare into his pocket. "Ten un buen tarde."

He wished me a good afternoon as well and sped off back to the ferry to try to get another fare.

I turned to where the Barbacoas watchman had already opened the gate for me.

"Buenas, Gabriel," I said, smiling at him.

"Bienvenido," Gabriel said, smiling back in welcome, revealing even more wrinkles in his brown skin, and a missing front tooth.

And after three hours and two buses, one canoe, and one moto-taxi, I am finally home.

CHAPTER SIX

A LOT OF LEARNING LEFT TO DO

I was falling in love with my new home: the people, sights, and the food (or, at least, most of the food). However, while Colombia's problems with armed guerrillas and drug traffickers might get most of the air time in the U.S. media, I was starting to add the public schools to the list of dysfunctional systems in the country.

My co-teacher, Pedro, was hopelessly uninterested in fulfilling his role as an educator, the heat was energy-draining, and the lack of supplies was frustrating, but the most exasperating thing about teaching at IESA was the school schedule. Actually, calling the randomness of when classes met a "schedule" might be a little generous.

The school's four different official schedules were posted on the office walls, and on paper we were supposed to start school at 6:30 a.m. sharp every morning with the last class ending at 12:30 p.m. (elementary school was held in the afternoon). This was inexplicably termed *Horario Normal* or "Regular Schedule" but there was nothing normal or regular about the fifty-five minute classes of Horario Normal: never did we have a week of "Regular Schedule," and I mean *never*.

Officially, our second "regular" schedule was *Horario Comunidad* for the normal morning gatherings on Mondays, Wednesdays, and

Fridays. Classes on the third schedule, *Horario B* (which actually had two separate versions with and without comunidad) were shortened to forty minutes each. Finally, *Horario C* had thirty-minute classes all morning and school ended at 9:30. Each day, I kept track of what schedule we had, and it soon turned into a long list of disruptions.

No class: student elections. Horario C because of Sports Day. Horario B because of a staff meeting (all the teachers sped back to Cartagena after school, so any staff meetings had to take place during class time). Horario C for the students to clean the school grounds. No school for a Monday holiday that was either St. Peter and St. Paul Day or the *Ascensión de Jesús Cristo* (no teachers seemed to be sure). Horario B: 11:30 teacher meeting on grades. Horario C: no water in the town. Second through fifth periods cancelled for school assembly. Horario C: the bathrooms clogged up again.

So was life on Colombia's coasts.

There were also random days when just one of my classes were canceled, such as when the local family planning organization Pro-Familia gave Sex Ed talks. With high rates of teenage pregnancies on the island (possibly simply resulting from a lack of things to do in town), at least I knew the school was using the students' time wisely whenever the ProFamilia folks showed up. It was actually pretty awesome that there *was* a Sex Ed program in the Catholic public schools, but it was still frustrating when another class was canceled for demonstrations of fabric models of penises and vaginas.

Even when class wasn't canceled for Sex Ed, I never taught all six periods a day, so I got a few breaks throughout the morning. However, my students only had a thirty-minute *descanso* when they finally got a chance to go to the bathroom, stretch their legs, and have some snacks.

During descanso, the two small snack sheds near the back end of the school would be swamped with students. Gripping crumpled bills and sweaty coins in their hands as they tried to force themselves through the crowd, they yelled out their orders for soda, chips, fried arepas, and sweet breads. Never much into health food, their favorites seemed to be any number of puffed corn packaged snacks and any flavor of the Colombian soda called Big Cola, which was frozen and slurped as if it were a soda slushie. The most coveted snack was a Colombian version of Cheetos known as Cheese Tris (when you say it out loud in Colombian Spanglish, it rhymes), and like its U.S. counterpart, it left one's fingers a radioactive orange for much of the day.

Besides eating, the other activity during descanso was to watch the inevitable soccer match held on the concrete *cancha*, which served as both the *fútbol* pitch and the basketball court (though despite the hoops on each end, I never saw it used for the latter). Sometimes it would be an organized match between grades, which was part of the year-long tournament P.E. teacher Tajan refereed, and the field would be lined with students watching the boys scuffling around the concrete. Tajan, wearing two baseball caps to shade both his face and neck, would blow his whistle on fouls, give out yellow cards, and even oversaw penalty shoot-outs. On non-tournament days, older boys played pickup games on the slick concrete while my sixth graders always hung around trying to join. Descanso would end whenever the guards decided to blow the air horn: thirty to forty-five minutes later.

Whether a descanso soccer match lasted well into fourth period or the teacher bus broke down and no teachers showed up until forty-five minutes into first period (besides Kassira and I, of course), classes were shortened with regularity. All of my six classes ended up meeting for different amounts of time and the classes that had periods on Mondays or Fridays were hit especially hard. Fridays were the day for any assemblies and special events, and Mondays seemed to be reserved specifically for holidays. There were certain Mondays after pueblo-wide parties the night before when I had five or less students in each class and I frequently had Mondays off due to the fact that Colombia has the second-highest number of national holidays in the world: eighteen of them (the United States has ten). I'm not saying that the number of holidays in Colombia wasn't a nice perk, but going to class once in a while would have been good too.

So rather than living and teaching by a set academic schedule, my life depended more upon when the bell actually rang, when teachers showed up, and when the powers-that-be decided to actually hold class that day. And whenever I could, I tried to fit teaching into that schedule.

The Cartagena School District had assigned a list of topics for each grade level and each quarter that Pedro and I were required to cover. But the English lessons were not as memorable as my students who would have fit into any middle school classroom anywhere.

In 6-2, the tall and bossy Huber Andrés would one moment have his eyes fixed on the board, while the next moment he would be flirting with the girls around him. Tiny and studious Mauricio and Jhon Jader, who were amongst the only students I never heard yelling, were best friends and both would sit with their notebooks open and be attentive in nearly every class. Arlin, with her shifting moods, refusal to work, and sullen manner, always needed extra encouragement.

Then there was Carlos, who stood out for two reasons. First, if you swept your eyes across all the rickety desks sitting on the concrete floor, you would immediately notice his light skin. He was my only true mestizo in a class of Afro-Colombians. More important, he mixed an eagerness to share with a patience that sometimes superseded my own; what I would have given for a class full of students with Carlos' drive.

In my other sixth grade section, class was held in a classroom that was almost half the size of the 6-2 room and approximately the same dimensions of the small armament rooms in Castillo de San Felipe de Barajas. The class didn't have a student like Carlos who I could count on to understand every new concept I introduced, but then again, it didn't have any students who enjoyed disrupting the class as much as Arlin did either. Instead, my two characters in 6-1 were two girls who were as different as the chilly Andes mountains and the scorching Caribbean coast.

Luz Daris was of medium height and thin, with frizzy brown hair, light brown skin, and wide eyes that gave her a bit of a crazed look. She likely had undiagnosed ADHD and loved running around the classroom or yelling—often at the same time. Sometimes she focused her enthusiasm on the class work at hand ("Teacher! Teacher! Yo puedo!" she would shout, running up to the board without an invitation) and sometimes she focused on things like a car driving by (she would stand on a desk, pressing her face against the open concrete tiles while yelling "Buenas!" in greeting to the passing car). Although getting her on task was a challenge, I appreciated any enthusiasm I could get.

In contrast to Luz Daris, a girl named Claudia had no enthusiasm for anything. Powerfully built, with dark black skin, a wide face, and short hair that she wore pulled back in a fuzzy bun, Claudia was also one of my few overweight students. Some days I worried she'd burst out of her tight skort that was the uniform bottom for all the girls.

She also had the annoying habit of ignoring me when I talked to her.

"Claudia, can you start working on your homework please?" I would say in Spanish, pointing to the board. She would stare at me for a moment, then look over at whoever was sitting next to her and laugh. Then she'd turn to look out the window at the school grounds.

Sixth grade certainly presented me with challenges, but seventh grade fast became my least favorite grade (a sentiment, I think, shared by many seventh graders around the world). My classes were frequently out of control, students refused to do their work, and nearly every student received abysmally low scores on homework and quizzes.

The worst of my two seventh grade groups, 7-2, was usually a small class—while slotted for thirty-one students, it had some of the worst attendance in the school. It was usually segregated by gender; the boys would sit on one side of the classroom, staring out the window or slouching with their heads on their desks, while the girls all congregated together in the front, chatting, laughing, and yelling.

One day, I finally asked them why they sat so clumped together.

"Los abanicos," Coraima—a somewhat pudgy girl sitting near the wall—responded, looking a little bored. She pointed to the ceiling.

I quickly learned that *abanico* meant "fan," and in the 7-2 classroom, only the ceiling fans in the front worked. The two in the back of the room hung pointlessly stagnant, and I realized there was probably nothing I could do to make students leave the faint but cooling breezes of the front row.

I wiped my forehead with the handkerchief I always kept in my pocket and sighed as I tried to get the class to copy a dialogue from the board.

Cenelia, a sharp-witted girl with piercing eyes, seemed to be the ringleader of the seventh graders and there was something about her that made her switch between bouncing off the walls and sitting quietly. If she was in the mood to pay attention, the rest of the class would also do their work or participate, but if not, mayhem ensued. The latter was unfortunately more common.

I looked forward more to eighth grade. While they also had bad, unmanageable days, 8-1 and 8-2 were my saving graces. There was

Marianela, Carlos's cousin, whose father owned the bakery in town, and her friend Maria Angelica, both who always greeted me at the start of every class and wished me a good weekend every Friday. They studied (actually studied!) for tests, almost never missed a homework assignment, and would ask clarification questions. Another student in their class, Luis Kevin, could have learned English if I had just tossed him a book and walked out, but he always asked me questions and helped students around him after he had finished his work.

One morning in 8-1, I was introducing jobs vocabulary and I started by asking students what they wanted to do after they finished school.

"Cantante!" a girl said, and I wrote both the Spanish and English on the board. We practiced together. "Singer," I said. "Singer!" they repeated.

We went on for a while, and most of the jobs were ones they could get in Santa Ana: "Bus driver!" "Chef!" "Fisherman!" "Farmer!" "Guard!" "Tourist guide!" and "Motorcycle taxi driver!" There was also a list of jobs that teenagers everywhere seemed to want ("Football star!" and "Model!").

"Presidente!" shouted Luis Felipe, always the class comedian, and the class laughed, but I wrote it on the whiteboard as well, adding it to our list. There's nothing wrong with high hopes.

But some students did have a specific dream. "Doctor," the usual joking Jorge said in all seriousness, which was the same response studious Luis Kevin had given me the day before. Keiner, another top student, carefully copied "engineer" into his notebook after shouting out, "Ingeniero."

As the class finished making a vocab list from the words on the board, a student named Katia came up to me, dressed neatly in her white and maroon uniform. Always holding her battered notebook, she would volunteer with a regularity I would sometimes find annoying and strive a little harder than needed to always be on my good side, but her intentions were pure and she just wanted to learn as much English as she could.

Katia stood posed with her pen. "How do you say *administradora de empresa?*" she asked.

I added it to the board. "Businesswoman," I said, and she repeated it. "And I think you would be a good businesswoman," I added, repeating it in Spanish. She gave me a wide smile and finished carefully copying the word into her notebook.

Katia, Luis Kevin, Cenelia... Knowing your students' names as a teacher is always a prerequisite to good classroom management, mutual respect, and knowing how to help individual students. Do they come from a supportive family? Do they have a job after school? Do they get any square meals at home? Are they being bullied at school?

Learning my students' names was a much more difficult task than I had originally foreseen. This was mostly due to the fact that I had never heard of most of their names before—and forget about knowing how to pronounce them.

The bane of my existence (and shame) were the unique names that I could only guess were African or indigenous in origin (or were simply made up by parents). Some of my girls were named Darledlis, Yajaira, and Damaris, and some of my male students were named Freidys, Yeison, and Yiminson. I had a Wanlin and a Wadis in the same class, and a Derlis, Delkin, Daimer, and Danilo all in seventh grade.

Besides the fact I couldn't properly pronounce any of these names at the beginning of the year, only about half of my students' parents were literate, and so the correct spelling of names always left me guessing.

And in Santa Ana, spelling seemed a bit flexible, with *z*'s and *s*'s switching spots on a whim, as did *i*'s and *y*'s. Letters were also constantly being added or taken off the end of names. Ana Sofia also wrote her name as Ana Sofi, Keith was also Keyth, Yaniriz was just as correct spelled as Yaniris, and Yenni was sometimes also Jennys and Yennis (though, strangely, never Jenny). An inability by many Spanish speakers to start words with an *s* sound (think the word "Spanish" versus *español* or "states" versus *estados)* created a few students whose legal name on the roster were Estefani (along with Estefanie and Estefany, depending on the day).

A short but always enthusiastic seventh grader may have won the prize for the number of ways he wrote his name throughout the year. Listed as Jancarlos on my roster, he wrote his name as Jhean Carlos on his nametag, and periodically also rotated through Jhon Carlos and Johncarlos depending on his mood. Adding the occasional times he wrote John Charles after learning the Anglicized version of his name, and I'd hate to be the guy at the DMV or social security administration figuring that one out. How was I supposed to learn my students' names if they kept changing them on me?

Then there was a tall, wide-eyed sixth grader who wrote his name down as Gil Flow. Strange, but I wanted to have the students choose which name to use out of their dozens of combinations, so when I called on him in class (or, as was more likely, said his name to try and get him back on task), I called him Gil Flow even though his name was Gil Cendris on my sheet.

What I did not know was that the "Flow" was in no way part of his real name. How students kept themselves from snickering for months whenever I called him that, I'll never know, because I was really calling him Gil the Cool. "Flow" was a word used in many reggaeton songs to refer to the smooth, cool style of singing, and had come to mean a trendy, urban guy who's got it all.

Not cool, Gil the Tricky, not cool.

I admit it took me an embarrassingly long time to learn all my students' names, but in my defense, they kept changing them on me.

However, I lived in a town that was spelled alternately as Santa Ana, Santaana, and Santana, so I guess it came with the territory.

"Teacher," Cenelia asked me after class one day. "Qué significa fucking you?"

I stared at her for a moment, but had prepared for the inevitable swear word questions that would come up.

"Uh... please don't say that, Cenelia," I responded, giving her the sternest look I could muster despite holding in a snort of laughter. "It is one of the worst words in English. Literally, it means to have sex," I felt obligated to explain to her in Spanish. "But if a student in the United States said that in a class, they would be in the principal's office *like that*," I emphasized, snapping my fingers.

Cenelia smiled her thanks, giggled, and walked over to her two friends eagerly awaiting the explanation.

When another seventh grade girl, Katy Luz (who was always quiet and polite), came up and asked me during class, "Qué significa fucking you?" I realized that the question wasn't coming out of the blue. After a little digging, I believe I found the source.

Back in January, while walking the damp streets of Bogotá, I had come across an advertisement at a bus stop for a new telenovela, the primetime soap operas popular throughout Latin America. The show was called *La Teacher de Inglés*.

The opening sequence to each episode showed a classroom with adults in the seats and a pretty English teacher in front. They all dance and sing the main title in a garbled string of phrases that sound vaguely English. If you look up the official lyrics, you will get something like this for the first part of the song:

Jelou mister
Esmoquin yu
Guachin drinqui o guisqui
O dans rumba o roncarol
O de colombia Merecumbe

I speak pretty good Spanglish and those lyrics certainly belong to no language I know of, whether Spanish, English, or even the weird accent of the Colombian coast. The show's long-running joke is that the main characters definitely needed an English teacher. After listening to the song around a dozen times, I finally came up with what I think was the English version of the theme (I've add my translations next to the official lyrics):

Jelou mister (Hello mister)
Esmoquin yu (And fucking you)
Guachin drinqui o guisqui (Why you drinking all whiskey)
O dans rumba o roncarol (Or dance rumba and rock 'n' roll)
O de colombia Merecumbe (Or the Colombia merecumbé)

I know, really? I challenge you to listen to it and try to hear something less offensive. You couldn't say the f-word on any television station, but my students were smart enough to figure out that "esmoquin yu" referred to a potent swear word that pops up all over in Hollywood films and hip-hop songs.

Always in the back of my mind was the fact that the English teacher that my students might be most familiar with was not anyone at their school but Pili, a dark-haired beauty teaching in a fancy classroom, who falls madly in love with her student Kike, who had hired her to teach him English so he could better run his... wait for it... lingerie factory.

Yes, that was the actual plot of *La Teacher de Inglés.* Thank you Colombian television for that.

To be fair, parts of the theme song were not offensive and contained both actual words in Spanish and English when Pili sings some vocab words and the class sings back their Spanish equivalents:

Lapiz? Pencil
Pluma? Pen
Pollito? Chicken
Gallina? Hen.

So there were at least four words my students knew—words much better than the four-letter ones.

As I dealt with strange questions, unmotivated students, and my own shortcomings in the classroom, there were a few days that made me want to practice my own four-word vocabulary.

It was a typical Wednesday. Comunidad had gone fifteen extra minutes into first period (and even longer for my boys who apparently didn't line up well, so they had to stay behind another ten minutes to practice). My seventh graders were especially rowdy and even getting them to take out their notebooks took painstaking effort and patience.

My double period with my sixth graders was going well as we practiced numbers, then Pedro decided to do his regular "I think I'll just wander outside class and maybe come back if I feel like it in five or ten minutes" routine and the class almost got completely out of control when I tried to give them homework. Two boys got into a fight when one took the other's pen and I had to get them to stop punching each other and take them to the office of the *coordinador,* which made me late for 8-2. Six boys I knew were at school that day weren't in class, and some of the girls openly chatted about how bad my jeans looked (comments on my shoes and clothing were commonplace, and I'm sure it didn't help that I was hand-washing all my garments). And after sitting in the back of the class for ten minutes, Pedro disappeared again.

I grumpily lectured the class on their poor behavior as they dragged out copying a few homework sentences from the board. Picking up on my sour mood, the always sweet Marianela and Maria Angelica asked me after class if I was okay while looking worried that my usual easy-going demeanor had disappeared.

Wiping sweat from my face, I felt ashamed.

I explained that I was sorry I had been late and wished we could get more done so we could practice, review, and play more games in class, and I told them I appreciated their concern.

Now even more disappointed in myself and in a bad mood, it was probably a bad idea to seek out Pedro and ask him yet again where he went during class ("I had to see the rector about something" was his answer this time), but I didn't want a bad day getting in the way of my attempts to improve how our co-teaching worked between us. I thought we should figure out our lessons for the next day; Pedro thought we'd have them "practice," and left it at that. I wanted to know what I could do to improve my teaching and my obviously strained relationship with him; Pedro told me everything was going great.

It went back and forth like that for another ten minutes before I gave up and told Pedro I'd see him tomorrow.

I went back into the teachers' lounge to grab some posters and noticed the usually boarded-up windows were wide open and it felt unusually warm inside.

I looked around quizzically, then addressed Ileana (still with her large pot belly), who was sitting and eating some chicken.

"El aire condicionante funciona ya?" I inquired, almost afraid to ask.

Ileana leaned over to the air conditioning unit on the wall and unenthusiastically twirled the dial with her greasy fingers. The unit gave a feeble hum and coughed.

"Pienso que ya terminó," she responded. Not that it was broken, or somehow not working. "Finished."

I managed to hold back some choice words of frustration, worried that with the popularity of *La Teacher de Inglés*, someone would actually know that the phrase "Are you shitting me?" and was probably something teachers shouldn't say.

The end of March brought about the end of Unit 1. Our first round of exams showcased the academic problems at IESA—and because our exams generally followed the national system of exams, I was not too impressed by the complicated Colombian system either.

Since Pedro's answers to my questions about the exams had made things more confusing, I asked the computer teacher, Norman, to explain the process to me.

"All exams will be done in two days," Norman explained in a hard-to-understand Spanish. "So five subjects each day."

We consulted the schedule together.

"So English will be the second day. And questions thirty-one to fifty." Seeing my confused look, Norman then backtracked. "All the subjects are on the same test and they need to be multiple choice. English is right after the religion section and you get twenty questions."

"And what happens if a student is absent the day of an exam?" I asked.

Norman shrugged. "Then they take the recuperación exam instead," he said, referring to the week after exams when students had a chance to improve their scores.

I checked the schedule again.

"So the tests are the first four hours. So, is there class on the test days?"

"No, no of course not." He paused. "At least I don't think so. Maybe after?" Another pause, then another shrug, but I didn't press the matter. No one ever gave me a reliable answer of the "when do we have class?" question anyhow.

Imagine being fifteen years old, sitting in an uncomfortable desk where half the wooden seat has broken off. It's about 88 degrees in your classroom. The teacher sitting in front is an art teacher and doesn't know anything about what you think may be a mistake on the chemistry exam. Your friend, who hasn't even been in class for more than ten days the whole quarter, has already turned in his test and is playing soccer outside. The sound of the crowd cheering after someone scores a goal pulls your mind further and further away from the passage of reading that you are supposed to be concentrating on.

Correcting the tests back in the Villa that night was depressing. Students had filled in bubbles for their answers and I—the human Scantron—put x's in the correct bubble if they got it wrong. It was a bit like walking through a minefield: it was as if my x's and the students' answers were trying *not* to line up. The average test score ended up being about 4.5 (the grading scale of the Colombian grading system goes from 0.0 to 10.0, which is similar to the 0 to 100% scale in the United States).

Considering that most classes only had fourteen of their scheduled twenty hours of class (which was officially thirty hours since we had 3 "hour" blocks each week), that Pedro's only goal seemed to be to waste as much class time as possible, and that it was my first few months teaching, perhaps it was not surprising that most of my students failed.

The weight of responsibility was sinking in as I handed back the graded exams to my students at school the next day, finalizing our first quarter together at IESA. I was already thinking of a myriad of activities and new strategies to try out for second quarter, but first it was definitely time for a vacation.

CHAPTER SEVEN

Thanking the Lord for Vacations and Drinkable Coffee

April arrived and although the heat did not abate, I looked for signs of spring everywhere I could. The jacaranda trees had started to blossom, their purplish-pink flowers spreading their petals wide before dropping to the dusty ground and giving our khaki earth a colorful corsage. Baby pigs raced to cross the street, dogs were in heat, and Palo, the local *perro* our group helped take care of, soon had a litter of puppies.

Another sign of changing seasons was the appearance of new fruit in town. One evening while walking back from a stroll through farms and fields, a man who I had never met—but who had children at IESA—gave me a paper bag full of tiny sweet mangos as a gift.

"Share them with all the English teachers," he told me, then swung up onto his horse and trotted down the road before I could say a proper thank you.

We had pucker-your-lips sweet pineapple juice with lunch a few days later, and I bought two small but succulent pineapples for 1,000 pesos each off a truck in town.

Spring also means it's Easter—in the United States it was time to put little girls in white dresses and take their photo with tulips and daffodils. Santaneros celebrated Easter with festivities marking the life of Jesús Cristo and a variety of sugary fruits.

Two Fridays before Easter, IESA celebrated *Día de los Dulces* (Day of the Sweets). In the coastal regions of Colombia, it was an Easter tradition to sell and eat sweet jam-like pastes that were made from every fruit imaginable (and some from non-fruits you wouldn't imagine could be sweet).

Different teachers at IESA organized the festivities, cooked and brought different dulces, and then students sold them at the Friday event. For 200 pesos you got a tiny cup filled with the soupy, sticky dulce, which was served with a saltine wedge and a half of a popsicle stick to eat it with.

My favorite was the *dulce de coco*, which tasted like the inside of a Mounds bar, with my runners-up the shocking sweetness of the dulces made from the local currents and, most surprisingly, from ñame. Posters at each table listed the nutritional benefits, though one had to imagine the healthier qualities were mostly offset by the sugar content. It was like saying Milo juice mixed with whole milk was good for you because of the calcium.

But the Día de los Dulces at the school wasn't just about getting a cheap sugar high. It was part of the religious celebrations at our school that commemorated *Semana Santa*: Holy Week (or the week leading up to Easter that commemorated the last week of Jesus' life). During the event, primary and secondary students held a reenactment that included togas, foam Roman guard costumes, and a Jesus played by an eleventh grader with a hairpiece that was stuck on with tape (I guess because Jesus always has long hair in all the paintings). They walked along part of the school grounds, telling the story of Jesus' entry into Jerusalem and his arrest, trial, and crucifixion. I was surprised, though, that with the ridiculously numbers of burros in Santa Ana, they didn't reenact the fact that Jesus arrived in Jerusalem on a donkey.

Although today Colombia is officially a secular state, the Colombia Constitution before 1991 stated that "public education shall be organized and directed in accordance with the Catholic Religion," and our school seemed to follow that tradition: many Catholic feast days (in addition to the days leading up to Easter) were national holidays, my students all had a religion class, and teachers often led students in prayer in the morning during comunidad.

This was because Colombia, like all former Spanish colonies in Latin America, was Catholic. Very Catholic in fact, considering 90% of the population consider themselves part of the Roman Catholic Church. Colombia is sometimes called the most Roman Catholic country in South America, although Colombians were much more likely to perform religious rites and hang a crucifix or poster of the Virgin Mary up in their homes (or buses) than actually attend Mass every Sunday. Colombians go to church for baptisms, weddings, and funeral rites, but otherwise, there was no apparent reason to talk with the local priest.

To be fair, in a poll that I read in *El Universal* newspaper, the readers voted on the number one thing to do during Semana Santa and chose "reflection and religious devotion." Coming in at number two was the chance to relax and spend time with their families and number three was the chance to travel.

And considering I had the whole week off for Semana Santa, that's what I did as well, heading north with my fellow English teachers Kayla and Alyssa in order to understand a little more about the new Colombia that was emerging from its problems in the last decades.

I sat on the back of a mototaxi and flipped the plastic shield on my helmet up, hoping to be able to see a little better, but instantly got six or seven large raindrops right in the eye, blurring my vision. I rubbed them with my wet hand and tried wiping off the shield again before giving up on adding to my visibility.

Water dripped from my arms, legs, and neck, and I could barely see through the deluge as my driver gunned the motor on the bike again, continuing up what used to be a road and was now a rushing stream of angry brown water.

My mototaxi was climbing the steep and winding roads of the Sierra Nevada de Santa Marta Mountains, and I hoped to arrive in the town of Minca before it became necessary to build an ark. Being the week of Semana Santa, I couldn't be sure that God didn't have something big in store for the world again that week.

If you shrink down Santa Ana (from 4,000 people to 800), substitute the dust for mud, and add a lot of steep hills, you'll get Minca, a tiny town forty minutes from the bustling coastal city of Santa Marta. Like Santa Ana, the way to get there is by mototaxi. As our moto climbed the steep road, clouds blocked the sun, shielding us from the coastal heat that we had suffered through since the end of January. The landscape was lush and green, which should have warned me about how often it rained there. Soon the clouds opened up—within two minutes it had gone from being partly cloudy to just a sprinkle to sheets of rain pouring down.

I struggled to put on my raincoat and my backpack's rain cover as the rain dumped down. Mud splashed up on my legs, then was instantly washed off by the rain and the water running down off my bag.

"Podemos parar para un momentico?" I asked my driver, realizing it would be best to stop for a moment to get my rain gear situated, although at this point I am not sure why I bothered.

He agreed, and we stopped on a part of the road that was more level, where I got off and finally succeeded in fitting the rain cover over my already wet backpack.

The driver eyed me for a moment, then must have decided I looked trustworthy and reached into the pocket of his soaked leather jacket. He handed his damp wallet to me, wondering if I could put somewhere safe. "Puedes cuidar mi billetera?" he asked, gesturing to my rain gear.

I took the wallet and placed it in my large travel bag, which sat on my lap. And with my rain jacket on backwards to better protect my bag and the front of me from the sideways rain, we set off again, following Kayla's moto, which had chugged by us while we stopped.

Our drivers plowed through what looked like rushing rivers, and whenever we came to an especially deep spot, my waterproof hiking boots (which had already been soaked from the inside out) were drenched anew by rushing brown torrents.

We finally arrived in town, hopped off our motos with a splash, and waded ankle-deep through another street stream until we could duck under the cover of a store. While the rain drummed on the tin roof and the cars parked nearby, we entertained ourselves by buying a few vegetables and watching some parents fitting their small child with a large trash bag.

Eventually the rain let up, and after paying our drivers (and returning my driver's wallet), we headed off to our hostel, Casa Loma, which the proprietors had promised to be a short ten-minute walk up from town. After passing through church grounds and crossing a concrete sports park (intelligently under cover) that was connected to the local school, we realized what "up" meant: a steep climb up the side of a hill, alternating between steps and switchbacks. With the weight of our backpacks and difficulty of the slippery mud, what would have otherwise been simply a sad reminder of how out of shape we had gotten while living in flat Santa Ana turned into a struggle to reach the top of the hill.

Next to where a house was being built, a man was using a machete to re-cut dirt stairs where the rain had washed them away, and a wrong step caused my shoe to sink all the way into spongy mud with a slurp. Not wanting to be eaten by the hillside, I quickly pulled it out again. After an embarrassingly large number of stops, a couple of slips, and Kayla finally giving up her flip-flops for bare feet, we finally arrived at the hostel. Soaked to the skin from the moto ride, sweaty from the climb, and muddy from the hike up, there was no doubt that we looked the part of weary travelers, and after only one day on the road.

The rain came and went that afternoon and we enjoyed it from under the cover of the cozy setup of Casa Loma (which translates to Hill House—a clue in regards to the way to get there). In the distance, layers of hills wrapped in thick clouds made us feel like we were in the middle of nowhere, and when it cleared a bit, we had a view of the city of Santa Marta and—if we squinted—the Caribbean Sea. Green and red birds flitted around, alighting on damp branches and causing leaves to shake off their water.

That night we were treated to a spectacular sunset with the clouds lighting up florescent pinks and oranges and bright spots of blue visible where the clouds parted. Nothing I had read about Colombia before I left prepared me for this tranquil scene and despite the struggles I had encountered, I was beginning to form my newer, more complete picture of the country.

That's not to say all the stereotypes about Colombia are always bad or untrue. The steep green hills of the Sierra Nevada de Santa

Marta Mountains were also a place where coffee was grown—Colombian coffee that was actually as good as its international reputation. In the mountains around Minca, as well as in the *Zona Cafetero* main coffee-growing region in central Colombia, coffee bushes lined the hillsides, farms spread out for acres along steep ridges, and escaped plants grew wild by the side of the dirt roads. The leaves of the plants were shiny and thick, shading the green fruit that would eventually turn a ripe red, before the hard interior would be separated from the fleshy coffee cherry, dried, roasted, ground, and brewed.

During our half week in Minca, we stopped at a small cafe to grab some breakfast and try some local coffee. The restaurant had a worn look to it—there was no menu, old calendars hung from the walls, and flies buzzed around the worn wooden tables—in my experience, all sure signs that the food must be good.

It did not disappoint. We got arepas and coffee, and it was the best breakfast I ever had in Colombia. In Cartagena, the streets were lined with vendors selling *arepas con queso*, but these were tall and gooey mixtures of barely cooked white corn flour and cheese, which was rarely appealing. Minca's arepas were thinner, with a crispy outside and the inside just soft enough. Instead of being baked with hit-or-miss queso costeño, they were served piping hot with a local cream cheese spread on top.

Que delicioso.

It was no surprise that the coffee was also excellent. The fact that it probably came from less than a mile away didn't hurt (nor that we were actually drinking it in cool air). It was the best coffee I had drunk all year, probably because most of the highest quality Colombian coffee is exported to roasters in the United States, Germany, and Italy. Almost eight million bags of coffee travel overseas every year. Still, that's not much compared to the first half of the 20th century when the Colombian economy meant coffee and nothing else. Today, petroleum and coal now make up almost half of the country's exports and the country ships out more gold and agricultural products (such as 46% of the world's cut-flowers) than coffee, which now constitutes only 5% of Colombia's total exports.

I had found $5 espresso drinks in Colombia in Bogotá and Cartagena; however, besides a few *pupí* city dwellers ordering lattes, most Colombians drink the sweet and hot, but mediocre, tinto when they're out and about. At home, I had resigned myself to the fact that the choice was instant coffee. Colombians might live in one of best places in the world to grow coffee beans, yet their cups of coffee come from dehydrated granules in tiny plastic packages. This is the definition of tragedy.

And since we were so used to coffee that was only really appropriate for long backpacking trips, astronauts, and people without taste buds, it was enjoyable drinking real coffee while being surrounded by the people and land that grew it. I took another sip of the warm liquid, breathed in its aroma, and appreciated the difference between instant coffee and the real thing. Legend has it that Jesuit priests were the first to bring and cultivate coffee in Colombia, and so drinking coffee seemed a fitting way to celebrate Semana Santa.

We would miss the region's lush, green hills when we were back in Santa Ana—of course, we had learned firsthand why everything was so green during our ride up. My shoes didn't dry for days.

The ride down the mountain was infinitely drier than the ride up as we headed along the coast and enjoyed the spectacular views and the crashing ocean at Tayrona National Park, with the green Sierra Nevada de Santa Marta Mountains rising from the rugged coast.

After stopping at the entrance gate (and failing to convince the attendant to give us the Colombian rate), we walked a few miles through the humid but nicely shaded forest, along the beach, and through sandy palm groves. Giant blue morpho butterflies flitted about and we had to constantly step over highways of leaf cutter ants, their tiny, dark red bodies following a well-cut ant road as they hefted bright green pieces of leaves to an unknown destination. The air smelled dank and sweet, with great wafts of salty breezes mixing with the abundance of greenery, flowers, and damp soil.

At one beach called Arrecifes, hammocks that cost only $8 for a night were strung up in an open-air netted room that was a three-minute walk from the ocean. And after relaxing on the beach and watching the movement of water and sand in Arrecifes' crashing waves, I headed in to sleep.

Though the hammocks were picturesque with the backdrop of the beach, they did require a bit of maneuvering before one could feel settled in. I stared at the length of my assigned hammock with its thick woven fabric folded in on itself and contemplated how to enter.

I debated between (1) sitting on one side and swinging my legs over it and (2) stepping over the hammock and straddling it before stretching out. I decided on the latter to minimize the chance that I would swing into Kayla, who was already asleep in the hammock closest to me. To step over the hammock, I bunched the thick fabric together and then sat down heavily on what now resembled a thick rope. As I attempted to tug the fabric out from under me, I started swinging precariously back and forth, my efforts to unfurl the hammock making me wonder if I should have consulted a user's manual or physics textbook before attempting this new mode of sleeping.

Managing to finally unfold myself and stretch out, my next task was to decide how far down in the middle to situate myself. I slithered down, but then I felt like a patient with a broken leg as my feet hung high above me. Inching up, I got too far to the left and swung back and forth again, nearly tipping over. I was able to just catch myself on the ground with one hand, but I bumped into Kayla. When I finally got my balance again, I looked over and saw that Kayla was still sleeping serenely in her own hammock. I begrudged her apparent ability to slide into the hammock and fall asleep with the ease of a person settling into a king-sized bed at the Hilton after dipping into the minibar.

Struggling, scooching, and swinging around, I settled into the middle of the hammock, finally in a relaxing position.

Of course, next I had to decide how to sleep with my bag and camera so I could make sure they didn't walk off during the night. (Should I use them as a pillow? A lumpy teddy bear?)

Despite my unpracticed hammock skills, I wrapped the sides of the hammock around me like a blanket and, now in my final relaxed position for the night, soon fell asleep while listening to the sounds of the wind in the palm trees, the chirps of frogs and insects, and the crash of the surf; my thoughts were a long way from worksheets, broken fans, and an unmotivated school.

But vacationing in a natural paradise does not always mean relaxation.

While the nearby beach of La Picina (The Pool) provided a beautiful and safe swimming area in contrast to the dangerous crashing surf where we were staying, further down the beach the area known as El Cabo was infested with a hundred or more foreigners, who were camped out in droves. We were not—apparently—the only ones who had discovered Colombia's Caribbean beaches or this slice of paradise.

It was hard to be a tourist again, and Kayla, Alyssa, and I took a quick dip in the water, then turned around and fled.

To counter the tourist infestation at Tayrona National Park, I caught a bus to the coastal industrial city of Barranquilla, and while I couldn't have been the only gringo tourist that day in the entire city, it sure felt like it. Walking around with white skin and a backpack, I got quite a few second glances. The guidebooks was full of phrases such as "little reason to visit" and "if you need to kill a day here..." Ouch.

There are really only two reasons why you've probably heard of Barranquilla. First, it hosts Carnaval every year—a celebration second only to Rio de Janeiro—but if you *truly* experienced Carnaval, there was a good chance the memories might be a little fuzzy. So it is much more likely you know Barranquilla as the home of the music superstar Shakira, who famously sang about Barranquilla dancing in "Hips Don't Lie."

No offense to Shakira's hips, but Barranquilla didn't look like it would become the happenin' spot in Colombia to rival Bogotá or Cartagena any time soon. But Barranquilla was Colombia's fourth largest city and the home of Norcy, one of the English teachers at Barbacoas who I had gotten to know a little. Norcy tried to explain the city to me as we walked the crowded streets.

"In Cartagena you have the Centro and then separate is the Mercado," she explained (by "mercado," she meant the hubbub of hundreds of outdoor vendors and shops).

"In Barranquilla, the Centro and Mercado are in the same place."

It was true: both of the cities were large Caribbean centers of commerce and Barranquilla felt like Cartagena if you took away the picturesque colonial Centro (and the tourists) and added more shops selling used clothes, books, locally-made furniture, tires or motorcycle parts, and who knows what. Barranquilla lay somewhere between the cleaned-up images of Cartagena's tourist spots and the negative stereotypes of war-torn cities. Barranquilla felt like any normal bustling port city and felt very Colombian.

Barranquilla may get fewer tourists than Cartagena, but its importance stems from its identity as a port city on the Magdalena River. For centuries, the river was the main route for transportation and communication from the interior of the country to the coast. The

Magdalena is 1,000 miles long and it provides drinking water to 30 million Colombians, though it faces threats such as overfishing, deforestation, and flooding that seemed to get worse every year. If you ride into the city by bus or car, you cross the expanse of the Magdalena near its mouth on an almost mile-long bridge.

Norcy and I walked around the Centro (and thus some markets) for much of the afternoon and visited the newly-refurbished Plaza de San Nicolás, which housed the gleaming white and orange Iglesia de San Nicolás de Tolentino. Much of the city landscape, such as the signs for *llamadas* on every corner, was similar to the Colombia I was getting to know. These booths had cell phones chained to them, which you could pay to use to call friends and family on any of Colombia's cell phone companies. You never had to hunt down a phone booth or get change to make a call in Colombia.

Less familiar to me was seeing foreign food restaurants, which reflected Barranquilla's high immigrant population. Next to the Estadio Metropolitano (home to the beloved Juniors fútbol club) was not only a Colombian restaurant with a yellow Aguila beer sign, but also a restaurant with green Asian lettering reading "Pao Pey." It had an upstairs balcony complete with a small pagoda.

After four months eating the various combinations of Colombian starches and oil, my mouth watered for some Chinese or Lebanese food. However, instead, I diligently followed Norcy to one of the large shopping malls in the city. In Colombia, malls are much more than conglomerations of clothing and electronic stores. They are places for families to hang out, grocery shop, and have a fast food (read: over-priced but brand-named) dinner out. Cartagena also had malls: three (Barranquilla has *fourteen*). I usually walked through the air condition-ing as quickly as possible—my backpack full of groceries—passing var-ious furniture shops, clothing stores, shoe stores, a Tommy Hilfiger, a McDonalds, a Subway, an Adidas, and a Home Depot-sized home store with the imaginative name of Home Center (yes, in English). So instead of indulging myself with sweet and sour pork or giant skewers of lamb, Norcy and I had mall pizza for dinner.

But it was eventually back to Cartagena for me, and the next day I arrived late in the evening, just in time to round out my touristy week with an evening of people watching and a night in a hostel in Colombia's most touristy city.

During my next morning's wandering around Cartagena's Centro, I happened to walk by one of the main churches at eight o'clock just as they were starting a Maundy Thursday service. Figuring both my students and I would need all the prayers we could get for the next three quarters of classes, I headed inside Iglesia de San Pedro Claver, one of Cartagena's most iconic churches and buildings. The church has a simple interior and a beautiful stone exterior, which is attached to a convent by the same name, named for Jesuit missionary San Pedro Claver.

Born in Spain in 1590, San Pedro Claver was the first person to be canonized in the New World for his work caring for slaves brought into Cartagena. Claver would enter the squalor of holding "pens" and slave ships, distributing food and medicine to the people within. While the city and many of his fellow priests profited from the slave trade, he argued that Africans, as fellow human beings and fellow Christians (he was also said to have baptized 300,000 people during his almost 40 years of ministry), were also entitled to personal freedom and civil rights. Claver died in 1654 in Cartagena and the old saint himself still rests at the church's altar in a glass coffin—with his skull still visible. Whether it was supposed to be a tourist attraction or a reminder to parishioners of the frailty of life, it certainly kept my gaze.

An elderly priest (who needed either a new microphone or a new larynx) led the service, which consisted of some Bible readings, an offering, and communion. And then it was over—perhaps in the running for the world's shortest Mass. After a short respite (maybe the priest was getting water, saying prayers for strength, or getting injected with stimulants), the priest came out again and the fifty or so people who had been sitting quietly in the pews suddenly rushed to the altar and stood in a line to get blessed. The priest put some holy oil on each person's forehead and said a few words, then the person bowed their head, clasped their hands, and headed back down the aisle.

It was a pretty diverse group of Colombians in church that morning (although I think I was the only one who didn't live in the neighborhood), with lighter-skinned, wealthier Colombians mixing with middle class blacks, younger couples, elderly women, and a few beggars. I watched a couple of men cross themselves continually as they ritualistically touched part of a statue of Jesus, the stone worn from so many people doing the same thing.

As soon as the last person who was in line for the priest's blessing got their forehead oiled, a lady standing in front of the two giant wooden doors shooed everyone out.

"Estamos cerrado. We are closed," she said, scowling at us.

Apparently they thought God was busy for the rest of the afternoon.

Good Friday (*Viernes Santo*) was the big day in Catholic Colombia, celebrating (if that is the correct word) Jesus' crucifixion. Large and small churches across Colombia held processions of relics and crosses through the streets, ending at churches that held more Masses in the morning and evening. Viernes Santo was the day most people had off, and I have it on good authority that it is the one Friday of the year when Colombia's upbeat nightlife slows down.

The Catholic Church was a large presence no matter where I was in Colombia, but Protestantism was more dominant with Afro-Colombian populations. Santa Ana had a Catholic Church like any other self-respecting Colombian town (it might be a law for all I know), but it didn't have a full-time priest, and I never saw Mass being held.

Once I was back in Santa Ana on Easter Sunday, I went to one of the successful evangelical startups with my across-the-road neighbors Eliza and Elfriem and their family. The service was held at the tiny church they attended every Sunday.

About an hour into the three-hour service (we chose to be about forty-five minutes late, which for coastal Colombians was practically early), the plastic chairs were full. About sixty people sang along with a man as he played an electronic keyboard, which was also providing the drum and horn section. This was followed by an enthusiastic prayer by the preacher, then another man led a few upbeat songs. He shouted into the mic, trying to be heard over the sounds of conga drums, a guiro (or as it is known, a *guacharaca*), and maracas in addition to the keyboard.

However, vacation had made me soft and I forgot the cardinal rule of choosing a seat in Colombia: make sure you are in front of the fan. I was kicking myself the whole time, or would have been if I was not constantly wiping my face. With sweat dripping down my back and legs and pooling on my forehead and chest, my religious experience that morning felt a little like I was getting re-baptized—and I'm not talking about the sprinkling of holy water, but the full immersion dunk-you-in-a-lake type.

I didn't get much out of the sermon. Instead, all I really did was take gulps of water (luckily I don't go anywhere further than my own kitchen without a water bottle), fan myself, and wipe sweat off my face, making it hard to concentrate on what the preacher was saying.

His accent was so thick and he was so excited by his sermon that it was hard for me to catch even a few words.

"Pero tenemos something something something something!"

"Aleluya, Jesu Cristo!" the congregation responded together.

"Something something, niños something something," the preacher continued.

"A sus hermanos!" the congregation shouted, raising their hands in the air.

"Y por eso, es necesario a something something something! Amen?"

"Amen!"

I was a bit confused by the sermon and by how the congregation managed to time their responses perfectly with the split second pauses the preacher used to take a quick breath before plowing on.

I politely declined Eliza and Elfriem's offer to return again for the evening service and prayed that the water would be on when I got back to the Villa.

And *gracias a dios,* it was.

CHAPTER EIGHT

A Walk About Town

While most of the unpaved, rocky beige road that passed through Santa Ana and connected the island posed no problems for trucks, motos, horse carts, donkeys, or gringo pedestrians, there was one part of the road that challenged all who tried to pass. Through some trick of nature there was always a spot where water sat in perpetuity, stretching across the entire road in defiance of the heat and strong tropical sun.

The Puddle.

It stayed there, day in and day out, shifting its shape with every rain.

Every day when I neared The Puddle on my walk to and from school, I would search for the best route around it. Should I jump over oozing gray-brown mud? Should I wobble on the broken-off slabs of concrete that orbited the water, creating a precarious set of stepping-stones? Some days The Puddle liked to disguise itself as solid-looking mud, but if you walked across it, it would grab hold of your shoe as if it was trying to start a collection. Other days The Puddle tried to hide under piles of rocks brought in on dump trucks, but it was still there, creeping and ready to make you slip and fall.

Despite the efforts of workers using backhoes, pipes, and shovels, The Puddle always remained.

Most days I made it across The Puddle unscathed. But I was not the only one who had to navigate the shifting waters.

On one particular day, it was nice and overcast due to a storm from the night before that had left behind clouds and cooler temperatures, making the walk back from school almost pleasurable. The rain had caused the entire area to be covered in mud and it looked like mudslides from Mt. St. Helens had just passed through. A thin man wearing a baseball cap was driving a backhoe, moving rock and dirt on top of the murky water, and trying to make the road look like, well, a road. The process seemed to be succeeding, and instead of the giant pool usually in the road, soon I could only see disembodied patches of water seeping up through the stones and soil.

But The Puddle was still there, lurking.

Then up came one of the Decameron Resort's large charter buses, full of Colombian tourists with sunburns and sun hats, heading back to the reality of their lives and jobs.

The driver knew the danger of this spot in the road (and even if he didn't, the backhoe should have clued him in). The bus paused at the edge of The Puddle's domain before going in with hesitation. At first, the bus seemed to have the upper hand, continuing forward despite loud sucking sounds coming from the deep mud.

And then the bus stopped continuing forward. Tires spun. The bus lurched a little to one side as it tried to reverse. But it could neither go forward nor backward and The Puddle was having a good laugh at the charter bus's expense.

It was not the only one that was laughing. With little in the way of entertainment in Santa Ana, soon dozens of people were watching the driver spin his tires. The looks of the tourists onboard were a mixture of excitement and worry that they might be perpetually stuck in Santa Ana. The looks of the Santaneros lining the street were mostly of mild amusement.

While I stood there, wondering if there was a Spanish word for *schadenfreude*, I realized I was living two lives: that of the people on the bus and also that of the people watching from the street. I was living in Santa Ana for just a year, with my return ticket to the U.S. already booked, and compared to most Santaneros, I was living in comparative luxury in the town until then. As for our bus, after failures with a shovel and a snapped fire hose, it was pulled free forty minutes later with a chain. But I was also part of the town, living some of the hardships and starting to understand what being a Santanero and Colombian was all about.

Considering this Bus vs. The Puddle bout was one of the highlights of my week, the excitement in my life was on par with the laid-back costeño attitude of town.

To get a little exercise and try to immerse myself in my surroundings, I would often go walking in the morning or the evening (not avoiding the heat, but at least avoiding the heat of the day).

Sometimes I headed down the side road that led past farms and hills until its terminus at the bright white gates of the Decameron Resort. Enjoying the green fields, trees, and usually an amazing array of birds, I would avoid the Decameron buses kicking up clouds of brown dust and greet men as they trotted to and from town on their donkeys or horses.

Other times, I would walk up the main road, climbing the small dusty hill past a small rock quarry and through an open forest. After about a mile and a half, I would sometimes cut down from the road and go through some trees until I ended up at what the Santaneros call La Cova, the cove that formed an inlet in Barbacoas Bay. This was no white sand beach. Here the Caribbean was gray-green and choppy, with rocks and coarse sand. I'd watch the waves crash against the gnarled rocks and look out as a one-sailed fishing canoe bobbed by.

I would walk back along the road, enjoying the evening air and occasional shade from the edges of the forest that lined both sides of the dusty track. And always without fail, a friendly mototaxi driver would slow down next to me and ask if I needed a ride into town. (Confusion about why anyone would choose to "just go for a walk" was rampant amongst Santaneros; "going for a jog" was an even weirder concept to most and Alyssa and TL got strange looks when they went for a run.)

But one thing I liked best about living in Santa Ana was I could walk through the streets of the town (careful to avoid the piles of cow dung and the rivers of sludgy green water trickling down the middle of the streets) and feel like I belonged despite my U.S. American-accented Spanish and pale skin.

My fellow volunteers and I were the only gringos in town and even kids who weren't my students would shout "Teacher!" "Howareyoufinesankyou!" or "Morning!" at me (even if it was evening) as I strolled past small shops and concrete houses, dripping with sweat. Tiny primary school students in their blue tartan Barbacoas pinafores gave me shy smiles. My middle schoolers would duck away with wide, wry grins and whisper their response to my "How are you?" worried their peers would think they weren't *bacano* (cool) if they greeted their teacher. Sullen high schoolers still in their red pants and worn uniform shirts would respond to my encouraging grin by breaking into smiles. I would briefly interrupt their games with a hello and then they would go back to kicking around old soccer balls, spinning old bike wheels down the streets, playing marbles, chasing animals, watching TV, helping their parents work, and taking care of their younger siblings.

Considering how small Santa Ana was, it was strange to me that four, six, and even eight months into living in Colombia I could still discover places that I didn't know about before. There was a tiny boathouse of sorts selling gasoline that was tucked into the northeast corner of town. A long open area (I can't quite bring myself to call it a street) followed the eastern edge of town along the coastline—a muddy tidal track strewn with trash but ending at a tiny inlet framed with tall trees. Narrow side streets led to muddy courtyards of small homes, which I passed through by jumping on broken pieces of concrete to try to avoid as much of the saturated mud as possible. At the southwest end of town, next to a small inlet, was an impromptu dump with heaps of garbage piled up: empty chip bags, plastic soda bottles, broken chairs, and a number of plastic flip-flops. Some of the trash floated in the murky water and nearby a heron fished.

I would walk a loop through town, passing Santaneros holding umbrellas to keep out the strong sun, or I would cross the street to avoid the dogs barking and snarling at each other. I always liked to swing by school to say hello to whichever guards were there and then might head across the street for a cold one—an ice cream that is.

Because few local women drank in public, I had sworn off beer in Santa Ana, and unfortunately no one sold Milo juice on the island, so if I was feeling overheated, craved something cold, or had had an unusually bad day at school, ice cream from the shop just across the street from IESA was my purchase of choice.

The store may have had an actual name, but our group of volunteers always referred to it as "The Pan."

In English, "The Pan" would suggest a kitchen store or perhaps a breakfast skillet restaurant. In Spanish, the word for "bread" would be obvious, but the foreign article would be completely... well... foreign.

The Pan referred to the Spanish name of the type of shop: *La Panadería*. That is, Santa Ana's one and only bakery. And it was *the* hangout spot for much of the town, including its party-goers, students, and already-carb-loaded volunteer teachers.

The Pan was run by the Olivero family. Javier was usually at the counter, but his daughter Marianela and his nephew Carlos also worked and I would enjoy running into them outside of class. The baked goods were courtesy of the baking prowess of a man named John (or Jhon, or maybe Jhean), who mostly stayed in the back with the oven, but good gosh, could he bake.

I would walk up the concrete steps of the outside patio and look over the selection in front of me. They had various loaves of bread (including my favorite whole grain rolls), breads with cheese, breads with guava or other fruit baked in, and breads made with *arequipe*, a caramel-like *dulce de leche* sweet spread. Croissants or Danish-like treats were also available (some even drizzled with chocolate) as were cookies and scrumptiously-decorated cakes.

Behind the counter, it turned into more than a bakery and ice cream shop. Waters, Gatorade, and soda were sold in varying sizes, along with bags of chips and snacks, cookies, lollipops, bags of milk, sausages, toilet paper, and laundry soap. Talk about one-stop shopping.

Javier or Marianela would unlock the ice cream freezer sitting to the side so I could see the selection for the day and I would pick out a coconut, guanábana, or chocolate ice cream bar.

"Como está la escuela?" Javier might ask me about school. "The students here are tough, aren't they?" Javier's tan rather than black skin revealed him to be a more recent resident of Santa Ana, having moved to the town a year ago from the northern coast.

"Yeah, they are difficult some days," I would respond, unwrapping my ice cream and tossing the wrapper in the trash. "But Marianela is never a problem. She and Carlos are great in all their classes." And it was true. Between Marianela's dedication to school, Carlos's sharp mind, and Javier's ice cream, the Olivero family was sometimes my saving grace.

You could usually find at least a couple of people enjoying the shade and a treat or beer under the store's sagging red awning. Santaneros would sit at The Pan's plastic tables, sometimes relaxed, looking out at the cars, motorcycles, pedestrians, cows, donkeys, and pigs going by. Other times they would shout out conversations over the deafening beats a salsa or *vallenato* hit pumping out of the wall-mounted speakers.

The Pan's decorative description, written on the outside wall above the hand-sprayed picture of a square pink four-layer cake, said it all: *para toda ocacion.* For every occasion.

And if my day at school was a disaster or the heat threatened to overwhelm me, or for those times I just really wanted a beer but could compromise with ice cream, The Pan (and the Olivero family) got me through the day.

If I was still feeling hungry or having an especially bad day, on my way back from picking up ice cream or bread I would make a detour to a house near Barbacoas, where I could pick up the best snack in Santa Ana (and Colombia): *deditos.*

The name of this food is not particularly endearing and is an unusual choice for an edible product sold to the general public: dedito means "little finger." So I should quickly make the assurance that deditos do not contain meat of any kind.

The pastries get their name from their tall, elongated shape. Sweet wheat dough is rolled around soft cheese or jam-like fruit, then deep-fried. Tender, with a flaky exterior, the cheese deditos are a perfect mix of sweet and salty while the guava *bocadillos* taste a bit like a jam doughnut.

You could get deditos all over Colombia, but in all my travels and sampling of street fare, it was no exaggeration that the best ones I ever ate were from a tiny pink house just down the street in Santa Ana.

It wasn't a shop per se, but simply the front kitchen of another concrete house along a row near Barbacoas. The family rolled out large plastic platters of deditos every hour and fried them up, selling them to Barbacoas students, hungry gringo teachers, and mototaxi drivers who stopped by.

If you were thirsty, they also sold juice, the flavors which changed daily: cherry, passion fruit, guava, and *jugo de arroz*—rice juice. Now, I've never personally attempted to squeeze the juice out of a grain of rice, but apparently it can be done—just in case someone wanted to drink even more rice with the inevitable serving of rice with their lunch. The juice was a milky white, mixed with sugar, and while it was not something I sought out, it was surprisingly refreshing.

Whatever type of juice they had mixed up for the day was handed to you in a thin, clear plastic bag which, needless to say, surprised me the first time it had happened. After having taken the bag, I looked awkwardly around for a place to set it down so I could free my hands and pay the 1,000 pesos for the dedito and juice. Unable to set the bag down without spilling it, I had to hand it back so I could fish out a crumpled bill from my pocket. But after some thought, I have come to the conclusion that juice in bags made sense.

While there was the problem with being able to set it down, it was portable and easily drinkable with the tall straw I was given. Bags were the norm for food, drinks, condiments—every kind of food or beverage you can think of in Colombia. If you ordered a soda to go at a store, they opened up the glass bottle, poured it in a bag, and handed it to you with a straw. Ketchup and jam came in squeeze bags at all the markets. Milk would stay in bags for weeks until opened. If you ordered salt, flour, eggs, or oil at a shop, it would come in a thin, clear baggie.

But the best thing you could get in a bag was drinking water. In addition to water bottles, vendors in city streets and rural shops all sold small bags of water, which were at least half the price of bottles (with my white skin and backpack, I would always be offered a 2,000 peso water bottle before I assured the vendor I wanted his 500 peso bag). I didn't have to worry about the seals being broken on the bottle, and since I couldn't recycle plastic bottles anyhow (Colombia is not exactly in the forefront of sustainability), bags created a lot less trash.

Of course, getting the thick plastic open took a little practice.

In the beginning of my year in Colombia, I would pull out my trusty Leatherman knife and carefully slit open one side. This would invariably cause some of the water to spill out before I could bring it up to my mouth to slurp up the refreshing liquid. Eventually I figured I might as well take my cue from the locals and open the bags with my teeth.

The first time I attempted this, I was successful in getting the thick plastic open by squeezing the bag as I ripped it open with my back molars, creating a hole that quickly emptied half of the bag onto my shirt. I looked around nonchalantly, as if dousing myself had been the game plan all along.

The next time I tried to open it with my front teeth, it sent a strong stream of water directly into my left eye. Blinking, I lost control of the bag and it slipped out of my hands and sloshed onto the ground.

My third attempt with my teeth opened a hole so tiny I started to feel light-headed while trying to suck the water out.

But after a few weeks of learning the timing and style of bag ripping, I could open one like a local, tearing a hole perfectly sized to take a deep drink or to dump its contents into my water bottle. The perfect balance of hand pressure around the bag, the speed of the rip, which teeth to use, the right angle on the bag—someone should do a scientific study.

So once I had enough practice, chilled bagged water was a sure way to try to beat some of the humid Colombian heat. Depending on how long my walk was around Santa Ana, I would either stop by The Pan to get water or ice cream from Javier or head to the house to give into my craving for deditos and bagged juice.

But usually my stops were not planned. One Sunday I passed a man painting the wall of a home, and he came down off his ladder as I walked past.

"Buenas," I greeted him with a smile and a nod.

He stuck out his hand in response, and asked, "He visto antes?" Had he seen me before?

"I live here," I responded in Spanish as I shook his callused hands. "I am one of the English teachers here."

"At Barbacoas?"

"No, at the public school," I was quick to respond to show my loyalty.

"But you are from the United States?" he asked, his eyes crinkling with either deep thought or the start of a smile.

"Yes, I am here for the year," I said.

"I lived in the United States," was his surprising next response.

The man, whose name was Victor, had worked on a boat all over the Caribbean, including in Miami. We chatted a bit and he expressed the usual surprise that somehow I was from the United States but had never been to Miami or New York, then he returned to his painting.

Not long after shaking Victor's gnarled hand goodbye, I passed the home of Jhon Carlos, one of my seventh graders, who was watching *The Simpsons*. It was dubbed in Spanish, was in black and white, and was apparently the acting ambassador for the United States that afternoon. Still, when Jhon Carlos saw me walk past, he left the show to run out and say hi.

"Enseño!" he called. I turned at the sound of his voice shouting out the now-familiar title for "teacher" and greeted him as I caught a glimpse of his TV.

From TV shows to music, Santaneros don't need to move to the United States or even attend my classes to connect to U.S. culture.

After chatting with Jhon Carlos, I headed to what was the closest thing that could be called Santa Ana's downtown and dropped into what we called the Everything Store, which was one of two stores in Santa Ana that sold clothing, school supplies, fans, kitchen utensils, and other random items you couldn't find anywhere else on the island. Once inside, I searched in vain for poster board for class. I eventually gave up and headed a few blocks up, and sat in the shade near a marsh on the north side of town. I enjoyed the shade and greeted two men who walked by with a thick log balanced on their shoulders, which had a boat motor strapped to it.

One of my eighth graders, the always-grinning Luis Felipe, showed up, wheeling his uncle's motorcycle. He was with two younger brothers (or cousins—the line was always a little fuzzy for me). Dunking a plastic bucket into the marsh, he then carefully cleaned the machine while the younger boys watched wistfully. A family walked by next, the mother balancing a giant plastic container on her head and the father holding a bucket filled with small, silvery fish.

The man looked at me hopefully. "Puede encontrar camarón!" he said, indicating the container on his wife's head. Apparently it contained shrimp.

"Sí, camarones," I repeated in a tone I hoped implied that I agreed and was happy for him, but I didn't want to buy any. "Y cómo se llama estes?" I asked, indicating the fish in his bucket.

"Gida," he responded, and Luis Felipe came over to check it out.

"Gida?" I repeated, unsure on the name of the fish.

"Gida," confirmed Luis Felipe, before he went back to washing his motorcycle and the family moved on down the street. Their young son, holding his mom's hand, peeked at me around his mother's legs, then didn't give me a backwards glance.

That was fine by me—I felt a little more like a resident now that the novelty of my white skin had worn off.

After saying goodbye to Luis Felipe and the other boys, I looped back to the middle of town, where I heard the unmistakable crack of a baseball bat and the cheer of a crowd as I neared the sports field.

It was an organized game of softball between the towns of Santa Ana and Pasacaballos, and women who could have been in high school or in their twenties were warming up for a game. A crowd sat in the shade, cheering them on as music blasted.

Each woman wore a uniform (red and white for Pasacaballos and blue and gray for Santa Ana) with "IDER" printed on the front, which stood for the sponsor of the league: Cartagena's Recreation and Sports District. They even seemed to have coaches and official umpires, though the players exchanged catcher's equipment and batting helmets between each inning depending on who was up to bat.

Like in much of the Caribbean, baseball was a popular sport in Cartagena and cable channels regularly broadcasted Major League Baseball games in both English and Spanish (there are a few Colombian MLB players as well, including the 2010 World Series MVP, Edgar Rentería). When I asked the IESA teachers from Cartagena what sports they liked, most listed baseball first. Pedro liked to imitate baseball players by pretending to swing a bat and guard an imaginary first base, trying (and failing) to look light on his feet.

Cycling was also popular throughout Colombia; the country won three cycling medals in the 2012 Olympics and Colombian Nairo Quintana finished as a runner-up in the 2013 Tour de France.

Then there was *tejo,* which has been played in Colombia for over 450 years and is sort of like horseshoes, but played with metal discs thrown at gunpowder targets that explode when hit. Luckily, it isn't a contact sport, except in the cases when the losing team decides they don't like the outcome (tejo is always accompanied by both teams drinking copious amounts of alcohol, which adds another interesting dynamic to the game).

But in reality, no sport in Colombia can compete in popularity with soccer.

In a third grade class at Barbacoas, TL was teaching a song that included the word "god" for the school's English Week and she asked her students if anyone knew what it meant. One energetic third grader replied by putting his arms up high over his head in a show of triumph and shouting, "GOOOOOOOLLLL!"

Who can fault him for confusing the two? Catholicism might be the official religion, but Colombia's favorite sport easily has more followers.

Boys and girls alike played soccer in the streets and in open fields. Every Colombian city, town, and tiny village I went to had at least one concrete cancha with a goal at each end. I often saw jerseys from teams from Spain and England on the streets, along with jerseys from Colombian clubs and the bright yellow of Colombia's national team, *Los Cafeteros.* The Colombian soda company Big Cola had pictures of the Barcelona team on its labels. Let's say it was a good thing I liked and followed soccer—I think I won a few points from my students by knowing a few players besides Lionel Messi.

Soccer, football, *fútbol:* it is easily the most popular sport in the world. Just compare the amount of people who watch and follow the

World Cup (or European championships, or club championships) with those who watch the championship games for any other sports.

And it is not hard to see why. Unlike football (the U.S. kind), basketball, baseball, cricket, hockey, and most sports that need specialized equipment, a game of soccer doesn't need much to start playing. You don't really need a field; just an open space and any street or vacant lot will do. You don't need goal posts as long as you have sticks or jackets or rocks. And you don't even need a ball. Tie together a bunch of plastic bags or use an empty bottle and hours of fun can ensue.

The Santa Ana dirt sports field provided an optimal place to play. Instead of the cramped and sometimes painful concrete canchas at Barbacoas and IESA, this field was full-sized, had a dirt surface, and actual goals. And thanks to the donation from a foundation a few years back, there was even a covered set of concrete bleachers on one end so the town could come out and watch the games in the shade. Whether people watched pick-up scrambles or organized matches played by teams of middle schoolers, high schoolers, or men in their twenties, soccer was some of the only entertainment Santa Ana offered outside of drinking and dancing, and families could sit in the bleachers and watch the young men of the town kick around a soccer ball. I'd always pause on my walks at the field to see what was going on, occasionally staying to cheer on my students, who would give me shy waves from the field.

Whenever the Colombian national team was playing a game, the entire town would erupt in collective cheers or groans whenever a goal was scored. All over the country, Colombians would crowd around fuzzy televisions to cheer on their team who dressed in the national colors: their large yellow jerseys, blue shorts, and red socks made the players themselves into human representatives of the tri-colored Colombian flag.

Colombia hasn't made a splash at the world level since the 1994 World Cup, where they went in as the top-ranked team (they had only lost one game in the thirty-four games leading to the World Cup). However, the competition was marred when the team received death threats prior to their matches from people linked to Colombian drug cartels, which may have been the reason they did not advance out of the group stage. Star striker and captain, Andrés Escobar, scored an own goal (that would be against his own team... whoops) while playing the United States, solidifying Colombia's failure at the competition. Upon his return to Colombia, Escobar (no relation to Pablo Escobar) was murdered, allegedly because of Colombia's loss. Still, excitement for soccer never waned, whether it was for Colombia's many club teams, the country's beloved Cafeteros, or the Santaneros in mismatched jerseys, kicking around a ball on their sports field.

Regardless of what I ended up doing in town, or how long I stayed to watch soccer or baseball games, I usually finished up my wanderings through Santa Ana's streets by swinging by a store to supplement my provided groceries. Dozens of small shops stocking produce, dry goods, and household items dotted the streets, interspersed with the concrete homes without any clear distinction. I had my favorite stores, and from Barbacoas I usually headed to the left, to a store we called the Green Store or simply "the store in urbanization," which was the name of the tiny neighborhood it was located in. The store had two official names of its own: Tienda Don Pedro and *El Condorito* (The Condor), a painted vulture head smiling happily on the green wall. Yet for all of its names, like the other shops in town, it consisted of a simple metal counter with tall shelves behind, where the worker would grab whatever item you pointed out.

I'd walk up and greet the young man working or fight my way to the front of a line of women and children as they waved crumpled bills or slammed a few coins down on the metal counter, shouting their shopping lists.

"Two eggs! Three potatoes! A bag of milk! Salt! Laundry soap! A bag of oil!" Small kids reaching only halfway up the counter would buy themselves suckers or ask for one or two cigarettes that an older relative had sent them to get (I never saw many kids smoking; it was a habit that was probably too expensive for most).

When I was able to catch the eye of the man behind the counter, I'd ask for tomatoes, cookies, eggs or whatever else I was getting (it would usually involve an unhealthy bag of chips or Cheese Tris), pay the few pesos, and head towards home, ready to traverse the last of the streets before entering the gates of Barbacoas.

Inevitably, I'd greet someone I knew, get a little too much mud on my shoes, eye a few donkeys or cows suspiciously, and pass The Puddle as I once again left the streets of Santa Ana behind.

CHAPTER NINE

The Sounds of Colombia

"Qué re ma' arro?"

I stared at Bleidis and blinked.

"Qué?"

"Qué re ma' arro?"

I stared some more. That could not be Spanish.

Bleidis repeated the phrase a third time and gestured; not with her hand, but in the typically Colombian manner of puckering her lips as if she was about to kiss someone in a comical fashion while pointing them in the direction of the thing she wanted to show me. In this case, Bleidis pointed her lips towards a giant aluminum pot, and I finally realized what she meant.

"Did I want any more rice?"

Apparently, in classroom Spanish Bleidis had not said "Qué re ma' arro?" Instead, it was "Quieres más arroz?"

While my answer was an obvious "no" (More rice? Are you kidding?), most things were not so straightforward to translate. So much for the adage that if you can pronounce Spanish you can spell it.

Bleidis and every Santanero spoke *castellano costeño* (coastal Spanish), which was heavily accented, especially among the Afro-Colombian community, and full of slang. So while my Spanish certainly was not up to par to follow most people's conversations, I felt consoled that people from Bogotá had similar problems when trying to understand costeños. The rapid-fire speech of my students usually left me bewildered. Somehow, it was both slurred and clipped and they used words that weren't in any *diccionario* I had brought with me.

Ironically, Colombia was known for having some of the clearest Spanish of any country, but that only rang true for the interior of the country and the people of Bogotá, Medellín, and any place that didn't border an ocean. Coastal Spanish was a whole different ballgame. In Colombia's far-off islands of San Andrés, Providencia, and Santa Catalina, Afro-Colombian residents even speak their own Creole language, Bende.

While most of the Afro-Colombians around Cartagena may not have had an official language of their own besides Spanish, they had a subculture of music, dance, and slang. African-originated dances and rhythms have an overwhelming influence on modern Colombian styles, and it was with music and dance that Santaneros celebrated the African influence in Colombia late one evening in May in Santa Ana.

The banner read "Mama Africa" and the town square in front of the Catholic church was bustling with people. May 21 was officially Afro-Colombian Day in Colombia (declared so in 2001), marking the anniversary of the 1851 abolishment of slavery, and it was an evening for celebrating the town's Afro-Colombian heritage.

I looked around the plaza, seeing perhaps 400 people crowding around what would soon turn into a performance space. Families dressed in bright t-shirts and students from Barbacoas sported colorful costumes. To get better a view of the crowd, teenagers climbed the monkey bars at the plaza's small playground, avoiding the most rusted parts. The only non Afro-Colombians present (besides all of us English teachers) were a smattering of mestizo Barbacoas teachers and one of the five policemen stationed in town. Looking around, I saw Marelis, Lilybeth, Norcy, and Bleidis, but no IESA staff members were in attendance, which was no surprise.

My eyes soon caught the face of a familiar woman in her sixties, sporting a white lace dress covered in what looked like tiny strips of colored crepe paper. The lady (whose name might have been Sugey) usually did not exactly stand out from a crowd, mostly due to the fact that she was shorter than many of my sixth graders. That evening, her tiny stature had been raised by a large homemade yellow and red hat with pieces of crepe paper and "Colombiano" spelled out in proud gold letters. I learned later it was not just any crepe paper, but a traditional paper made from—what else—but rice. I grudgingly appreciated how versatile the grain was turning out to be.

I stepped aside to allow a group of kindergarten students, who were barely shorter than Sugey, to walk by. The girls wore long white skirts and blouses and had enough mascara on to qualify as Little Miss Sunshine contestants. They had large fake red flowers in their hair and were paired with tiny kindergarten boys who wore all white, except for red kerchiefs around their necks. The boys held large straw hats, which they periodically took on and off as they shuffled around the girls, dancing shyly.

The Mama Africa Barbacoas celebration had begun.

Different-aged students read poems, told jokes, and danced to the beats of their fellow students' drums and singing. Our theories about the artistic talents of our students (and Santaneros, really) gained further evidence when the students singing were very, very bad and the many groups of dancers were very, very good. A couple of boys showed off their impressive breakdancing skills by the light of a flashlight as the festivities lasted past sunset. Bodies twirled and leaped, feet shuffled and pranced. The crowd smiled and cheered. And the music blasted.

The most popular act was some middle school students who did choreographed *champeta* dances to the popular Afro-Colombian music of the same name.

Champeta is West African music sung in Spanish—or, that is, costeño Spanish—and was born of the poorest of Afro-Colombian neighborhoods in and around Cartagena, which was why it was so popular in Santa Ana. Some songs seemed to come directly from West African traditionals, while others were a mix of African undertones and Caribbean beats. Champeta is both a style of music and a dance and because champeta is only popular within a small culture in Colombia, it also can become an identity. I am not sure residents of Isla Barú had a choice: everyone had to like champeta. It was the music always played during breaks at school, and at dance parties in the town.

While champeta is not well liked in all parts of Colombia, Afro-Colombian day was celebrated in other ways in many parts of Colombia. In Cartagena, like in many cities with significant black populations, the actual day was marked with conferences, cultural activities, marches, and street parties.

As Marelis described it: "They'll be celebrations and events in the streets with singers and dancers. And of course it is different when the event is not connected with a school, so it is a big party."

I am not sure what cultures invented rum and *aguardiente* (the ubiquitous anise-flavored Colombian liquor that translates to "fiery water"), but those two things certainly bring together Colombians of every race and heritage.

Besides having drinks present, I believe it is also a federal law in Colombia that every celebration with over twenty people must include a beauty pageant.

So after the excellent dancing and painful singing, the main event at the Mama Africa celebration was a hair and model competition for a girl from each grade. Their hair was made up in all sorts of creative ways and was graded on whether or not it looked African. The criteria for this was a little ambiguous considering 250 years had passed since most Santaneros had ancestors that actually lived in Africa. The irony was not lost on me that although I was one of the whitest people there, I was probably the only person in the crowd who had actually been to Africa (I spent five months in Tanzania during college).

In the beauty contest, contestants had intricate braids, afros and headbands, cornrows, and long tresses. The winner for the high schoolers had tied up her short hair and added small pointy sticks, which made her look a little like a porcupine, but it was certainly creative and a labor of love. Her dark face broke out with a wide smile as she jumped up and down with excitement.

The sign in the plaza may have celebrated "Mama Africa," and the students may have been laughing, singing, and dancing around to deep Africa beats with smiles on their faces, but in years past, celebrating their heritage was looked down upon and sometimes impossible.

The history of blacks in Colombia has traditionally been ignored by most of the country—similar in many ways to other African populations in the Caribbean and in Central and South America. (I myself was surprised to learn that Brazil is the country with the second-largest black population in the world, after Nigeria.)

Colombia has the second-highest black population in Latin America and the third largest Afro-descendent population after Brazil and the United States, though no one seemed positive about the actual numbers of Colombians of African descent. Estimates on the percentage of Colombians that are black vary from about 10% to 25% with some believing it to be as high as 35%. (While a 2005 survey only categorized 4% of the population as Afro-Colombian, 14% of the population had a mix of African and European heritage, 3% had a mix of African and Amerindian, and around 11% of people self-identified as Afro-Colombian. No wonder there is confusion.) A high percentage of Afro-Colombians live along the Pacific and Caribbean coasts, but they also live in large populations in all of Colombia's major cities and regions.

In the 1500s, the Spanish first brought blacks to Colombia to the very area where I was living because the colonizers needed another population to exploit after killing off most of the indigenous population with disease and by forcing them to work in mines and on plantations. The Spanish looked overseas for their next source of free and morally-dubious labor, and boatloads of Africans arrived on the Caribbean coast. Cartagena had the largest slave market in the Americas, a market located in the plaza right behind today's iconic clock tower that signaled the entrance to the Centro. In fact, African slaves were the main labor force used to build the wall that surrounds the historic Centro, and both the products of their physical labor and their additions to Colombian culture were everywhere, especially on the coasts.

Nueva Granada, as Colombia/Panama was named until Panama declared independence in 1903, officially abolished slavery on May 21, 1851, the date we marked with so much celebration even in the 21st century. The newly freed population joined with already-established communities of *palenques* (consisting of freed and escaped Afro-Colombians) all along the coasts, but the struggles of the former slaves didn't end there. In the 1800s, the Colombian government had an official policy of *blanqueamiento* (or "whitening") under the premise that whitening the population would "improve" it, and create a unified mestizo population.

Even in the year I was there, Afro-Colombians still faced more hardships than white or mestizo Colombians. Like so many other predominately-black communities in Colombia, Santa Ana was poor. On average, Afro-Colombians only made $500 a year while white or mestizo Colombians made around $1,600 (indigenous peoples faced even lower numbers). Representation of Afro-Colombians in the government was pitifully low. Afro-Colombians were disproportionally displaced by the decades-long civil war, yet had little voice when negotiations between the government and factions like FARC took place. Afro-Colombians in the more underdeveloped Pacific region had it even worse, and the government, paramilitary groups, and multi-national agriculture corporations have all admitted to collaborating to force Afro-Colombians off their land (many times with violence) to create the new plantations of today for growing bananas and palm trees for oil.

Since few Afro-Colombians lived in the most remote jungle sections of Colombia, Afro-Colombians actually attended primary school at a higher level than the national average. However, Santa Ana was richly blessed with two schools—throughout the country secondary education is only available to 65% of Afro-Colombians. With that, almost 70% of schools in Afro-Colombian communities receive a "poor quality" or "very poor quality" result based on students' scores on the annual eleventh grade end-of-year exam. IESA was one of those schools.

But Afro-Colombian Day gave the students and staff at IESA a chance to celebrate their achievements rather than just focus on their failures. While the Barbacoas teachers had the time and money to host the pueblo-wide event, IESA marked the holiday with special events during the school day. Our multipurpose room was decorated with a large banner denoting the *Día de Afrocolombidad*, the yellow, red, and blue of a large Colombian flag, bright cutouts of some

African dancers, and a map of Colombia filled in with magazine cutouts of people of every color. There were speeches, poems, and dancing. Of course our celebrations also meant a few shortened planning days, a full day of class missed, and another beauty pageant.

Seven girls, dressed in bright sarongs with their hair braided, competed to be the Queen of Afro-Colombian Day by walking around the front of our multipurpose room to loud cheers and whistles. A few boys in tight jeans, t-shirts, and gelled hair joined in as well, strutting in front of their peers, their barefoot feet dusty. Katia was one of the representatives for the eighth grade and she ducked her head bashfully as she grinned, turned, and joined the line of the rest of the contestants. She applauded the pageant's winner, Estafani (or maybe Estefany), who our *coordinador*, Abram, presented with a picture frame wrapped in bright turquoise tissue paper.

Of course, not every student in town or at our schools was black. I didn't exactly go around taking a census and asking the skin color of everyone's great-great grandmothers, but I assumed the majority of Santaneros probably had a mix of European and African ancestors; my students were every shade of black, brown, beige, and tan. There was one indigenous family and a couple of students were so pale that their ancestors must have come from Spain rather than Africa. But at both schools, every student was participating in Afro-Colombian Day celebrations, no matter their heritage. Both Carlos and Marianela, who were some of my lighter-skinned students, read parts of Afro-Colombian history at IESA's celebration.

Under a 1996 law, the Colombian government was required to protect the "ancestral territories of Afro-descendants" and to invest in these areas and help protect and promote Afro-Colombian culture. This law may be one of the reasons that all my students took Afro-culture as a required class, where they learned about African heritage in Colombia and the struggle persons of African descent have faced around the world. They learned about famous black Colombians and read plays, poems, and political writings from prominent Afro-Colombians. And hopefully students across all of Colombia did so as well, because, from fighting in the ranks of the Independence armies, to their artisan work, to food to music, Afro-Colombians have played a major role in the culture and history of Colombia.

Heck, even coffee is from Africa.

While my students mostly listened to the distinctly African beats of champeta, all of their favorite songs owed a lot to the music of Africa. Everyone in Latin America, whether black, white, mestizo, or indigenous, dances to the beats of Africa: salsa, cumbia, samba, tango, cha-cha, and pretty much any Latin dance you can think of were originally African rhythms brought over to the Americas by slaves. These influences are now simply "Latin," and no matter where I went in Colombia, I couldn't escape the catchy Latin rhythms.

Literally, I couldn't escape.

Music pumped out of cars and buses, blasted from speakers in people's homes, spilled into neighborhoods from clubs, and emitted—a bit muffled—from cell phones or small portable speakers carried by people as they walked down the street. Radios blasting from doorways would compete with each other, sometimes causing the beats of one song to mix in with the melody of another. Taxis played music, shopping malls played music. And Colombians loved to randomly break into a few lines of a song, whether they were cooking, working, or sitting with you having a conversation.

Thanks to the traditions of African immigrants, Colombia music has distinctive beats, and the country has a musical heritage to rival any country in Latin America. And like the different regions, ethnicities, and cultures in the country, music exhibited diversity in Colombia.

Anyone listening to pop radio from the 1990s onwards has mostly likely heard Colombian music, thanks to Isabel Mebarak Ripoll, who you probably know as Shakira. It's debatable whether it was her voice or rock-hard abs and hips that made her famous, but there's no denying that her catchy rhythms are danced to all over the world.

Some of Shakira's songs were popular in Colombia, especially at *discotecas*, but these days she is more of an international pop sensation than a hit in Colombia. However, I *did* heard "Waka Waka" in pretty much every town I ever visited.

On the flip side, there is Medellín-born Juanes (or as his mother calls him, Juan Esteban Aristizábal Vásquez), who is just as successful (both of Colombia's most famous singers have two Grammys, though if you are keeping count, Juanes has twenty Latin Grammys to Shakira's eight). In general, Juanes is much more popular in Latin America than Shakira and his Latin style is more rock than pop.

In the interior (or in Bogotá-owned supermarkets anywhere), you might hear some of Colombia's newest pop, whether it be Shakira, Juanes, or one of the other flash-in-the-pan stars while I was there: Fanny Lú and the slightly longer lasting Fonseca, a 2012 nominee for best Latin Pop album. Apparently to make it big in the Colombian music industry you either had to only have one name or you had to sound like a southern belle from the 1950s (though to be fair, Fanny Lú does have a degree in industrial engineering—go figure).

There *is* one type of music popular in every corner of Colombia: salsa, which should always be said with flair (as in salzzza!) so it doesn't get confused with the sauce that is squirted on hot dogs or with the Tex-Mex tomato recipe used to dip tortilla chips into.

First introduced in the 1960s, salsa has become one of Colombia's most popular dances, and salsa music continues to be a favorite on the radio. The city of Cali, in the southwest interior, is the undisputed salsa capital of Colombia, but clubs, radio stations, bars, and homes—

from the Guajira deserts in the north to the Amazon rainforest in the south—blast it. Today both salsa dancing and salsa music have specific Colombian styles.

Certainly one of the most popular and famous *salseros* (salzzzeros! to you) was Joe Arroyo, an Afro-Colombian from Barranquilla and Cartagena whose fame and ability to crank out hit after hit continued from the 1970s until his death in 2011. His hit "La Rebellion" was the unofficial anthem of Cartagena, and I will go out on a limb here and say it may be the world's most danceable song about a 17th century slave. The refrain keeps repeating the line "Don't hit the black woman," which may rhyme in Spanish but only sounds mildly better (*no le pegue a la negra*). Still, it always got the crowd going in a discoteca and it's undeniably catchy.

Joe Arroyo may have had the monopoly on popular slave-related songs (I won't dare use the word "hits" here), but still it was champeta that seemed the most popular among Afro-Colombians. I didn't know any champeta singers or bands though, so thought I should do some research.

"Who is your favorite singer" I asked Katia one morning after class when she wanted some extra practice on the English phrases for likes and dislikes.

The always calm and conservatively-dressed Katia thought a moment before replying. "My favorite is Da' Yinki."

"Who? Quién?" I asked (my attempt to understand costeño Spanish failing me again). After I was unsuccessful trying to understand a second time, I handed Katia my dry erase marker to write the name on the board. Excellent, I thought. Katia could practice her English, and I could learn about a local artist.

What she wrote was "Daddy Yanke," which despite missing the last *e* was certainly no local singer, but one of the world's most popular reggaeton artists, who was, in fact, not from Cartagena, but from Puerto Rico. And who definitely did not sing champeta.

There were Colombian reggaeton artists (J Balvin was the most popular; after all, the hip-hop-meets-reggae-meets-Latin beats of reggaeton actually originated in nearby Panama), but Puerto Rican artists dominated the market. Whether listening to the radio or at a discoteca, Don Omar, Pitbull, Angel & Khriz, and Daddy Yankee could be heard in all corners of Colombia.

Along with reggaeton, other styles such as Latin pop, Rock en español, reggae, bachata, and pretty much anything else with a beat streamed over from Puerto Rico, the Dominican Republic, Mexico, Argentina, and Spain. And it was always hard to escape U.S. American music. I heard the hit "On the Floor" quite a few times before I realized it was Jennifer Lopez singing with Pitbull in a strictly mainstream pop hit (however, the reoccurring opening melody was from the 1989 hit "Lambada," a song about a Brazilian dance sung by the French pop group Kaoma, so I felt a little better and worldlier for liking it).

You could rely on some music being on wherever you went in Colombia, and you could also rely on the fact that you never knew what genre you were going to get. I was once listening to the Tropicana radio station coming in from Cartagena, and when the morning news came on, it was read with "Eye of the Tiger" pumping out in the background. "Bum---ba-ba-bum. "[Announcer's voice] A bus crash occurred this morning in the northern neighborhood of... Ba-ba-bum, bum-bum-bummmm... [guitar continues]." Dramatic to say in the least.

When it was not pumping out early 1980s rock hits, the Tropicana station played a mix of salsa and *vallenato*, another typically costeño style popular with everyone from Cartagena up through the Guajira Peninsula and well into Venezuela.

It's a bit difficult to characterize the upbeat rhythms and melodies of vallenato. When I first heard it those first days walking around Santa Ana, I simultaneously envisioned it being played next to some fountain in Bavaria while being accompanied by some 14th century troubadour serenading some royal court. Turns out this wasn't too far from the truth since vallenato is a mixture between the traditions of West African traveling musicians (who played flutes and drums) and European accordion music. Now it is considered a folk music—a bit like Mexico's *mariachi*—and tells the stories and poems of the people on the Caribbean coast. Playing vallenato with guitars is common, but traditionally a vallenato band must include a *guacharaca* (like a guiro), an accordion, flutes, and a small drum called a *caja vallenata*.

Vallenato bands were hard to miss in their coastal black-patterned straw vallenato hats. If you ever visit a Colombian Caribbean town, you will soon notice that the hats are popular tourist souvenirs as well. I advise you not buy one: in my opinion, they should only be worn at soccer matches or while you are actually playing an accordion.

Vallenato's repetitive rhythms constantly blasted out of Santa Ana's homes and businesses, but it was also played by shops and restaurants in the bigger cities. Unlike champeta, which was still looked down upon by the elite and middle class, the folk music of vallenato was much more accepted along the entire coast—but like champeta, I could go an hour or two inland and find few people willing to buy tickets to concerts.

Vallenato's ability to sound both laid back (it was perfect beach music) and intense (which was also the usual way Santaneros would converse) fit well with life in Colombian's Caribbean. However, as I tried to concentrate in my room one afternoon as vallenato pumped out from the houses across the way, I finally figured out what my problem with vallenato was. Its heyday was the 1970s and '80s, so you would hear the same songs repeated over and over. In addition, many of our neighbors blasted the same mix of songs from their homes, which caused vallenato to slip from my personal Top 40 list. When the power would go out and cut off an accordion bridge mid-note, part of me would appreciate the silence (of course, approximately 1.2 seconds after that, the last breeze from my fan would stop and I would have willingly suffered through whatever songs my neighbors wanted as long as the air got moving again).

In the 1990s, Carlos Vives (one of the better named of Colombia's singing stars) became the ambassador of vallenato to the world by combining traditional vallenato songs with pop and other Latin rhythms to appeal to a wider audience. Which means, of course, there were a lot of on-stage gyrations with guitars and accordions. His music became popular around the world for many reasons.

The preschoolers at Barbacoas' celebrations in the plaza danced to another folk music that originated with African slaves on the coast: *cumbia,* a rhythm now ubiquitous to many types of Latin music and still popular in Colombia. Then there was the European-influenced Andean music called *bambuco* (sort of a Colombian polka), *porro* (like Colombian big-band jazz), and *joropo* from Los Llanos (the eastern plains in Colombia), which sounded to me a little like flamenco guitar being played on the harp. Which, by the way, meant it was awesome.

Music played from every corner of Colombia. When the power went off in town, it was peaceful for those two seconds, but then felt almost eerily quiet. Only a power outage or the Armageddon would stop Santaneros from blasting music. Of course, to make up for the quiet on those days without power, there were Fridays, Saturdays, and Sundays when the music blasted across the field and through my room's walls while I was trying to work, watch a movie, or sleep at night. I would have turned it down if the dial had been within reach. I knew how loud it was for those who sat next to the speakers and I tried to avoid being too close to them. How people held conversations by shouting at each other and standing a foot apart I'll never know. And I've never figured out how my students weren't deaf by the time they graduated from high school.

But after I learned reggaeton singer Daddy Yankee was Katia's favorite, I had to learn more. "What is your favorite type of music?" I asked her, ready to translate something like "ra'gon" to "reggaeton."

Katia didn't hesitate. "Champeta, claro." Of course.

Despite music from all over the globe spreading to Santa Ana, champeta and its African origins still had a hold on my students. It was played more than anything else, blasted from speakers, mp3 players, and buses. It was their music. Something Colombians of every heritage could dance to and celebrate—not just once every May—but every day out of the year.

CHAPTER TEN

In the Amazon

A month and a thousand vallenato songs later, I peered out of a tiny airplane window as we broke through the clouds. Below, trees and jungle greenery stretched to the horizon until they merged with the pale sky and faded out in a blue-green tinge. There were no buildings, roads, water tanks, or huts; nothing to indicate humans lived anywhere around. There was also no indication that there was an airport nearby, which was disconcerting considering we were descending lower and lower towards the jungle canopy.

Then suddenly a clearing appeared, then a small road. One house, then a second. And the plane's rubber wheels hit a concrete tarmac as we landed at the Alfredo Vásquez Cobo Airport in Colombia's southernmost city of Leticia. I had arrived in the Amazon.

Stepping out of the door of the plane, the air hit me like a curtain. It was dense and damp, full of flowers and bugs and pollen and smells. I watched a yellow butterfly flit through the two people in front of me and realized there was something familiar about the way the air felt: it was like stepping into a hot and dank butterfly house at a zoo, with its smells of mud, scent of orchids floating past, and that all-to-familiar muggy heat.

I fought my way through my first swarm of Amazon mosquitoes and soon found my hotel at the edge of town, set on a small pond in an open forest. With mosquito net up over my bed, I put on long pants, covered myself in bug spray, and set off to explore Leticia.

The population of Leticia was listed as 33,000, but I didn't see enough buildings to qualify for that number. I assumed smaller towns and villages a few hours boat ride away (Leticia was not connected to any road system) were considered part of Leticia as well. But there just weren't that many people. The entirety of the eastern lowlands of Colombia—the plains and rainforest that made up 54% of Colombia's land mass—house just 3% of Colombia's population.

Leticia's streets were laid out in the center in a methodical grid, with a few restaurants, hotels, and shops of every ilk. On one edge of the city near the river, sat rows of shacks that had been put together with mismatched boards and metal roofs—they had been raised on rows of stilts to try to escape the mud (and during the wet season, a few feet of water).

In the evening you could stand in the middle of downtown Leticia, and if you closed your eyes it was easy to imagine that you were the only human for miles, standing in the middle of a dense jungle. Tiny green parrots screeched in giant flocks, the wind whispered through the trees, frogs and insects seemed to be having a battle of the bands, and if you listened closely, the sound of the gentle waves from the mighty Amazon River drifted in the evening air. No matter how you looked at it, Leticia was just a tiny island within an ocean of thousands of miles of rainforest.

However, there was one side of Leticia without any jungle: I followed International Avenue past a small white sign that read "Bem Vindos ao Brasil" (it was easy to miss), and suddenly realized either someone's spelling had gotten creative or that I just entered Portuguese-speaking Brazil. I glanced every which way to check to see if any border patrol agents were running after me for entering a foreign country without a passport or paperwork, but the only person on the street was a boy kicking a soccer ball around in a puddle. Welcome to Brazil.

I spent most of my time in the Brazilian city of Tabatinga that afternoon darting under overhangs to avoid the worst of the rain that was crashing down from the heavens, reminding me that although there was concrete under my feet, I was still walking around a rainforest. Residents on motos tried to stay dry in all manner of methods: coats on backwards, covering up the handlebars; children wedged between parents; drivers trying to navigate with one hand balancing an umbrella; and passengers covering themselves in trash bags (only their torsos were covered, however, making their legs looked disembodied). You would think that in a city that receives 130 inches of rainfall a year, everyone would have invested in a raincoat (they live in a rainforest for goodness sake). Apparently not.

The cities of Tabatinga, Brazil and Leticia, Colombia weren't even the wettest places in South America. That distinction goes to the small Colombian town of Lloró on the Pacific coast, which receives an average of 523 inches of rain every year (equal to over forty feet and more than four times what Leticia gets), making Lloró officially the wettest place in the world. Lloró translates to "it rained" but also "it cried," which might be your reaction when you wake up every day to gray skies and another flood. I hope that in Lloró, at least, they have all invested in ponchos.

It wasn't raining every day in Leticia however, and one morning I wandered over to the river not long after sunrise. An island across from the city tricked me into thinking that the Amazon River by Leticia was narrower than it actually was, but provided a bit of a harbor away from the choppy open river. Boats, carrying loads of bright green plantains, sharply cut halves of giant striped fish, plastic containers full of papayas, and crowded full of dozens of people moved in and out of the hubbub. Some of the wooden canoes were piloted by families, and young girls, in beige smocks and rubber boots that swallowed their legs, navigated the traffic with wooden paddles. Once out of the dock area, the families lowered small motors on the end of long metal rods into the muddy water, the sputtering sound of the motors giving the boats the name of *peque-peques*. The putt-putt of boat traffic mixed in with salsa music and the sounds of cars and motos from the streets above. If I listened closely, above the chatter of greetings—in Spanish, Portuguese, and different indigenous languages—and over the sound the birds and insects chattering, I could hear the squelch of boots on mud and the soft lapping of water from the river.

Sets of ten or more stairs down to the deep mud of the docks were a testament to June and July being part of the Amazon's dry season (though with all the rainstorms, this seemed yet another tropical climate misnomer), and during the actual rainy season, the river rose to almost street level.

Tired-looking porters bent over with the weight of large bunches of plantains as they carried them on their backs via a strap around their heads, heading up the steps to the indoor market a block away. Men and boys tugged pigs away from the shore, stomping around the mud as ladies behind tables served up Styrofoam containers full of rice, fish, noodles, and plantains. Vendors on the street called out the names of their wares: sweetened juices, *arroz con pollo*, and phone minutes. Others advertised currency exchange between Colombian pesos, Peruvian *soles*, and Brazilian *reales*.

I sat and watched these comings and goings, munching on a few bananas and taking photos. Few tourists were out and about in the early morning, though there were others at the port for reasons other than work. A stooped man named José Sanchez told me stories of his twelve children, lamenting that none of them wanted to stay in Leticia, and a short black man in a starched shirt handed me a pamphlet from the Jehovah's Witnesses. Four young guys in jeans, sitting under a larger-than-life bronze statue that looked like the Amazon rainforest version of Hercules, also watched the comings and goings. My eyes drifted up to the statue. The bare-chested local hero had a massive anaconda wrapped around his body and his muscular hand gripped the throat of the snake. I wondered who or what I might actually meet when I ventured away from the city and into the actual jungle.

It was time to head up river and explore.

The army-green vinyl of the hammock surrounded me on all sides, its built-in bug net letting in the cold night air and preventing claustrophobia as I listened to insects and frogs chirping loudly and an unrecognizable animal crying off in the distance. I shifted, unable to fall asleep as a strange feeling overcame me. Great leaping fish, I realized, I was cold! I reveled in the sensation, which after six months I had thought was impossible in Colombia.

My enthusiasm slowly waned. I had forgotten how uncomfortable being cold was. I curled up as best I could, my hammock swaying from side to side as I shifted.

I was attempting to fall asleep in the jungle, two hours outside the small town of Puerto Nariño. Earlier, an hour and a half boat ride had brought me up the Amazon River from Leticia, past Amacayacu National Park, past worn wooden signs denoting village names ("Arara," "Santa Sofia," "Zaragoza"), and past the seemingly endless jungles of Colombia on the right and the jungles of Peru on the left. We eventually docked in Puerto Nariño, a town of no more than 3,000 people with small concrete sidewalks laid out in a grid and no motor vehicles.

Puerto Nariño was a great place to lean back with a book and a beer and watch blue and yellow macaws fly around, but I also wanted to get a feel for the Amazon rainforest itself. After all, no matter how you looked at it, the Amazon is one of the most amazing places on the planet.

The sheer mass of the Amazon is impressive. The Amazon rainforest covers over 1.4 billion acres; not just in Colombia, but also Ecuador, Peru, Bolivia, Venezuela, Guyana, Suriname, French Guiana, and of course Brazil. The sheer amount of trees (an estimated 390 billion) and other plants have given the Amazon the nickname of the Lungs of the World and produce 20% of the world's oxygen. Take a deep breath and thank an Amazon tree.

The rainforest is home to 10% of the world's known species. Search around and you'll find 475 species of reptiles and 500 species of mammals. And scientists believe they have only identified 10% of the species in the Amazon. There are frogs hopping, insects crawling, birds screeching, mosses growing, and flowers budding, and we have no clue that they even exist. Although scientists have named around one million different species of insects in the world, they estimate there is likely more than two and a half million different types of insects in the Amazon rainforest alone.

The river itself is no less impressive. The Amazon is debatably the world's longest river (some say it's the Nile), and by far the largest by volume. It is over 200 miles across at its mouth, although in the Colombian Amazon, the river is only about a mile wide (only!). Think about how big the Mississippi and Missouri River systems are: North America's largest rivers (by both volume and length) have an average discharge of 16,200 cubic meters per second. The Amazon's average discharge? 209,000 cubic meters per second. That is a lot of water.

And because of a strange protrusion of geography that juts Colombian land down south to the border of the Amazon River (a result of land gained from various treaties and a war with Peru in 1932-33), Colombian territory is integral to both the river and greater rainforest. Brazil might get all the Amazon press, but the Amazon covers 25% of Colombia. With slightly less than 1% of the total land area on Earth, Colombia has 14% of the planet's biodiversity (second only to a much larger Brazil, making Colombia the most biologically dense country in the world).

A desire to explore this diversity led me to take an overnight hike with two guides named Sergio and Esteban—who were locals of indigenous heritage—and a couple from Switzerland for whom I served as an impromptu translator. Late in the afternoon we set out from the north of town, past a school, across a large soccer field, and then along a narrow and very muddy tract into the forest. As we gradually climbed in elevation, walking in the deep gray-brown mud became a challenge (I was grateful that my hotel had loaned me a pair of rubber boots when I couldn't avoid stepping into an almost calf-deep puddle—tall boots were the practical fashion statement of everyone in the Amazon and every *campesino* who worked in a muddy field or tramped through Colombia's mountains). Eventually, we left the human-planted forest—which included yuca and bananas in addition to native plants—and entered a virgin forest with taller trees.

We wobbled across small streams on rickety logs and kept an eye out for monkeys, birds, and poisonous creatures. We set up camp a little over two hours later, lighting a fire and eating some spaghetti mixed with canned tuna—perhaps an odd choice for jungle fare, but it tasted delicious after the humid walk. Night fell quickly within the thick canopy of trees, though during the day, the canopy can block around 80% of the sunlight. Evening insects started up their orchestrations, adding to the sounds of our crackling fire. A bright quarter moon shone through some of the leaves high above us.

After scraping the tuna pot clean and dumping the water a ways from our camp so we wouldn't attract jaguars or other friendly beasts of the forest, we geared up for our night hike. "Gearing up" basically meant I turned on my headlamp, slung a water bottle and camera over my back, and covered myself in bug spray.

Twenty minutes in, we crouched down to see a faint green glow emitting from some mushrooms. One of the more than seventy types of bioluminescent fungi (or glowing mushrooms) in the world. Who knew?

The answer, of course, is probably the people indigenous to the area where they grow. Scientists might be "discovering" uses for plants and naming new species in the Amazon practically every day, but just because western scientists don't know about something doesn't make it unknown. Unfortunately, indigenous knowledge is shrinking as fast as the rainforest, even though the medicinal potential of the Amazon rainforest alone should be enough to protect it. Already 25% of western medicines are derived from plants in the Amazon.

Plus, let's face it: knowing there are glowing mushrooms growing on the jungle floor is just awesome.

The path was thin (actually, calling it a path was, in most spots, a little generous), with thick underbrush on both sides. With little to see in the dim jungle around us, I focused mostly on my feet, making sure I was following the person in front of me and not tripping on any logs. I forgot to also be on the lookout for jungle creatures.

"Ojo!" said Sergio in a tense voice behind me. I turned around to see a snake crossing the path where I had just stepped, slithering off into the undergrowth. It paused briefly, perhaps disoriented by our lights, and I caught a good look at its yellow (or maybe white), black, and red banding. A coral snake? Milk snake? King snake? Which were the poisonous ones? I gulped and tried to remember how to tell if it was venomous or not. "Red touches white, you're all right. Red touches black, you're dead, Jack," I quietly recited, pulling the phrase from who knows where. Or was the phrase "Red touches black, you're okay, Jack. Red touches yellow, you're a dead fellow?" I couldn't remember.

"Serpiente coral. Peligroso," Sergio said, ending my third-rate poetry debate. (For future reference, you want red to touch black whether your name is Jack or not, though this apparently doesn't always hold true with South American coral snakes—go figure. A little research when I got back revealed that coral snakes are not very aggressive, but they are deadly poisonous and tend to bite when stepped on. Timing is everything.)

The bright moon was scaring off most of the nocturnal animals, so we decided to head back to our camp for some shut-eye. I then crawled into my hammock in my sweaty clothes, zipped myself in, and tried to fall asleep.

Besides the cold night (okay, it was 71 degrees, but much colder than I had been in for a while), I also had to go to the bathroom badly. After debating it for a while, I unzipped myself from my hammock, found my headlamp, and ventured off in the pitch dark. There is just something inherently scary about the jungle at night, and my DNA reminded me that the consequence for those who set off by themselves in the middle of the night thousands of years ago was that they tended not to make it back to reproduce. I walked behind a tree, sure I would see the shine of jaguar eyes. Luckily I did not seem to disturb any large predators, snakes, or spiders and I crawled back into my hammock, zipped the net back up, and tried to get warm.

The next morning, some locals gave us strange looks as we went back to the concrete walkways of Puerto Nariño, so I glanced down. I looked quite worse for the wear. Besides what I am sure was a bleary sleep-deprived look on my face, I was yet again soaked in sweat, with mud spattering across my pants and completely covering my rubber boots almost to their tops just below my knees, and I had a few scratches on my arms from traipsing through the underbrush.

Perhaps I needed a more peaceful way to explore the jungle.

Three days later, I looked down at our mode of transport for going to nearby Lake Tarapoto with more than a little apprehension.

It was a typical Amazon wooden canoe: two small seats and low to the water. Very low to the water, especially after we put the food, water, and my backpack in.

"Lista?" asked my companion Otto, flashing me a wide grin. Ready?

"Vamos," I said more confidently than I felt. We got in the canoe (the water level was now about two inches below the wooden sides) and pushed off. Otto handed me a wide wooden paddle that had been carved and polished, and we were off, heading away from the Amazon, west up the Loretoyacu River towards Lake Tarapoto.

I had met Otto where he worked at the local museum in Puerto Nariño. The Centro de Interpretación Natütama was a local education and research organization, and when I arrived I was greeted by a short and wiry man in his late twenties with tousled hair and a wide smile. Otto introduced himself as a museum guide and said he would show me around the exhibits. He spoke about the relationships between plants and animals and passed along stories of his Tikuna people as we looked up at carved, life-sized animals and paintings representing the river habitats in the region.

Otto's Spanish was textbook, sounding amazingly clear to my brain that was tired of trying to pick Spanish words out of costeños' speech. We ended up chatting for a while after the tour had finished, talking about the Amazon and my plans for the rest of the week. We soon agreed to meet up early the next morning to rent a canoe and head out to the nearby lake.

Otto's calm demeanor and genuine smile put me at ease, and once we were on the water, heading slowly but steadily upstream, the peace of the river soon pushed any last apprehensive thoughts from my mind. Unlike the brown, muddy water of the Amazon River, the water we skimmed across on the Loretoyacu was called *agua negro*: black water and it shimmered from the dark river bottom below. An occasional plant floated by, but for the most part we could have been floating on a dark mirror, with the water reflecting the tall trees and grasses on either side.

The river was wide at first, then narrowed before we reached the first lake and cut through a forest—which I can't say I had done in a canoe before. We could see the dark line on the trees maybe another ten feet up, evidence left by the high water of the rainy season. Even during this season the trees and plants appeared to grow out of the lethargic dark lake. All I could do was stare as we quietly skimmed through trees with braided trunks and under overhanging vines on that still, black water.

Then I realized I was like a lazy passenger on the back half of a tandem bike and Otto was doing all the work, so I dipped my oar into the lake again as the smooth wood of the paddle strained a little against my palms. The paddle made a soft slap as it hit the water, then it whooshed in a way that sounded more like a passing breeze than water, and we floated through the jungle almost unnoticed. The rhythm of our paddling added to the sound of insects, birds, the occasional monkey, and the passing showers of rain plip-plopping with a shimmer on the lake water.

About five miles and two hours later, we spotted people on the shore of our destination, the small Tikuna village of Santa Clara, population 40. As we passed over a little mud and grounded up on the shore, I could see a small crowd was gathered around something on the grassy bank, and we hopped out to take a look.

A fish the size of a small shark lay on the grass, its mouth gaping open to reveal sharp teeth. From the reddish tail to the gray stocky head (a length of more than five feet), there was no other way to describe the fish but as prehistoric. I realized that its stiff mouth was big enough to fit my head into.

I wanted to ask Otto, "What the hell *is* that thing?" but decided on more polite Spanish wording.

"Un pirarucú," Otto replied. "El pez de agua dulce más grande en todo el mundo." In this case, local hyperbole wasn't too far off: the *pirarucú*, or arapaima, *is* pretty much the biggest freshwater fish in the world.

The crowd around the fish turned out to be a family, a father and his six sons, who were all gutting the fish, having successfully maneuvered the body onto the bank from their wooden canoe. With the son holding the fish, the father, named Luis, cut away its armor-like scales and then sliced it down the middle, revealing hot pink flesh. Otto helped as they filleted a body-length chunk of pirarucú meat and separated the spine, entrails, and head to use later. A woman who I assumed was also part of the family soon joined in, whacking the spine with strong swings of her machete as her younger sons put the pieces in old plastic rice and corn flour sacks.

Luis' older sons washed the meat in the river, attracting the small ugly piranhas that populate the waters in the Amazon (they flopped into their canoe but no one gave them a second glance), and they bagged the fish to sell in Puerto Nariño for 6,000 pesos a kilo.

No need to exaggerate the size and success of this fishing trip. My arms weren't long enough to demonstrate how big the fisherman's catch was.

"How big do you think this fish is?" I asked Luis as he watched his sons finishing up.

He stared down a bit, contemplating. "Posible 60 o 65 kilos. Posible más." I wasn't too good at mathematical conversions but knew I weighed around 64 kilograms, or about 140 pounds, which was pretty much the same size as the fish. This pirarucú was on the larger size, though in years past pirarucús had been known to reach 450 pounds. Though the Tikuna and other tribes have fished and eaten the pirarucú for generations, sports fishermen and more locals selling the meat have threatened the pirarucú with extinction, and it was rare to find any fish that big anymore.

I shook hands with Luis and headed into the tiny village of Santa Clara, where we would string up some hammocks and spend the night. The village was trying to attract a few tourists but its inhabitants were still making a living off fishing and horticulture. The people of Santa Clara, other indigenous villages, and the jungle itself were all living in two worlds: of tradition, nature and old ways, and of modernity, consumer goods, and new ideas. Even Otto was a mix of those worlds: knowing how to speak Spanish in addition to Tikuna, wearing cotton shirts with western designs (like everyone I met), but also carrying a machete in an ancient leather case and wearing traditional necklaces.

Although Otto had lived in and near Puerto Nariño for all of his twenty-nine years, I was not alone in my constant desire to take in everything around me. Otto was continuously staring up at the trees or out over the water from our view in the canoe and saying, "La selva es una maravilla, no?"

Yes, the jungle was certainly something special.

As we explored that afternoon, we got out of our canoe to hike a bit and looked at the glue-like latex sap of a rubber tree, which oozed a startling white from the brown bark. Other trees, many with thick roots acting as buttresses around their trunks, created a canopy far above our heads by stretching more than a hundred feet into the sky. One tree was called the *árbol de fertilidad* (or the fertility tree) and its wood was traditionally burned as an incense to help women get pregnant. Why? Its sticks looked strangely phallic.

We saw butterflies, eagles, kingfishers, giant ants cutting highways across the thick forest floor, and giant gray millipedes disturbing dry leaves as they slinked with snake-like movement across the ground. Thin brown and white monkeys stared at our canoe from atop trees with their large black eyes. A lizard darted away from the shoreline as we skimmed past, but not before I caught a glimpse of his scales, which started orange on his tail, changed to red and yellow by the middle of his body, then switched to green before fading to gray on his head.

That night we sat with two Germans and a local named Pedro in a large canoe, silently paddling up the lake under a bright moon to look for caimans, the nocturnal crocodiles of the Amazon. The night was even louder than the day, with the calls of all the insects and frogs carrying across the water.

Pedro started flashing his light into the jungle. Cool air lifted off the water as we looked along the slowly moving shoreline for caimans.

Then I heard a strange sound. I looked around for jaguars, tapirs, or a hurricane, but then felt a drop of water hit my cheek. The sprinkle soon turned into a downpour. My rain jacket was trying to hold its own, but soon I took up Otto's offer to share his poncho, and the both of us bent over as the rain pelted down.

The rain let up for a few minutes, but then the sound that I couldn't place began again: more rain was coming. There was a quiet roar: the sound of drops hitting a million leaves and the trees grumbling about being pushed around by the wind and rain. Pedro decided to call it a night and we rowed back, occasionally stopping to cover ourselves while another downpour lingered. I could just make out the flash of Otto's teeth in the moonlight as he smiled, and we started laughing at the absurdity of us trying to paddle as we shared the poncho and attempted to stay dry.

We made it back to Santa Clara, where the rain continued on and off throughout the night as I lay comfortably in my hammock under a wooden roof. The next day, after a thanks to the families of Santa Clara, Otto and I headed off in our canoe into the gray morning. It was quiet (especially after the hubbub of animals and rain of the night), with only a few bird calls piercing the misty morning air. A loud splash interrupted the peaceful lake and we spun around to see a gray river dolphin surface not five feet away.

For more than an hour we observed tiny gray dolphins leap above the calm waters and larger pink dolphins (*boto*) who breathed loudly as they came briefly to the surface before disappearing beneath the dark water. According to Tikuna legends, the boto were actually shape-shifting humans, usually handsome young men who would seduce young women at night. The dolphins, who were a grayish-pink to a stunningly red, had prehistoric snouts that made them look exactly like the now-extinct *Ichthyosaurus* who lived in oceans around the time of the dinosaurs.

A few dolphins followed us as we paddled steadily back through the submerged forests and river channels towards Puerto Nariño, and we greeted a few fisherman and their families as they passed in their peque-peques.

Muddy from the hikes, soaked from two days of rain, and smelling of sweat, dirt, and lake water, I stepped onto the muddy soil of the Amazon shoreline with mixed emotions. I felt a great sadness about returning to life outside the peace of canoes and jungles.

Two days later, as Otto saw me off on my boat back to Leticia, he handed me what looked like a painted plastic disk about the size of my palm and curved on the edges. On one side he had painted the lake at sunset and on the other, a dolphin. *Lago Tarapoto Julio 2011,* he had written. I flipped it over again and realized he hadn't just painted on a piece of plastic.

"Es del pirarucú de Santa Clara," Otto explained. The fish scales from the pirarucú were big enough to paint a scene on.

In addition to my photos, more insect bites than I cared to count or identify, and my memories of the sounds, sights, and smells of the jungle, I treasured Otto's gift and the memories of Colombia's Amazon.

I ran my finger down the sharp edge of the pirarucú scale, and if I closed my eyes, I could still hear the sound of jungle insects and monkeys calling to each other, and the sound of rain hitting the tops of a million trees.

CHAPTER ELEVEN

SAINTS AND SINGERS

I could have spent another month or two or a couple of years in Leticia and the rainforest, but as I rode into Santa Ana on the back on my mototaxi, narrowly avoiding a collision with a giant bus, it was good to be home. Back to why I was in Colombia.

However, teaching never took up more than half of my day, even on those rare days when we had full classes. While I did what every self-respecting young expat does in their spare time and watched my share of TV shows and movies, I was also keeping busy with other more productive tasks, including writing, getting to know my Colombian neighbors, and teaching language lessons to students more receptive than your average Colombian middle schooler.

Every Tuesday and Thursday I did a Spanish lesson with fellow volunteer Kayla, who had already surpassed me in her ability to understand conversations but had never had a formal Spanish class. I reviewed what I knew of Spanish grammar, went over vocabulary, and had fun making difficult sentences for Kayla to translate such as "When it is hot at school, my students are thirsty and lazy" for practicing adjectives and "I would wash my face, but there is no water" for some conditional tense practice.

Wednesdays I would meet with Barbacoas teacher Marelis and we would go over English idioms. I had a book of U.S. American expressions, would introduce and explain five, and then Marelis—who was much more bilingual than I'll ever be—would decide if there was a Colombian equivalent. There were a surprising number of idioms that were the same as the U.S. expression, but mostly the class proved why I would never become bilingual. Besides all the slang words involved in the expressions, there was the problem of actually remembering the new and strange phrases, such as the fact that *es tiró la pata* might translate to "the leg is pulled," but was more akin to "he bit the dust." Colombian idioms that were just slightly different from my U.S. ones existed in surprising numbers: similar expressions with cultural twists. My favorite example: *con la mano en la masa*. Instead of being caught with your hand in the cookie jar, in Colombia you are caught with your hand in the corn flour. When I first heard it I was just surprised it wasn't something to do with rice.

There was also a serious problem with some idioms reading the exact opposite of what I was used to. The phrase that translated to "butterflies in the stomach" was nothing to do with being nervous before asking someone out on a date or getting up your courage to cross the street in Bogotá. Instead, it meant the more romantic "my heart gives a leap." Instead of the phrase "the calm before the storm," Colombians had the phrase "after the storm comes the calm." It's a lot more optimistic, which perhaps isn't surprising when you look at the average Colombian's attitude. Despite guerrilla warfare, unsteady politics, and all the problems associated with the country, a 2012 poll showed that Colombia was the happiest country in the world. Hopefully for Colombia, the storms of the last decades were turning into a new calm.

I was settling nicely into that happiness and calm myself.

Monday nights, I went back over to school to help out with an English class for community members. I usually referred to this gathering as "Adult Class," a name that always elicited a few winks from my fellow volunteers.

The G to PG-rated Adult Class was led by a local teacher named Alvaro who lived in Ararca, the town on the north of the island on the way to the ferry. He was practically bilingual and actually cared both about his students' progress and the students themselves. The class was mostly made up of recent high school graduates, with some in their mid to upper twenties, a mixture of men and women from all over Isla Barú. Other classes took place at night at IESA throughout the week as well, most sponsored by local foundations to help residents get what seemed to be the Colombian equivalent of the GED.

The English class, however, seemed to be made up of students who wanted to be there—a refreshing change from my mornings with the middle schoolers. Most worked at the Decameron Resort on the island, sold goods at Playa Blanca, or were pursuing technical degrees in tourism. The exception to this was Ubadel, who would hang out in the back of the classroom in his IESA uniform whenever he had an evening shift, taking notes and asking questions.

While the class was different every time I went, I got into a routine before each session started. Even though I knew the scheduled 7:30 p.m. start time meant that it would start more like 8:00, I had lived too many years in punctual North American Time to *plan* to arrive late, so I would usually walk through the dimly lit streets to arrive at the school before any of the students or teachers. As I slapped at mosquitoes and wiped sweat from my face, whichever guards were working would grab a chair for me as they finished eating chicken and rice out of plastic containers. Students would slowly trickle in, some greeting me and starting conversations, others standing shyly outside. Eventually Alvaro would show up and we'd head to one of the classrooms.

Every class was different. A few times I was just a resource for Alvaro to bounce questions off of (such as the easy vocabulary task of coming up with "flip-flop" to describe a sandal and the more difficult grammar request of a list of verbs you cannot put in the future continuous tense—the answer to which I am still not sure). Other times, Alvaro had the students ask me different types of questions in order to practice certain grammar concepts and listen to my native accent when I responded. (Where were you born?... California... What is your favorite food in Colombia?... Patacones.... When are you going to have a family?... Uhhh....)

One evening, the class split into groups to present a "fashion show" about clothing. Each group had an announcer who described and interviewed the other members of the group. As they prepared, I passed through the groups, helping and enjoying the presentations. It was strange to see creativity embraced in my classroom. Chance had it that our fashion show was the same evening the coordinador showed up and stated that because class was held at school, the adults students also needed to adhere to a uniform: white polo shirts and no flip-flops. Luckily the coordinador would rarely be around at night, Alvaro didn't care, and after much discussion, the students decided to ignore the decree, which would have made the fashion show a bit boring.

Class would end around 9:30 or 10:00, which to my grandma-like schedule felt like the middle of the night. Alvaro was always concerned about me walking back alone, so I would walk with one or two of the male students on my way back to Barbacoas. Sometimes Alvaro would volunteer a student named Oscar, who sold his artisan carvings at Playa Blanca, to take me back on his moto, and the cool night air would rush past as we sped along the road.

As productive and creative as the adult classes were, they were victim to poor attendance and a regularity of cancellations just like my regular classes at IESA. For instance class was always canceled for the almost-monthly street parties and the students traded grammar for a little *cerveza* and *baile*. Back in class, these parties brought up the questions of "Do you drink beer?" and "What kind of dances do you like?"

At least these students had a large vocabulary that was applicable to their daily life.

I lay in bed one night, the event across the street completely drowning out the usual cacophony of music and night sounds of insects and frogs. This event also was causing my bed to move rhythmically, shaking it ever so slightly.

The cause: a Santa Ana *picó*, a giant dance party of sorts with towering speakers pumping out champeta, reggaeton, vallenato, and more champeta music at an incredible volume.

This particular picó was right across the way, hence why the heavy bass rhythms were causing my bed frame to vibrate. Picós are loud—a decibel level that made me think more of the level of jet engines than parties.

Picós in Santa Ana happened every month or so, but in the last week of July, picós went to a whole new level to celebrate the patron saint week in Santa Ana.

Every town in Colombia had a week of big festivities centered on a festival or saint day, and it was finally our turn. Besides giving people the excuse to take what felt like every other Monday off, celebrating saints in Colombia was yet another excuse to party. There was the saint of the school, saint of the region, Colombian saints, saints for travel and vacation, saints for mothers, fathers, brothers, and dogs. There were probably saints for every fútbol club and type of beer as far as I knew. After all, according to the Catholic Church, there is an official saint for grocers (Michael the Archangel), goiters (St. Blaise), two patron saints for glove bearers, three patron saints for gall stones (though I'm not sure if this is for the stones themselves or those who suffer from them), and a saint of greeting card manufacturers (St. Valentine. Seriously, it is).

And nowhere else was there a bigger excuse for a raucous *rumba* in the street of a town than the patron saint festival of a pueblo. It didn't take a rocket scientist to figure out who the patron saint of Santa Ana was (I'll give you all a second...), who was apparently the mother of Mary, so was consequently the grandmother of Jesus (Santa Ana did not have a monopoly on her patronage: St. Ann is also the patron saint of various places in Spain, Canada, and the Philippines, as well as the patron saint of Detroit). She was also the patron saint of many different types of people, including housewives, unmarried women, women in labor, and grandmothers (not surprising). However, that list also includes miners, horseback riders, and cabinet makers (perhaps more surprising). That seems to cover a lot of people—whether you were on that list or not, July 26th was the feast day for Ann, and so Santa Ana got down to business.

Throughout the week there were a variety of different events, such as footraces, Masses, Barbacoas-led competitions and games, and a best-dressed donkey competition that, unfortunately, I couldn't find to get a photo of.

And luckily, our classes were more or less normal until Friday (when only half the students came). And the Monday after the weekend of parties, both schools canceled classes, which was an unprecedented event (for Barbacoas to do at all and for the teachers at the public school to know of ahead of time), which gives you an idea of know how big these *festivos* were.

From Tuesday to Friday the town celebrated the festivos with the events during the day, but Saturday through the following Tuesday morning was a never-ending party, with food vendors, games, live music, and multiple picós blasting music at the same time. The picós paused for an hour or so around seven or eight in the morning before starting up again, a hubbub of activity beginning again.

As dusk fell on Sunday, I walked through the usually lazy streets, which were now crowded with so many pedestrians that motos were having a hard time navigating through. The crowds in the street were not just from Santa Ana, but—as the rows of motorcycles and strange sight of parked cars attested to—people had come from the two other island towns of Barú and Ararca, from Pasacaballos, and from Cartagena itself. There were even a few gringos who looked like they stopped in on their way back from the beach.

I stepped deftly around a moto that had just come out of a side street, then breathed in deeply. Mixed in with the usual odor of dank mud and dust was the smell of street food. The spice of sausages, the smoke of roasted meats, and the always-tantalizing smell of frying oil filled the town for a few blocks on both sides of the plaza.

I perused my choices carefully, passing up the hot dogs cut up on a stick, French fries, chicken legs, and some fried cornballs on a stick (think a corn dog, just without the dog).

Regardless of what I decided to order, I also had seven or eight different types of sauces I could choose to smother my dish with. The sauces were lined up in mismatched squeeze bottles and old water bottles with holes punched in the tops. These were in addition to the combo of mayonnaise, sweet ketchup, and the pink sauce that the vendors usually squirted artistically on everything ordered. I watched one of the ladies layer fresh cheese and four condiments onto a plate of French fries and hand it to a young boy who took it slowly, his eyes wide.

The smell of a grilled stick of what was likely beef wafted enticingly and I got one, then headed over to order a giant *patacone*, a twice-fried plantain starchy banana the size of my face. As I ordered my patacone, I held up my hand as the vendor reached towards one of the sauces.

"No, gracias, sin salsa," I said, unsure if I would be able to taste the patacone under the layers of added flavoring. It was also doubtful that I could walk around the rutted streets while eating it without getting sauce on my shirt.

The vendor stared at me, his hand still in the air, hovering over a white squeeze bottle that probably contained mayonnaise. I held out my money for the patacone, and he slowly moved to take it. But no sauces? Gringos really were crazy.

I grabbed a few pinches of salt from a plate, sprinkled it onto my patacone, and bit into the crunchy, fried goodness. Delicious. In my opinion, you should never mess with secret sauces when you're eating fried street food. The amount of oil I was consuming was enough for my arteries anyway without the help of mayonnaise.

I turned from the food stall and nearly ran into a man with a towering pole of cotton candy, a painfully fluorescent pink that rose at least five feet above the crowd.

Everywhere I turned, there were vendors selling snacks and drinks. The men perhaps making the most money were those with homemade Styrofoam coolers slung over their shoulders, doing a brisk business of cold beer. Aguila, Aguilita (an Aguila in a tiny bottle), Cerveza Poker, Club Colombia, Costeña, and every other brand of beer I had ever run into thus far seemed available, and few festivo attendees were walking around without some kind of drink in their hand.

Beer (as well as rum and aguardiente) may have been the focus for everyone who was a teenager and older, but there was also plenty for kids to do, which I found out when I finally made it to the street bordering the plaza. Game stands swarming with my students and many adults lined the plaza and streets, with people playing a roulette-with-a-dice-type game, trying to throw darts at a target, trying to get a coin to land in the middle of a line, and more. Maybe they weren't the flashiest of carnival games, but people were certainly entertained.

The church doors were also open, but the only thing that reminded everyone about the religious reason for the festivities was the Mass earlier in the week and the apparent popularity of taking photos in front of the decorated statue right inside the church (I didn't know if it was the Virgin Mary or St. Ann).

A concert stage involving lots of yellow Aguila beer banners had been set up in the plaza. Dancers, bands, and recorded music entertained the people passing through the plaza throughout the day. Late in the afternoon, as I meandered through the plaza's crowd, the stage was occupied by an energetic band, rocking out to their own live music.

They played, without a doubt, the worst music I had ever heard in my entire life.

There were two guitarists who wailed and screeched, a bassist slowly bobbing his head to the elusive beat, one guy on a drum set, two young guys hitting bongo and conga drums while mouthing enthusiastic lyrics, one guy in the back on *timbores* drums and cowbell, and two guys just sort of hanging out on the stage, trying to look cool. (I didn't stick around to find out whether or not those last two guys also played instruments in later songs—when I was there, one just stood in the back looking bored while the other sat up front near the drums, wearing thick-rimmed glasses he obviously thought looked trendy, and swigging an Aguila.) Out of all the instruments, I could mostly only hear the off-tune noise of the guitars, which was surprising considering the band mostly consisted of drummers.

If it wasn't for the scratchy microphones making static noises, often accompanied by high-pitched feedback, maybe the band would have at least been able to play half-decent music. Although the musicians (a term I use loosely) may have managed to play something resembling music, the lead singer (an even looser term) could not. He was dressed in jeans, giant shades, and a t-shirt that stated (in English): "Ay! Awesome is somethin' on my street, this is how we feel this big beat."

He sang out, "Llorarahhhhh... (quick breath)... ahhhhh... Llorarahhhhh... (another pause for breath)... ahhhhh," his pitch falling and rising as the notes went on and on. When the singer held out the warbling notes of the Spanish word meaning "to cry," his choice of lyrics seemed to be the only fitting part of the show.

Besides two ladies in the front row who clapped along enthusiastically (girlfriends? groupies?), nearly every single other person watching the group reacted in a way that was similar to me: they either looked bored, angry, or were staring off into space as if they were trying to find a happy place far away from this affront to garage bands everywhere.

If this was the best band the festival could bring in, it was no surprise that picós were the main attractions of the patronage festivities rather than live music.

Instead of live musicians, picós consisted of a small group that "performed" together as glorified DJs—singing along, sometimes playing drums or adding electronic music, providing commentary like a pumped-up radio announcers, and running the recorded music. Picós sounded like actual music, were definitely danceable, and were less likely to make you run away screaming in search of earplugs. And so instead of a typical band name, the group is named after their speakers.

That's right, the speakers. Amplifiers. Sub-woofers. Whatever you want to call them: the focus of a picó was the fifteen to twenty-five foot tall speaker system towers. In fact, the word picó comes from the English term "pick-up," meaning your speakers and party can be moved to whatever neighborhood needs a little excitement. Picó also means "peak," and looking at the mountain of speakers involved, it seemed like a good choice. One formal definition of a picó translates to something like "a sound system of giant proportions that is used to animate/spice up festivals." And we certainly had speakers of giant proportions.

Santa Ana's picó was called Pibe and each of its block of four tower speakers had a bright green letter: P-I-B-E. Painting the speakers was a common practice to let people know the name of the group. I think our live band was named El Braw, but they had mixed up their left with their right, so the name read "Le W Bra."

In Santa Ana, "Pibe" was synonymous with festivo, rumba, or any word meaning "to party," and it could be used in all sorts of ways in a sentence. For example, you might say, "What a great pibe last night!" or "We're going to pibe tomorrow!" or "Man, another pibe? Guess I won't get much sleep tonight."

Signs went up everywhere—including in Cartagena—with the dates of the event, and which speaker/group would be putting on the show. At the patronage festival, we had Pibe, with visits from El Imperio, Fredy, Messy (which presumably was supposed to be "Messi"), and El Rey de Rocha.

I meandered around the festivities, passing the entrances and signs for the different picós, making my way back to the plaza where thankfully the band had packed up and families were swarming the games, which were now lit up by bare bulbs and lanterns.

Though the band had gone, music was still everywhere. Besides the noise from the picós, some individuals were trying to make inroads with their own speakers in all the hubbub, blasting music from their stores and homes. Trying to compete with all the noise to have a conversation was a losing battle.

Some of the Barbacoas teachers, including Norcy and Sergio, were sitting around the games section with plastic cups and a tall, covered pitcher of Aguila. They kept offering to share it with me, and thinking it was rude to continue to refuse, I squatted down on the cool concrete and took a cup.

Aguila is not a strong beer. It tastes similar to Corona, which was no surprise, and it is more refreshing then filling. The teachers kept throwing ice into their pitcher, which kept it cold and also watered it down to such an extent that by the time I let them fill my glass a fourth time, I still hadn't felt a thing. It was probably keeping me hydrated more than anything. Still, it was nice to just sit, watch all the activity, and hang out with colleagues and friends. I was getting very used to life in Santa Ana.

Feeling cooled down from the evening air and the ice water (pardon, beer) I had drunk, I eventually said my goodbyes and wandered down the street towards school and The Pan.

Ubadel had guard duty that night and he sat in his usual chair right outside the front gates, watching the revelers totter by.

"Whee," he said, whistling a bit through his teeth. "The festivo is how you say, crazy, no?"

We were interrupted by a loud laugh, which I recognized. Then one of my eighth graders, Rosiris, stumbled on a piece of chipped concrete and her wide smile dropped a bit when she turned and saw me.

"Hello, Rosiris," I said in what I hoped was a friendly, nonchalant tone that was perhaps mixed with a little disapproval. I decided following up with my usual "how are you," might have been awkward considering it was obvious how she was.

"Buenas, teacher," Rosiris responded a little shyly, then quickly turned away.

Ubadel just shook his head and I shrugged and wished him a good night as I crossed the street. This was another reason why I didn't usually frequent the picós: none of my students were over eighteen (the legal drinking age) and I didn't really want to see them in a tipsy state.

As a regular hangout for drinkers, it was no surprise to find The Pan hopping during the festivities. Marianela and Carlos were both working alongside Javier, all kept busy by a steady stream of customers buying beers, aguardiente, rum, coke, waters, and snacks.

I waited behind the crowd and finally found my way to the counter.

Marianela looked a little surprised to see me. "Good night, teacher. Qué quieres?" At least I though that's what she said. Because of the din from the picó across the road and the shouted conversations of the patrons at The Pan, she could have said something in Bulgarian for all I knew.

"Ice cream!" I shouted, giving her time to translate.

"Helado?" She scrunched her eyes, thinking.

"Helado," I repeated, and commenced with picking out my flavor for the evening.

The tables were full and groups of people stood around with beers, some talking and laughing, others nursing their drinks and looking mournfully at the flashing lights of the picó across the street. I leaned up against a post, watching the activity in the street as my quickly-melting chocolate dripped on my sandal.

The vacant lot I always cut through on the way to school was walled up with maybe seven or eight foot-high plywood and metal barriers. A crane-like speaker system also towered overhead in the middle. Amplifiers painted with florescent green, pink, and yellow proclaimed that EL REY was the name of this picó. Flashes of blue, green, and red lights pulsed to the music, and fireworks occasionally burst ten or fifteen feet above the speaker set.

El Rey was the crème of the crop out of the five different picós happening during the patronage festival, but each picó had their own walled area, flashing lights, and blasting, thumping champeta music with the occasional reggaeton song thrown in. Some were free, but being the best picó in town meant a higher price: El Rey cost 10,000 pesos a person to get in (other picós were 5,000 pesos for men and 3,000 for women). Despite the lure of the flashing lights (I guess it works in Vegas), I was content to stand on the outside patio of The Pan, where I was still able to enjoy the lights and music of El Rey.

With a bit of mystery meat, a patacone, four beers (okay, four glasses of liquid equivalent to one beer), and an ice cream mixing around in my stomach—and with my ears already ringing from the picós—it was time to call it a night. The picós might only start slowing down around seven in the morning, but I was on a teacher's sleep schedule, so after finishing my ice cream and slipping through The Pan's crowd to throw away my trash and say goodbye to Marianela and Carlos, I headed back to the Villa.

And yet a picó is a party that never stopped giving. I was able to enjoy the music all the way back to Barbacoas—passing rows of cars and motos and the more common spectacle of cows that were on the road—as the music got slightly fainter with every couple feet; though when I arrived back at the Villa, I was still able to hear the music quite well.

I went into my room and I lay in the dark for a while, and although the picós were no longer physically shaking my bed, I heard a mix of champeta, reggaeton, laughter, and the shouts of the picós' DJs. The party would go on for quite a while.

CHAPTER TWELVE

Rainy Days, Sick Days

I was in Cartagena for the day, ambling beside a newly redone waterside park and was momentarily distracted from eating a dedito by a policeman running pell-mell past me with one hand on his hat and the other gripping the gun in his holster.

Thoughts flashed to the FARC, bombings, and drug busts. Or maybe another tourist had forgotten to put their toilet paper in the trashcan.

Yet I realized, as I stood there motionless, that the police officer did not appear to be chasing anyone; and consequently, I couldn't see anyone chasing him either.

Approximately two seconds later, rain drops the size of bullets started falling and the danger the policeman had seen coming hit the street. It took me a good seven seconds or so to run for cover toward the kiosk that the policeman had just made it to, and during that time, I felt rainwater soak through my shirt. After a few distracted moments of trying to get the latch of the wooden gate undone, I managed to take cover under the kiosk's overhang and finally got another bite of my now-damp dedito. Three policemen who were now in the same kiosk watched me flirtatiously.

Soon, a couple, clutching damp shopping bags, came over to me from the other side of the kiosk (where the policemen were still grinning at me).

"Que aguacero, no?" I commented, pointing to the sheets of rain and the last people running for cover across the street.

"Aya, esta es la verdad," agreed the man as he rubbed his hands over his hair, trying to get the water out.

Soon we were talking about other things. They were traveling from Medellín, but it was their first time in Cartagena and they wondered if I was a tourist too, which of course led to my inevitable explanation of what I was doing there and where I lived. By the time the rain let up ten minutes later, one of the policemen had joined the conversation and he and I had sold them on the merits of Playa Blanca and walking around the Centro at night.

Rain brings people together—when a monsoon suddenly starts coming down and you have to huddle under the tree until it stops or all-day showers mean you have to spend the day inside with friends, colleagues, or strangers, you start conversations that you might not have had under different circumstances.

And there is something to be said for talking about the weather. It is an old fall-back for when topics go dry (if you'll excuse the expression), but I don't resent it for that role at all. Instead, time and time again, I've had good conversations that started with a comment about the weather. It is rarely controversial (global warming debates aside) and it's pretty much always safe to say, "Boy, it's hot today," to a stranger next to you.

It is also the one thing you and the person standing next to you who is drenched from a downpour have in common. Your backgrounds, language, and social status could be as different as a Sahara Desert sandstorm and a North Pole blizzard, but you share a common experience regarding the weather. It can lead to conversations about the different places you've been to or where you're from. Rain, or any weather, can bring people together in more than just a physical sense.

I am no stranger to rain. Growing up north of Seattle, gloomy days between October and May were the norm (add in most of June and September as well, when you get right down to it). Some of my best memories happened on rainy days, which was helped I'm sure by the fact that there were so many of them. So I was excited by the prospect that the rainy season would break the monotony of the daily "sunny and hot" forecast in coastal Colombia.

Rain transforms the air, causing it to smell newly washed: that refreshing scent that wafts even through concrete classroom walls. It definitely cuts down on the dust. And those shocking moments when the temperature dips below 80 degrees were gifts from God.

And we knew the rain would eventually come. All tropical countries experience wet and dry seasons instead of winter/ spring/summer/fall cycles. A rain belt of moist air fluctuates between the northern and southern tropics during the year, bringing rain to whichever area it is over. Near the Tropic of Cancer or the Tropic of Capricorn, the land experiences one wet season and one dry season, but as close to the equator as we were, the rain belt passed us over twice (once heading north, the other time heading south)—so to be technical, Colombia did have four seasons as well: wet, dry, wet, dry. Or maybe it was dry, wet, dry, wet. I'm not really sure.

The short rainy season in March and April (winter number one) mostly consisted of blasting hot mornings followed by torrential downpours in the afternoons, which were usually accompanied by lightning and thunder (both rumblings in the distance and heart-stopping cracks indicating the lightning had struck nearby).

The good thing about the season was the rainy afternoons were much cooler than our sunny days, and a nice respite from the heat, although we usually had to close our windows so the rain wouldn't come through the screens.

All the rain also meant that water was everywhere.

The walls would get damp and moldy. Deep puddles covered our kitchen floor. Walks through town were impossible. Getting to school meant carefully surveying the land to determine a path around puddles and mud trenches (and my students snickered at my muddy shoes upon my arrival). Doing laundry (when I had to hang it outside to dry) became a bit more difficult. Even being on the internet was more challenging, since the wireless signal was on the Villa's open-air veranda or in the open-air teacher's lounge.

The rains that came in October and November (winter number two) were different from those earlier in the year. These rains usually started at night—and continued all night long. The sheets of water from earlier rainy days now changed to heavy showers: rain that fluctuated between the deep thud of large drops and the patter of thousands of smaller sprinkles. Continuous lighter rains were only rarely accompanied by the distant flashes of lightning that we had been getting so used to.

And during the last week of October something else new happened: a rain day.

In the United States, when there is a snow day (or wind day, or flooding or whatever), teachers generally activate a phone tree. The principal calls a couple of people, who then call another couple of people who are on their list until all the teachers, aides, secretaries, custodians, and guys who might have been subbing know the plan for shortened or no classes (this works rather efficiently). Then TV and radio stations are informed for the students to check to see the schedule.

At IESA we didn't exactly have a phone tree.

One Tuesday night (after yet another Monday holiday), it started raining and was still going the next morning, so Kassira and I called various teachers to try to figure out what was happening with school (Kassira had to leave a message for Arelis, and unsurprisingly, I couldn't get a hold of Pedro). Previously when it had rained in the morning, teachers arrived late, then students showed up and we missed first period but continued normally after the rain stopped. The problem that day was the rain wasn't stopping. Finally Alyssa—who also taught for part of the morning—got a hold of her kindergarten co-teacher, who confirmed that the teachers weren't coming and school was canceled.

The next day I woke up to clouds but no rain, so I got up, relieved that my short vacation was over. However, by the time I made it down to breakfast, a light had rain started. But sprinkles weren't going to stop me, so I geared up for the walk to school by collecting my umbrella, raincoat, and my backpack (with its rain cover), then I put my trustworthy Chaco sandals on and rolled up my pants to accommodate any puddles.

As soon as Kassira and I opened the door to walk outside, the deluge started. It was as if someone was standing on our roof with a fire hose. It was only 6:15, and with comunidad most likely canceled, first period wouldn't start until 7:00, so back upstairs we went to try to wait it out.

The rain fluctuated between monsoon conditions and a heavy shower. After making many phone calls, we finally got a hold of the coordinador, who said we'd still have class if the teachers—who were coming from Cartagena and were apparently at the ferry—got there. So we put our coats on and with our umbrellas up, off we went.

We made it about fifteen feet.

The new strength of the storm forced me to duck under the roof of one of the teacher's houses and wait for it to let up a little. A half hour later and there was still no change as far as the intensity of the rain erupting from the heavens, so I gave up and left anyway.

This time I got twenty feet.

That twenty feet was through a growing lake where a path used to be. It was knee-deep and I trudged through it, soon taking shelter under the roof of an empty classroom whose floor was being flooded as the water level outside spilled (or more like flowed) over the edge.

After a shorter wait, the rain actually let up a little more (it was just heavy now rather than torrential) and I went to the cafeteria, dropped my bag, and, armed with a camera, cell phone, umbrella, and one dry erase marker in case I made it to school, headed out the gate to the road.

Except the road had disappeared under a rushing river, with muddy brown water flowing at a good clip past homes, through trees, and down the road.

"It's a river!" I exclaimed to no one in particular.

Alejandro, dressed in a bright yellow rain slicker instead of his usual Barbacoas guard uniform, was preventing trashcans from getting washed downstream by rolling them away from what was now the riverbank.

"Ay, que aguacero, no?" he shouted above the sound of the rain and the rushing river, and pointed a dripping hand at the torrential downpour.

I could just nod as giant drops of water flew off my hood.

Determined to try to make an effort to hold class, I decided to make an attempt to heads towards town, and entered the river. The water was just under my knees and I actually had to fight the current a little as I walked to the high ground towards the spot where The Puddle always sat.

Of course, The Puddle was gone—it had been integrated into the new Santana River system. I watched as a moto came up. The driver paused to figure out which route looked the shallowest, then he dove in. Halfway through the crossing, it got too deep and he fell over and had to push his moto out of the nearly waist-deep river.

Waist-deep. Needless to say, I didn't make it to school, but neither did the other teachers and it wasn't going to be easy for most of our students. So I decided to call school a bust for the day (and when we did finally have school, we got confirmation that it *had* been canceled), snapped some more photos and videos as I balanced my umbrella under my arm, and waded back against the current.

I returned to my cozy room, tried to dry off, and spent another day inside, eating soup (since it was a wintry 80 degrees), working, and wasting time in all the best rainy day ways.

If Santa Ana was some rural U.S. town that got flooded, it would have made the news in the United States regardless of whether or not it was a slow news day. We had trees uprooted from the saturated soil, cars and a bus stuck in the mud (which happened on the first day of rain, thankfully before the formation of the river), and water rushing around tree trunks and telephone poles. And unfortunately many people's houses got flooded, with ankle-deep water ruining furniture, making the rain day a day full of cleaning for some.

Luckily, while we had many days of torrential rains, we only had the one week of flooding.

The rainy season had arrived with both positive and negative changes. If only I could have had the cool weather without the flooding, the cozy feeling of being inside without my students having to miss another day of class, the refreshing smell and comforting sound of raindrops without having to worry how it would affect plans to work, walk, travel, and go to the store.

Few in town actually liked the rain because of all the problems it caused. Colombians would stare at me in horror if I went outside while it was raining.

"Si te mojas con agua lluvia te resfrias!" I heard more than once (you were asking to become ill if you let rain get you wet).

I didn't take much stock in that, having walked around in rain most of my life. In fact, the first time I had gotten sick in Colombia was back on the last day of a hot and dry February.

Luckily it had been a Tuesday—when I only taught two periods—and the light-headed nausea didn't begin until near the end of my last class. My stomach and pride managed to make it back to my room by 10:00 and I barely avoided losing my breakfast in the street. For the next thirty hours, I tried to keep down saltines and sips of water, knowing I had exactly 4.3 seconds to make it to the toilet.

Diseases seem to flock to the tropics for the same reason tourists do—its year-round warm weather and abundance of sunshine causes a diverse array of plants, animals, and microorganisms to thrive. These diseases continue to cause incredible amounts of widespread suffering each year: malaria, yellow fever, typhoid, hepatitis A, dengue fever, cholera, and even dehydration (killing at least three million people per year, mostly through diarrhea) are more prone to the hot tropics. Some of these are more common in tropical countries because the tropics house some of the world's poorest countries and also because these viruses, bacteria, fungi, and other microorganisms like it in hot, humid places.

We like to think of ourselves as these indomitable beings who have conquered nature and live in man-made environments, comfortable no matter the climate, weather, or if we happened to be living in the middle of a barren desert (I'm looking at you, Las Vegas and Dubai). But if you get a head cold or a couple of microorganisms party it up in your intestines, you'll quickly remember how vulnerable you really are. Who knows what I actually had? Anything could have been to blame from food poisoning to dangerous microbes in the water, but it was definitely an interesting experience.

Since lying horizontal and sipping water was apparently too much for me to handle, I missed a day of school and Kassira brought the lesson plans I had written to IESA, only to find Pedro was absent as well (why wasn't I surprised?).

But though a little weak from my diet of saltines, I was back at school the day after, whatever I had had in and out with a bang.

I woke up and tried to say good morning to Shannon, but was alarmed to hear a grating rasp emit from my throat.

Months after my first sick day, my next illness was just a plain, ordinary, cold. In Colombia, the word for a cold was *gripe* (pronounced gree-pay), but it was also used to describe any sort of flu thing, so when I rasped out what I had to a Colombian, they could have thought I was fighting anything from a bad sore throat (true) to life-threatening influenza (less likely, thankfully).

I didn't have to go to the clinic, but the painful sore throat turned into laryngitis, a slight fever, and a raspy cough.

That would have been the week to use a sick day or two, call in a substitute teacher, and make sub plans—if only Colombia had such things. Unfortunately, it seemed to be the week for medical problems: I woke up with the laryngitis one week into what turned into a two and a half week absence from Pedro (he reportedly had a stomach hernia, and okay, I'll take the cold over that, but he was gone a suspiciously long time). So if I didn't show up, my students would completely miss out on a day or more of English (we actually were having full classes that week with, shockingly, no scheduled holidays or meetings) and I would need to figure out how to catch them up with exams three weeks away, so I felt I had to show up.

"Good morning," I whispered to my students, then pointed at the board, where I had written a message stating something like "I cannot talk today because I am sick but we are still going to have class. Get out your notebooks and do the activity on the board." I should have added, "And you better behave because I feel like crap and can't talk loud enough to be heard above a chirping frog." My feeble whispers sounded like they were coming from a scratchy record being played on a 1920s Victrola record player. I kept pointing to the board and going from student to student explaining the plan for the day.

The sixth graders stared at me as I coughed into a bandana.

"Estás enferma?" Jhon Jader asked me, worried. I nodded but couldn't respond with a, "Yes" or an, "Of course I'm sick; read the board and hope I don't sneeze on you."

Instead, I again pointed to the board and had Mauricio read the message aloud as I shushed students with hand gestures.

Finally, I saw looks of comprehension on the faces of most of students though most also looked confused—I don't think they ever had a teacher come to class sick before. Others looked excited, as if anticipating having to pay even less attention than usual that day. Arlin just sort of stared at me as if she couldn't believe I had that much desire to be in the classroom.

"You shouldn't be here," said Mauricio kindly as I coughed again and wiped sweat from my brow, and quite a few students shared his look of concern.

"Sí," piped up the always unmotivated Dilson with a half grin. "You should go home."

I shrugged at Mauricio and a give him a look of thanks and stared at Dilson and shook my head, hoping he realized it meant I knew why he thought I should go home.

But through pointing, gesturing, and acting out the directions of the activities I had written on the board, the students were soon working. I made sure I didn't lean in too close to anyone (I definitely didn't want any of my students to catch my cold), but gave out a lot of stern looks and thumbs ups as class went on. When the level of conversation began to rise, I realized how often I usually raised my voice to be heard over their chattering. Of course, I had no way of doing that this day, but I held up my hand as I usually did and gestured to a few of my most studious sixth graders in the front row to help me out.

"Cállense!" Carlos shouted over the noise. Huber Andrés actually pushed a student back into his desk. I told him (with my new version of South American Sign Language) to ease up a little, but was surprised how much the class actually settled down. The boys didn't seem to know what to do with the new situation and the girls seemed to feel sorry for me.

Perhaps it was because the dynamic of the class was forced to change (or because I had to come extra prepared and had planned on Pedro not being there), but it turned out to be one of the best weeks of teaching I had had all year.

I got through my laryngitis thanks to the fact that I never had to actually do anything after 12:30 except revert back to my childhood sick days: drinking Gatorade (though here it was passion fruit flavored), making homemade chicken noodle soup, and watching *Toy Story*. It wasn't a bad way to spend an afternoon, although I would have given up Milo juice for the year for a single mug of hot herbal tea with honey. However, on second thought, perhaps nix the tea; while it might have felt good to my throat, I also discovered I had a fever.

Having a fever in Santa Ana was a new and interesting experience. I first had to go through the stages of "do I feel regular hot or extra hot" and "okay, am I feeling extra hot because it is actually just ridiculously extra hot out there today or do I actually have a fever?" When I took my temperature and it read almost exactly what it was outside (99.7), I felt a little better about why I was dripping with sweat so much (an extra excuse!). Plus, if I didn't have a thermometer next time, I could maybe just ask, "Do I feel exactly like the outside temperature or hotter?" And if it was the latter, I would fill up on chicken soup and electrolytes.

Fevers and laryngitis are not the funnest things ever, but since I didn't have malaria or dengue or anything that was actually serious, my class and I pushed through and had one of our best weeks at school.

But later, maybe because of the rains (who knows?), I got hit hard again with Colombian Sickness Part III as October turned into November and rainy season officially started. I spent another day in bed, jumping down my ladder to the bathroom whenever I needed and getting sympathetic looks from my fellow volunteers, who brought me cool bottles of Gatorade that tasted good going down but less delicious when they inevitably came back up.

I think Colombia was testing me—the heat, bugs, disorganized teaching schedule, and floods had not stopped my explorations or the fact that I had slowly fallen in love with the country, so Colombia had decided to give me the rite of passage of a doctor's visit.

Still, compared to what some of my friends and family were predicting might happen to me if I went to Colombia, getting sick for a few days was something that could be easily dealt with.

One evening, I woke up from a long nap long after dark, and in the stillness of the night, I decided to just lay there before going looking for more saltines. Not moving, I took assessment of my current state. I was hot, of course, but didn't feel like I had much of a fever. There didn't seem to be a need to jump down the ladder to rush to the bathroom, which was definitely a good sign. I slowly sat up, scratching an itch on my arm. Then I scratched again. And I looked down.

The reason for the itch was immediately apparent. I had pink bumps all over the undersides of my arms and, as I looked and felt around, I discovered more on my legs, back, and ears.

I groaned a little as I looked over at the clock—which read 10:45 p.m.—as Shannon walked in. It seemed I had developed hives in reaction to my fever (if you had forced me guess to before I came to Colombia what might have given me hives, I probably would have gone with weird foods, crazy bugs, or dangerous spiders). After much debate, I walked downstairs and had a chat with one of the *medicos* who was in for the night. We decided I should probably head to the clinic, just in case.

So I walked to the gate of the school, wishing I could enjoy the almost-cool night air a little more, and I explained to the guards what was going on. I wanted to find a moto to take me since I didn't relish the fifteen-minute walk to the clinic on a more-than-empty stomach. This led to Gabriel searching for someone with a moto who was willing to take me across town. Although it wasn't far, it was nearing midnight and finding a driver who was still up and about for a reason besides late-night drinking was a bit difficult.

After twenty minutes, Alejandro, the other guard up on night duty, finally borrowed a moto from one of the teachers (I didn't asked if the teacher knew it was being borrowed or not) and volunteered to drive me. I tenderly swung onto the seat, Alejandro gunned it, and we were on our way, slowly bumping through town. It was exactly midnight on Halloween, and the best thing about the experience was that my nausea had lessened to the point where I was only slightly worried about the possibility of expelling whatever was left in my stomach all over poor Alejandro.

The clinic was actually quick and easy—the lateness of the hour meant there was no wait and that only one other person was in the clinic when I arrived. A nurse, looking grumpy enough to make me wonder if they worked 24-hour shifts in Colombia, handed me a form to fill out. While I did not have to put down any insurance plan or sign any privacy statement, I did have to write in my religious preference. I could appreciate how this information might be helpful, but it was a little alarming all the same; did I look so bad they thought a priest might be needed? Still, I was surprised and grateful that a Colombian clinic listed options other than Catholic. Luckily no priest, pastor, rabbi, or imam was needed.

After only having to answer a few questions (which I found disconcerting), I was back with the grouchy nurse/receptionist, who told me to remove my pants. After a good old shot in the butt and second shot in the arm, I was back outside (pants on) and hopped a ride back to Barbacoas with Alejandro, who would have been my number one choice for moto driver anytime (unfortunately for me, it didn't pay as much as a guard). Gabriel opened the gate for us, I expressed my heartfelt thanks with a big tip to Alejandro, and finally headed to bed.

Needless to say, I did actually take the next day off from school. The country showed me I could fight against schedule changes and class cancellations all I wanted, but regular life problems sometimes take precedence.

I just wish I could have called a substitute teacher to fill in.

Of course, one of the benefits of co-teaching was supposed to be that two teachers were attentive to the students, but I had given up on Pedro for that long ago.

CHAPTER THIRTEEN

In Class (and Out of Class)

It was a normal hot day in 8-1, and my students were working fairly quietly, creating sentences about three things they liked and three things they didn't like by using a set of vocabulary words on the board. I walked through the haphazard rows, making sure they were on task and answering their questions.

I looked to the back of the classroom where Pedro was sitting in a desk, zoning out. This was normal for him during work time, which he saw as a chance to sit back and relax while the students completed the tasks at hand.

Then I looked closer. Pedro wasn't just relaxed. He was asleep.

Jorge, a skinny boy in the front row, followed my gaze to the back of the room to where Pedro was leaned all the way back in his desk, taking slow, deep breaths.

"Pedro se durmió?" he asked with a half-laugh, turning back to me. I didn't want to be involved in making Pedro the butt of another joke, but neither could I deny that Pedro *had* in fact fallen asleep, so I decided to shrug and give Jorge a half-smile, tapping his notebook.

"Posible. Pero necesitas terminar sus oraciones," I told him, and he returned to his notebook and homework sentences, though he occasionally glanced back at his dozing teacher. I looked around the room to see if anyone else had noticed Pedro's soporific state.

Of course they had noticed—teachers sleeping during a class was novel to Colombian students as well.

Katia looked both worried and as frustrated as I felt. Rosiris took it as a sign that she was allowed to put her head on her desk and try to fall asleep herself. Luis Felipe couldn't seem to stop laughing.

When I asked the class to share their sentences a few minutes later, I turned around and saw that Pedro's eyes were open again. Apparently he was either unaware or unconcerned that he had been the center of attention.

When it happened for the second, third, and fourth time as the year went on, the students started to treat it like an ongoing joke.

At least Pedro never snored.

I finally decided to confront Pedro, but debated with myself about how to go about it. I was deciding between "So... I noticed that you've been tired in class lately. Everything okay?" and "Since we don't allow sleeping in class, I was considering having the students doodle on your face in Sharpie. What do you think?"

When I finally brought it up in what I hoped was a nonchalant tone, that it probably wasn't a great idea to fall asleep during classes, he dismissed my worries with a wave of his hand.

"I do not sleep. I am resting my eyes."

Right.

While being a teacher is a difficult task anywhere, teaching at IESA had a few extra challenges. Besides sleeping co-teachers, there was the rain, the "flexible" schedule, power outages, lack of support from teachers and administrators, and lack of supplies.

For instance, a teacher might want to give out a worksheet to their students. Because of the extra effort it took, handouts were such a novelty at IESA that students would work harder and longer on a printed sheet than on something copied from the board. So occasionally I would create a worksheet about vocab or grammar or as a review for an exam.

I would bring a flash drive over to the Barbacoas office where the always-helpful Barbacoas coordinador, Gregorio, had a printer. If I was lucky, he would be in his office and he'd print the sheets I needed. Then, with copy paper I bought the last time I was in Cartagena, I would head off to the library, where hopefully the librarian, Juan Carlos, was around and the copy machine was working. If all went well, I would pay Juan Carlos 50 pesos a copy and emerge into the open air, wiping sweat off my face. If all didn't go well, the process could take all afternoon, or a week if my luck was really bad (and of course it was not possible at all if the power was off).

Gregorio would always help me out, but unfortunately he was not part of my school's administration. The IESA coordinador, Abram, was around most days and would talk to a student about their behavioral problems if you asked (though this usually involved yelling at them as flecks of spit flew from his mouth). He was nice enough, but he seemed physically incapable of talking in anything less than a raspy shout. It wasn't his volume that made him sound like he was talking over an especially loud picó, but simply his matter of speaking and intonation.

He would greet me and Kassira with a "BUENOS DIAS!" as we waited for the other teachers to arrive in the morning, and follow it up with a "COMO ESTAN?"

I always wanted to respond with a raspy shout of my own ("WE ARE GREAT!"), but we'd usually reply with a meek "Bien, gracias."

We had two rectors (principals) during the year. Jorge, who was tan with short-cropped gray hair, was the first, and he was gone at least two days a week. He would say the right things (Study harder! Have pride in your school!) when he was around, but I never saw him actually sit down and talk to a student. Jorge left halfway through the year for what was apparently a more lucrative position (all the teachers and administrators were trying to get to a better school as soon as they could), although I wasn't sure how he earned a position at a more successful school. Then our new rector, Alaberto, came, and I realized that maybe our first principal *had* been one of the better ones.

In the more than four months Alaberto was rector, I saw him a grand total of six (yes, *six*) times at school. And it was hard to miss him, since he usually strode into the grounds wearing all white (which wasn't too unusual), with the first four buttons on his shirt unclasped (unusual, but it was hot) and pimp-like bling dangling down his chest (more unusual).

But the haphazard way IESA was run wasn't one person's fault— we could blame the curriculum, the Ministry of Education, the teachers, the culture of students, civil conflicts drawing away education funding, and even the heat. And of course I was to blame for not being a better teacher.

Some, like the English teacher Arelis, were trying to change the culture, caring about their students and trying to raise expectations up from what seemed the current standard of mediocrity.

Pedro, on the other hand, seemed to have made a commitment on being a role model for his students' mediocrity (and worse). For him, learning a language was not about communication (heaven forbid), but grammar rules. Having failed in other methods of co-teaching our classes, I relented to Pedro's desire to present all the grammar himself while I taught vocabulary and pronunciation. But after a semester of trying everything and making excuses for him, I had nearly given up on the hope that he would do anything that resembled teaching. In Pedro's world, a well-ordered classroom meant coming up with a task that would keep the students busy for as much of the period as possible.

He might sketch detailed drawings of different food items on the board—a whole chicken on a plate, a double scoop of ice cream, a bowl of rice—drawing and erasing for ten or fifteen minutes straight until he completed the sketches to his satisfaction. The noise of the class would grow louder and louder before Pedro would turn to a student after putting the finishing details on his drawing of a bowl of soup, including garnish, and steam and ask, "Do you like soup?" (pronouncing it "soap"), then he would repeat his question loudly a second time. Pedro would then head to the back of the room, leaning back with his eyes closed while the students spent the next thirty minutes copying his drawings.

Maybe you had a teacher in sixth grade who was sixty-seven-years-old, close to retirement, and who rushed home to watch reruns on the Hallmark Channel with an entire bottle of liquor every night. Pedro had a similar commitment to teaching (though I can't speak to his liquor consumption and unfortunately for everyone involved, he was nowhere near retirement).

On a normal day, I would get out of my seat in the library about two minutes after the bell sounded, and stretch theatrically. Pedro, who was usually sitting across from me with his hands resting on his large stomach and his head tipped back, would maybe open one eye. I'd make a fuss of gathering my things, then finally say something, always trying to sound cheerful.

"Time for third period," I would say, then I would pause. "We have 7-1 now, Pedro."

This usually elicited a yawn or a nonchalant, "You have class?"

My tactics to get Pedro to go to class with me changed day-to-day as I tried different methods as the year wore on.

Some days I just sat and refused to budge unless Pedro came too. "I am ready to go when you are ready," I'd tell him in English and Spanish. Then I would feel bad that this meant the students would lose at least fifteen minutes of class time before Pedro would finally get up and shuffle off to the class (plus I'd have to round the students up off the playground and break up all the scuffling that the lack of supervision had created).

So I occasionally shifted tactics and just left without him. He'd meander in five, ten, or twenty minutes after I'd start. Sometimes, he'd just head to the nearest chair and go back to his natural state of slouched relaxation. Occasionally he would walk in and interrupt me mid-sentence with a "Good morning, class!" and follow it up with a loud "How are you?" which always elicited snorts of laughter from a few students.

A few times as we sat in the library, with the minutes ticking away after the bell had sounded, I would just keep arguing with Pedro that we needed to go. "Okay, you go," he'd say. "I will be there in a few minutes."

"No, we are a team," I'd respond. "I want to teach together."

Pedro would usually just ignore me, apparently also happy to ignore the fact that we were supposed to be co-teaching.

Some days it would get so bad that other teachers who were also sitting in the library would try to shame Pedro into going to class with me.

"You have class," Luis would say. "You should go." Then he would address me. "You have class now?"

"Yes," I'd respond, looking at my watch. "7-1."

Pedro's response, yet again, would be "I'll be there soon." Luis would argue with him more, then maybe Gérman or Norman would join in. They'd laugh, cajole, and try to shame him into going to class, becoming more incredulous as the minutes wore on.

It was like he was another student who I needed to motivate to work, except he had actual authority in the classroom, which he used and misused whenever he felt like it depending on the day. Sometimes instead of class, he would hold an hour-long lecture on the students' behavior. Or, instead of presenting an activity, he would sit in the back sleeping (sorry, not sleeping: resting his eyes). Once he sent a student out of the room in the middle of a lesson to go buy him some food.

"Estamos un equipo" ("We are a team") was a phrase I tried repeating in both languages as often as I could whenever I discussed school with Pedro. I didn't want to come off as a crazy, inexperienced white girl barging into his classroom and telling him what to do. And yet it didn't seem like he wanted to be included in our classes. He was happy to split his time between letting me take over so he didn't have to do anything and his brief grammar lessons which he did to try to prove that he was competent in English—despite never having a conversation with me in English that lasted more than a few sentences.

Because of all these difficulties, it was actually a relief when I learned he could be absent for over two weeks due to surgery because of a stomach hernia. This was after he had been absent three days in a row. Did I hear this from Pedro (who had both my email and phone number)? Of course not. Did I hear it from the rector or coordinador? No, because apparently Pedro didn't turn in his necessary paperwork and they had no clue either. The phone number Pedro had given me was out of service, so I tried to track down some way to contact him. With the help of Arelis—who asked about five teachers and finally got a working phone number from the librarian—I finally called and asked Pedro when he thought he might be back (he didn't know).

I would finally be able to have a routine and at least I could rely on Pedro for something, even if that something was the fact that he wasn't going to show up.

With him gone, I ended up doing most of the third quarter grades myself, which I didn't actually mind so much since I had the records of all the homework and test grades anyhow. When he came back with sixth grade still left to do, I pulled my laptop out in the library and offered to sit down with him so we could do it together.

The most subjective grade was something called *autoevaluación*, a sort of "effort" grade. I started at the top of our list.

"Irina. Si, ella participa mucho y casi siempre hace sus tareas. Qué piensas, Pedro?" I asked him. "Ocho?"

"Okay, si ocho is good," he said, trailing his eyes over her other grades.

I marked down an eight in the column. "Okay," I continued to the next student whose effort wavered a bit more than Irina's. "Jesus Maria. El es una mezcla. Qué piensas?" I wanted to know what he thought and to get his input.

Pedro stared at Jesus Maria's row of numbers, which denoted the one to ten scores I'd given him on quizzes, written work, participation, attendance, and the final exam.

"Él participa bien?" It came out as a question.

"Si, no todos los días, pero más o menos bien," I responded with a sinking feeling, then took a slow breath that ended in a sigh. "Conoces a Jesus María?" I asked. Do you know him?

"Pues, si, lo conozco," Pedro responded quickly, then paused. "Pero me confundí las caras."

Pedro didn't know who Jesus María was. To paraphrase him, he "couldn't put the name to the face" of the student who he had been "teaching" for eight months.

We had to stop there. If Pedro didn't know the names of his students, then there was no point in doing the grades together. I just shook my head at Pedro's ridiculousness and the other teachers gave me conciliatory looks. We ended up wasting all of the next class in

6-1 by calling students up one by one so Pedro could see who they were, and we assigned the grades on the spot.

How Pedro decided the grades for Quarters 1 and 2 when he refused my help, I'll never know. And he had never mentioned it being a problem or seemed awkward about the fact that he didn't know his students. Even the students knew teaching could be so much more than what Pedro offered.

One especially hot morning, Pedro had come into class thirty-five minutes after it had started, caught Gustavo, who was one of my quieter boys, tossing a pen to his friend, and started verbally attacking him.

Ten minutes later, Pedro left with Gustavo to take him to the coordinador's office, and I was back to a subdued class. After giving some homework, class ended, and I headed out into the bright courtyard.

Marianela caught up to me, her notebooks under her arm. She paused, then commented in English: "Pedro is crazy, yes?"

All I could do was wipe sweat from my face, applaud her for her excellent grasp of English adjectives, and give yet another half-hearted argument in Pedro's defense, all the while wishing I could give Marianela a giant hug and tell her to write a letter to the Secretary of Education.

The only bright side to all of this was that Pedro was the worst teacher at IESA and there were many, many good teachers, Arelis being at the top of the list. At least I knew that if a student survived Pedro for three years, there was the reward of being able to take a course that actually resembled a genuine English class once they reached ninth grade.

After I left at the end of the year, the other teachers tried petitioning the Cartagena school district to fire him. That was unprecedented.

But there was a benefit to having a co-teacher who showed such a lack of dedication to teaching. I knew I had a good reason for being there: for the students. Even on days when they went crazy and didn't listen to one word of English—when whatever semblance of a lesson plan I had in mind had fallen apart—I knew I may have been the second-worst teacher in Colombia, but I couldn't have been doing worse than Pedro.

Was Pedro certifiably crazy? Perhaps not, but should he be teaching middle school students English? Personally, I wouldn't have trusted him to teach a fish how to swim.

As part of the readings I was doing throughout the year to earn my TEFL certification for Teaching English as a Foreign Language, I came across an article that stated "Ultimately, you want your students to see misbehavior as a disruption to their learning."

A good thought, but misbehavior was actually pretty far down on the list of disruptions. It was more like misbehavior resulted from outside disruptions that became the norm for a typical class, including other students poking their heads in the door or their hands through my classroom windows, a repairman working on the broken lights or installing cords while I was teaching, another teacher coming in the middle of class to make an announcement, students being pulled from my class to help another teacher, an iguana crawling through the ceiling—the list went on and on. Just as soon as we got into a groove of teaching, the week would be interrupted by another Monday festivo, another week of vacation, or a special event that canceled Friday classes.

Despite the school's (and Pedro's) attempts to have as little class as possible, by the time the third and fourth quarters came along, lessons were starting to improve. My classroom routine (or a semblance of one) became more established and I was finally doing more creative things with my classes.

The eighth graders presented dialogues about ordering food in restaurants by working off menus I printed out for them. I drew, cut out, and laminated (with packing tape) different household items, which students tried to place in the correct room on the board. And I was most proud of the labeled drawings my students made of a "Clean Beach" and a "Polluted Beach" while all the grades were working on beach and ecology vocabulary.

The students' drawings of the polluted beaches were filled with garbage, dead leaves, and large, nuclear-looking power plants, which were labeled "air pollution." Carlos's drawing had some of the palm trees chopped down. Claudia's had a sad-looking sun to counter the happy sun in her clean beach. In his clean beach drawing, Jesus María gave the sun trendy shades and a big grin. Ana Sofia's had two stick figures walking hand in hand. Daison's had a figure labeled "mother" tending to a plant labeled "flower." Camilo had a hilarious depiction of an upside-down snorkeler.

Huber Andrés even wrote about each of his beaches in Spanish—his polluted beach's description translated to: "The pollution of the most beautiful beaches in Colombia is no good. Leave them clean to reflect their beauty and your paradise."

And I couldn't help but walk home whistling cheerily the day when student after student came up to me continuously to ask for new words that they could add to their beach drawing.

"Enseño, how do you say lancha?" (Boat) "Profe, what mean nube en inglés?" (Cloud) "Teacher, cómo se dice arco iris?" (Rainbow). The rainbows may have been my favorite—maybe a quarter of my sixth graders decided to add a rainbow to their clean beach drawing. Instead of the usual spectrum of colors, these featured only three:

yellow, blue, and red. In that order, their rainbows were the Colombian flag.

Claudia even ran up to show me her drawing, which had a matching rainbow and Colombian flag flying on a boat to round off her clean beach. It brought a big smile to my face and I complimented it, then pointed out a misspelling of "polluted." I was both shocked and proud as she quickly ran back to her desk, calling out for the ubiquitous *liquipaper,* the Colombian version of White-Out, and, after commandeering her neighbor's bottle, she corrected the word. The brief smile she flashed me on her usually sullen face remained in my mind for weeks.

Learning and creativity were happening.

For an extra adventure, I volunteered to help chaperone the sixth and seventh grade field trip to Cartagena, which Tajan, the P.E. teacher, had organized. This meant I spent a long time on a bus with dozens of excited middle schoolers, came up with random English translations for the different sports-related destinations we went to, and was a crossing guard for students who were apparently unconcerned about the trucks that were careening around Cartagena's busy streets.

A lot of things were similar to U.S. field trips I had taken as a kid. Students had to pay ahead of time (13,000 pesos, which I found out meant many students couldn't afford to come). The morning of the trip, we loaded a bus and headed to the big city of Cartagena. Two of the students' mothers also came along to help supervise, though the ratio between students and adults certainly wasn't ten-to-one like many U.S. schools required, and I am not sure the thought of nametags or permission forms had ever crossed anyone's mind.

The bus ride was similar to what I remembered from my own middle school field trips, although it was much bumpier and somehow even louder. My students had a continuing problem of being unable to talk in anything less than a shout, which was a cultural tendency of all costeños, and problematic to the eardrums. The students frequently sang out snatches of song, deafening all those we passed. I couldn't make out the words through all the ruckus, but I guessed it was a Colombian version of "The Wheels on the Bus."

After visiting different sports fields and stadiums, we had lunch (which the students ate with amazing gusto considering the fact that every time we stopped they bought treats that weren't available on the island, including packaged chips, drinks, cookies, meat kebobs, and shaved ice). We took over a roasted chicken restaurant, where my students bought pieces of deliciously greasy chicken and more soda as the other teachers and I tried to corral them to make sure no one ran across the street.

This turned out to be a bigger job than I had envisioned since even after the students had finished their chicken, most of them still wanted to buy more snacks (really?) and water (this I could understand). Santa Ana kids weren't well-practiced in keeping track of traffic though, so finally I let them cross in groups while I looked in all directions to make sure the road was clear of motorcycles, trucks, buses, taxis, and horse carts. Luz Daris was excited (her normal state) and she was especially difficult to corral. She started to step out into the street while talking excitedly with her friend, and I threw out an arm to stop her from getting an up-close look at the side of a taxi. Learning to look both ways is a lesson lost when you live in a place where the biggest traffic problem was cows sitting in the middle of the road.

My students and I were progressing with creativity and actually learning something day-to-day. My sixth and eighth graders even got rewarded for their hard work by watching a copy of the animated feature *Rio* that I had (I also gave seventh grade the option to watch it, but unfortunately the students continued to be their usual less-than-cooperative selves, so they missed out on the movie). The sixth and eighth graders read the Spanish subtitles, half-listened to the English dialogue, and thoroughly enjoyed the songs. Katia had moved her desk up to the very front—sitting right in front of the speakers to better pick out any words she knew—while other students leaned back in their desks, just enjoying the film. When two characters careened around the narrow streets of Rio on a motorcycle, the students roared with laughter.

After the movie and class finished, a few students stayed behind.

Katia's pen was poised over her always-open notebook. "How do you say pájaro, moto, aula, y caja en inglés?" she asked, listing off things she had seen in the movie. I started to write the words on the board, adding to the vocabulary list I had introduced before the movie.

"Teacher, otra vez!" I turned to see Jorge, Luis Felipe, and a couple of other eighth grade boys still in the classroom as well.

"We don't have time to watch it again," I explained to them, though I took the fact that they didn't rush out as soon as the bell rang as a good sign.

"No, profe," Luis Felipe said, shaking his head. He explained that they wanted the credits back on.

I was still confused, but as I started the credits over, I realized what they wanted.

"La canción, teacher!" they shouted with glee. English dialogue was interesting, but songs were better. I turned it up. Katia bobbed her head to the song as she copied her new words off the board while Luis Felipe and Jorge started an impromptu dance party.

"Let Me Take You to Rio, Rio," the song sang out, and I leaned against the wall, laughing, not wanting to be anywhere else.

CHAPTER FOURTEEN

SURVIVING THE GUAJIRA

I tried to rest against the back cab of the truck, wedging myself into the corner for a little comfort as I sat in the bed of the pickup. However, I soon realized comfort was not an attainable goal. Between the jarring ride over dirt roads and the food poisoning trying to ruin my vacation, it was looking to be a long ride.

I was on vacation, and in the back of the pickup, because just as we were getting in the groove with classes, the Colombian school system had dictated another week off for all public schools. So while I would have preferred to be teaching, I was told to take the second week of October off and, in lieu of taking more long walks around Santa Ana, I headed north along the coast to the Guajira Peninsula, which was the northernmost tip of both Colombia and South America. The Guajira was notably different from much of Colombia in that it had a high population of indigenous peoples (mostly members of the Wayúu indigenous group) and that it was a desert. October through December may have been Colombia's rainy season, but that didn't mean all of Colombia was a lush green jungle during those months.

It also proved that rain wasn't the only thing that made me sick in Colombia.

My bus arrived in Riohacha in the early afternoon. Now it may have been because I arrived on a Sunday, but for the Guajira's capital and largest city, Riohacha was disconcertingly empty. One main market street had a little hustle and bustle, but otherwise the narrow streets of gray-brown concrete were devoid of any activity. There was little evidence of the 150,000 people that apparently lived in the Riohacha municipality as I headed away from my hotel to the center of town. As I walked, I became less and less sure I was headed in the right direction.

The road ended at the beach and I was happy to see signs of life (I was getting a little worried that there had been some mass alien abduction or the rapture or something). Riohacha's waterfront actually had people. It also had a few shops and restaurants, a short boardwalk stretching into the choppy waves, and a few dozen beach-goers lying around or playing soccer. Wayúu women dressed in simple tan dresses (the Guajira version of muumuus) watched over rows of brightly-colored cloth bags that they had woven, attracting a few customers walking by with ice cream.

But this was no Cartagena. I could step one block away from the water and the streets would became eerily desolate again.

The city itself didn't have much in the way of tourist activities, and I spent my first full day in the nearby town of Camarones, which was also right on the Caribbean—though I was far enough east to argue that the Caribbean had ended and the open Atlantic Ocean had begun. Camarones means "Shrimp," a name which drew me in, unlike the off-putting translation of Riohacha ("River of the Axe"). There was a bird sanctuary in Camarones, and I headed there Monday morning. The journey involved walking from my hotel to a nearby traffic circle to ask around for a *colectivo* to Camarones. Colectivo cars were common transport in Colombia. They were cheaper than actual taxis, had a flexible general route, and would leave whenever they had three or four passengers. It was usually a bit of a tight fit, but at least five times cheaper than a regular cab. The car might not have to pass a safety inspection, the driver might not have to pass any special driving test, and you might not get dropped off right in front of your door, but it was a cheap and logical way for people to get around.

I waited for my colectivo to fill while talking to a toothless character named Alejandro. His passion was vallenato music and he thought today's music had no message or poetry (apparently the best year for vallenato was 1978). I then listened as Alejandro sang me his favorite song.

If I thought Santa Ana played a lot of vallenato, it had nothing on Riohacha, where every taxi, shop, and house seemed to be tuned into the same tropicana radio station that was blasting the same few songs. No other region on earth could have had as many accordions belting out songs as the northern coast of Colombia, of this I was certain.

More passengers finally arrived at the colectivo stop, I gave old Alejandro a quick peck on the cheek goodbye, and we were on our way to Camarones, with vallenato (of course) playing on the radio. Fifteen minutes later, we got dropped off in the small town and I asked around for a mototaxi to the sanctuary. I soon found a willing driver and found myself on the back of a rickety moto, driving past a lush lagoon, salty air blowing on my face.

At the sanctuary, I took a gondola-style boat tour with a seventh grader named Joinel, then staked out a place in the shade on the beach and ordered some lunch from the makeshift restaurant. There were few people on the beach and the view was spectacular. Since the name of the place was Camarones, I decided to order some rice and shrimp, which I was excited to learn came with a side of patacones. I enjoyed the meal in the shade with sand underneath my feet and waves crashing not too far in the distance. I scraped my plate clean, leaving a sheen of oil.

The beach was a strange mix of the usual Caribbean staples of a crisp, blue sky, palm trees, and sandpipers—paired with cacti and goats. After walking along the shore for a long time and letting some of the local boys use my camera (note: if you give ten-year-old boys a camera to play with, they are guaranteed to take pictures of themselves with silly faces and pictures of a dead bird they find on the beach), I returned to Riohacha on the back of another mototaxi.

On the way, we stopped to pick up the driver's young daughter, who climbed on with us and sat wedged in front of her father.

Like in Santa Ana, Cartagena, and everywhere in Colombia, having multiple passengers on a motorcycle was common. A family of five could all squeeze onto one bike as long as everyone took care when they got off and the kids were small enough. Three adults created a tight fit, but a shortage of mototaxis sometimes necessitated this extra-friendly journey. I always questioned the law of physics when I watched motos whiz by carrying large pieces of furniture, baby carriages, or roof siding, but it was not an uncommon sight.

All three of us managed to arrive safely and I slid off the moto and found another colectivo back to my hotel in Riohacha. Inside, I packed for my next day's journey further north into the peninsula and enjoyed having a television at my disposal. I flipped through a couple of telenovelas, a baseball game, and the news, and realized many of the stations were Venezuelan because of how far east in Colombia I was. One began doing the 7:00 news, and I glanced down at my watch, which read 6:30. I leaned over to my alarm clock, which also read 6:30 p.m. (and 89 degrees). Strange as it seemed, the half-hour difference was correct. In Venezuela it was in fact a half hour later: official Venezuelan Legal Time, which was implemented by then-President Hugo Chávez in 2007 for a number of reasons, including an attempt to improve Venezuelan education. Chávez was quoted as saying "These children have to get up at five in the morning... they arrive at school dead tired. And why? Because of our time." So now they all get up a half hour later.

I'm pretty sure the root of South America's education problems was not that the sun just starts rising when my students are scheduled to begin class. But who knows? Maybe it would improve a few things.

So I enjoyed a variety of Colombian, U.S. American, and Vene-zuelan TV programs, and finally went to sleep around 10:00 (that's 10:30 to you, Chávez).

I don't know what time it was when I first woke up, but I blamed the rain that beat loudly on my windows. The storm caused water to stream down the windows, thunder crashed, and I then felt a familiar unpleasant feeling in my digestive tract. My lovely beach meal was exacting revenge on my stomach.

When morning dawned, I walked out into the fresh air (and predictably quiet streets) and made it to a store to buy my new favorites, saltines and Gatorade, which I drank with an Imodium to try to quell the diarrhea. The debate was whether to continue my planned journey north or if I should stay in Riohacha and weather the storm. Could I make the trip without the convenience of an en suite bathroom? Would I get worse before getting better? Was it possible that I would become even more ill halfway through the colectivo ride and my fellow passengers would feel the need leave me on the side of the road? I debated for a bit of the morning, but finally, with a small bag packed full of my saltines and extra toilet paper, I set off.

Another colectivo took me to the town of Uribia, which was about an hour and a half north into the peninsula. The air condition-ing felt good, though the man in the passenger seat chatted away in a voice that was better suited for shouting over a picó. The well-dressed lady and overweight man who were with me in the back seat didn't seem too happy to be so squished together—I didn't tell them they should have been grateful I wasn't throwing up on them.

In Uribia, I jumped out and quickly asked around for a bathroom. At the back of some market stalls, a man pointed me to a wooden door on the side of his house and I made good use of the toilet paper I had brought. I was grateful that I had found a place to use the bathroom, but if it hadn't been an emergency, there would have been no way I would have set foot in that room. I have used many a pit toilet in my day, but that outhouse took the cake. And it cost me 1,000 pesos, which was the worst cash-to-cleanliness bathroom stop ever. I'll refrain from describing it further.

Safely out of the bathroom, I found a colectivo that was headed to Cabo de la Vela, the town I hoped to make it to that afternoon. This would have been a good time to ride in a charter bus with a bathroom in the back, but I had no such luck. The colectivo was not even a regular car. Instead, it consisted of a white 1990s Ford F-150 pickup truck covered in a fine film of red-brown dust. In the back bed, bench-like seats lined each side, with a hard top secured by bars to give us some shade along the ride and provide an extra rack for cargo and spare tires.

Unsure when the truck was leaving and deciding it best if I didn't remain standing too long, I climbed into the bed and found a seat in the corner, after navigating around some blue plastic barrels that left one wanting in the leg room category. At first this extra cargo seemed like a good idea. We were, after all, heading deep into the Auyama Desert, and my first thought was that the barrels contained extra water, so I didn't begrudge them too much for giving me leg cramps. Then I realized the barrels were emitting a potent and rather unpleasant smell. Gasoline? Perhaps they were being delivered to small communities that we might be passing or carried as an extra precaution of riding through the desert?

But then a man in his sixties, with a wide smile and many missing teeth, came up and unscrewed one of the caps on the barrels. He took a tube from his pocket, pulled out an empty coke bottle, and siphoned off some of the clear liquid.

"Quieres un poco?" he asked me, holding out the now-full bottle. The look I gave him, full of confusion and illness, caused him to explain further. "Es vino de arroz," he said, grinning. Then he held up his bottle again and took a long swig.

Apparently the jugs contained the Colombian version of sake, and I finally realized the smell wafting from the barrels was most akin to rubbing alcohol. Rice wine... is there no end to how rice haunted me? Technically, the liquid may not have been gasoline, but I had a feeling that if our gas gauge started to head towards empty, we could have put some of that stuff in the tank and it would have powered us just fine.

With what I hoped was a friendly smile that didn't reflect my queasiness, I told the man I didn't want any moonshine and I leaned back against the truck. The man started taking large gulps of the stuff, and a little while later, I was happy to discover that he was not the one who climbed behind the wheel of our colectivo.

In addition to the plastic jugs and the unpleasant smell, three other tourists soon filled the bed of the truck, joining me along with six or seven locals, including a young girl in a red dress who sat on the barrels and would spend the entire trip staring at me, chewing gum, and popping bubbles.

We set off, leaving behind the hustle and bustle of Uribia, which had an economy based almost entirely on contraband goods going to and from Venezuela, and sped along a paved road. I closed my eyes, wishing I could enjoy the ride, but the road soon turned from asphalt to dirt, and the combination of the bumpy seats, my cramping legs, the smell of the *vino,* and the clenching battle between my stomach and intestines made the journey a test to see if I could survive it. We jolted and bumped out of town, and I realized that given the opportunity, I might even have eaten a whole bowl of mondongo cow stomach soup to get rid of my stomach problems (of course, as I considered this wry thought, the very idea of mondongo threatened to make me lose whatever was left in my stomach, so I quickly turned my thoughts to other things to distract myself, such as the fact that the remote Guajira region had on average one FARC attack a month. I prayed that wouldn't disrupt my trip either).

I opened my eyes when I felt us turn into what appeared to be a sparse forest. Feeling discombobulated, I looked around for the road. As we weaved around low-lying trees and thin saguaro-like cacti, I managed to spot a tire track or two up ahead. We went over a rocky bit, causing our four-wheel-drive to kick in and dust to billow up behind us.

Apparently the route (it certainly could not be called a road) we were driving on was an actual path that other vehicles took, and we stopped briefly at a stick and mud house to stretch our legs and drop off one of the giant jugs of alcohol. Then it was off again, twisting between trees with branches that occasionally brushed against the truck as we bumped along the sparse landscape. All the jolting caused me to close my eyes again, feeling that if I had made it this far without vomiting or needing to have the driver stop for a bathroom break behind the nearest cactus, there was hope of arriving in Cabo de la Vela unscathed.

After a bit (my sense of time was completely out of whack), I felt the wind pick up and our speed suddenly increase, and opened my eyes again. Trees lay to our right, ocean was to our left, and we were now speeding along a strip of sand near the shore on an expanse of dry plains. As we neared Cabo de la Vela, we stopped a couple of times to let off passengers—sometimes at a clustering of wooden dwellings, other times seemingly in the middle of nowhere. We unpacked their cases of soda and whatever else the passengers had bought in Uribia and finally moved on until we arrived in the actual town with only a few tourists left.

Cabo de le Vela had around a thousand people and may have been the most stretched-out town I had ever been to: the whole community was spread out along a five-mile stretch of beach and was only one or two houses deep along both sides of the sandy road. While most people translated the name of the town to the "Cape of the Sail" (apparently the land looked like a sailboat to Spanish sailors, though I question the creativity of men who hadn't seen anything but their own ship for a few months), its other translation of the "Cape of the Candle" also worked since the town was thin and followed a near straight line, with a lighthouse at its far end. Most of the buildings were made of wood and had roofs thatched with palm fronds, though some did have a concrete wall or two.

I hadn't researched places to stay, except to learn that there were dozens of tiny hotels to rent hammocks from, so I just stayed in the truck until we looped away from the more touristy parts and past advertisements for windsailing. After much debate, I picked a place where I could sleep in a hammock under an open-air hut on the beach side of the road for 10,000 pesos a night. I paid my 12,000 pesos to the driver for the bumpy ride and settled in.

In some sense, my two days in Cabo de la Vela were what a beach getaway should be: lying around in a hammock a few feet from the waves, munching on snacks, reading, napping, watching black-eyed crabs scuttling around in the sand, and staring out at the ocean. Of course, my time in the hammock stemmed from my inability to do much walking around and my snacks consisted of saltine crackers and sips of Gatorade. Still, Cabo de la Vela—with its fresh air and lethargic pace—was a good backdrop for my battle with whatever microbes were still partying it up in my digestive tract.

Of course, I couldn't stay in the hammock forever, and I soon found myself dashing off to the bathroom stalls, where I found a row of squat toilets and no running water. There was a large rain barrel sitting outside with a makeshift bucket next to it—obviously the manual flush on the toilets. I leaned over the barrel and looked down: it was empty. We were in a desert after all, but it meant I would end up owing an apology to anyone who had to use the bathrooms over the next two days. By the time I scrounged up enough water to flush the toilet the next day, it might have been able to beat the outhouse in Uribia in a Filthiest Bathroom competition.

I was eternally grateful that I had stocked up on toilet paper before I had left Riohacha.

I woke up to sunshine and a breeze that was causing my hammock to sway back and forth ever so softly. The motion didn't immediately cause me to run for the bathroom, which I took as a good sign, and I got in a short walk along the beach in the stiff salty breeze.

Mothers and daughters walked along the beach with bags slung down their backs and the straps around their foreheads as they chatted in their native language of *Wayuunaiki*. One family came up to ask me in Spanish to buy some of their brightly-colored woven handicrafts. Their dark skin and broad faces were typical of the town, where almost everyone claimed the indigenous heritage of the Wayúu Amerindians, a group descended from the Arawak group in the Caribbean, which was one of the few groups the Spanish failed to defeat in their colonization of Colombia. The Wayúu were one of Colombia's most prominent indigenous people and made up a full 20% of Colombia's indigenous population. Though that population isn't exactly gigantic, however: indigenous peoples only make up 1%

of Colombia's population (in contrast, their southern neighbors, Ecuador and Peru, have indigenous populations of around 25% and over 30% respectively). In fact, as much as Colombian Wayúu Amerindians were able to maintain much of their culture, there were many more Wayúu over the border in Venezuela.

Through an interesting quirk of the calendar, I was in Cabo de la Vela on Columbus Day. Strangely enough, Columbus never landed on or even saw the country that now bore his name; the closest he got was seeing other countries that were once part of Bolívar's Gran Colombia. Columbus sailed down the coast of Panama (trying in vain to find some sort of southwest passage) and, in 1498, made landfall in what today is Venezuela. But he spent most of his voyages in the Caribbean, frightening American Indians, establishing colonies, and thinking he was in Asia (until a brief land expedition into Venezuela finally made him realize he had found a new land rather than just a collection of Asian islands).

Despite naming their country after the guy, Colombians don't have a Columbus (or Colón) Day. Instead, they celebrate the date in October when Columbus first spotted Caribbean land as *La Día de la Raza,* or The Day of Race or Roots. And it made sense to celebrate it: most Colombians had both indigenous and Spanish roots; 50% of Colombians were mestizo and many more some combination of Spanish, indigenous, and black.

And at least this far east in Colombia, I was finally near an area that Columbus had actually seen.

Cabo de la Vela was sacred to the Wayúu people, but they also were trying to attract tourism, hence all the tiny businesses with hammock space to rent and the persistence of the women trying to get me to buy their bags and headbands. As the mother and daughter who had approached me walked off and switched back to speaking in Wayuunaiki, it felt like I had stumbled upon yet another Colombia.

It was a new view of the country. The dry rolling hills and tiny shrubs growing in the rocky soil reminded me of the expanses of Nevada; that is if Nevada had been located right on the Caribbean Sea. In one direction you had all the desert hills covered in red-brown rock, low green shrubs, and cacti. In the other direction was the open ocean, surf crashing on rocks, sandy beaches, and water as far as you could see.

Despite it being a desert, I awoke from a mid-morning nap to a few raindrops. The lady from my hotel (to use the term loosely) hurried over and helped me take down the hammock and restring it in the indoor courtyard as the rain blew in in sheets.

Few people were out in the uniquely wet weather, though there was one man in front of us who had grabbed a long-handled brush and commenced washing his truck, scrubbing the sides and tires as the rain washed the desert dust away.

The man, whose name was Jorge, soon finished cleaning his truck and came over to join me under the cover of an open-air hut with a roof made from palm fronds. Jorge was an interesting enigma. He loved to talk about movies (his favorites were Bruce Lee films), wanted to learn Japanese (which made me try to recall Bruce Lee's heritage—note to Jorge: Bruce was a Hong Kong-raised, Chinese-American), and he was the first Colombian over twenty-five I had met who didn't have kids. We passed the time by watching the rain together and trying to remember different actors in a wide variety of Hollywood films.

After the wet weather let up, Jorge headed off to see if he had missed any spots on his truck, and I realized I was actually feeling hungry. I ventured down the now-muddy street to see if I could find a house I had passed that morning that had a sign advertising soup. I successfully found the sign, but didn't see much in the way of a restaurant.

"Buenas," I greeted a woman walking out of the kitchen. "Tienes sopa?"

At first the lady looked apologetic, then she paused.

"Pues, si quieres esperar, puedo cocinarla." If I could wait, she'd cook me some soup to order. Apparently the sign was a bit of false advertising for a ready-made menu, but I agreed on the spot, then thought I'd ask what type of soup she was going to cook. Please, not mondongo, I prayed.

"Pescado," she instantly replied. Fish—what else on the beach?

I breathed a sigh of relief, told her it sounded great, and settled into a chair at a table outside.

About a half hour later, out came the bowl of soup: delicious broth with plantains, cassavas, bell pepper, yuca, cilantro, other spices, a lime on the side, and an entire fish sitting in the liquid, its middle bending down and its head and tail sticking out of the broth. Despite it staring at me, the need to scrape its pink scales off, and me accidentally swallowing a fish bone, the soup was salty and delicious and it hit the spot after two days of saltines and bananas. Fresh, made-to-order soup for only 6,000 pesos was a decision I was happy with, especially when it all stayed down.

"Cómo estaba?" the lady asked, as she cleared my dishes.

"Rico," I responded truthfully, rubbing my calm stomach.

"Viajas sola?" was her next question. Are you traveling alone? This was a common question I had gotten all over Colombia. Regardless of their gender, Colombians rarely headed to another room without their wife or child or friend with them for companionship.

"Soy de los Estados Unidos, pero enseño inglés cerca de Cartagena," I responded, and I could tell her interest was instantly peaked.

"Roberto!" she called, and soon her husband appeared from the back. The lady, who I soon learned was named Rosana, explained with some excitement to her husband Roberto that I was an English teacher.

We ended up chatting for almost an hour, throwing in a few English words as we discussed my teaching, the Guajira, and their desire to learn English. We exchanged contact information, firm handshakes, and a kiss on each cheek before saying our goodbyes.

Before I left I also bought some bags of water from Rosana and Roberto. To top everything off, I had somehow caught a cold (maybe there *was* something to this rain-causing-illness thing). So considering my diarrhea, head cold, the amount I usually sweated in the Colombian sun, and the fact that I was in the desert, I wanted to make sure I was ready for whatever Mother Nature had decided to throw my way next.

It was another night of little sleep, this time for reasons other than a few bathroom trips. Once, I woke up because I was actually hungry. A couple of times I was startled awake because of mosquitoes that had appeared out of nowhere after the rain. And I also woke up in the middle of the night because I had set my alarm for 3:30 a.m. to catch the colectivo back to Uribia.

The trucks always left at around 4:00 a.m. (apparently to make it there and back in one day), and so I stood along the road in the quiet, moonlit morning, munching crackers and looking out for headlights. Soon a truck pulled up, other passengers arrived, and we all climbed into the bed of the truck. A few men chatting in Wayuunaiki tied bundles to the metal rack on top of the truck and loaded a few sacks into the back of the cab (I sniffed at one container apprehensively, but there was no rice wine on this trip, thankfully).

Everyone got in the back and we looped through town, riding right along the water and waves on the beach, picked up more people, and finally were off through the dark desert, our tires wet with seawater. Bright blue flashes of lightning revealed the landscape and ocean as we bumped between tress and cacti on our path through the terrain, which now included large puddles formed from the recent rain. A baby wrapped in her mother's arms didn't let out a peep and two kids who looked about my students' age gave me shy smiles. Others slept, and one couple, their faces wrinkled with age, leaned against each other the whole ride, wrapped in a thin sheet to try to block the cold wind.

After joining the main dirt road again, we stopped for a coffee break (tinto, of course) at a random crossroads, where the morning light made everything—from the road to the expanse of rocks—a rosy pink. After about fifteen minutes, we were on our way until we stopped back in Uribia about two and a half hours later. I got off and the truck rumbled away, continuing to the town of Maicao and the Venezuelan border.

As for me, after a night (and shower) in Riohacha, I went back south along the coast, the dry shrubs turning into green fields and forests of palm trees, the flat horizons turning into the towering green of the Sierra Nevada mountains. I went past tiny towns, impoverished fishing villages, stone churches, concrete police stations, and expanses of countryside, back to my island.

CHAPTER FIFTEEN

Not Yet a Paradise

I turned down the road to IESA and it was obvious that it was not another quiet Sunday in town.

Our six Santa Ana policemen were standing around with reinforcements: at least three army guys dressed in full camouflage were gripping machine guns as they stood guard around the school.

It was Election Day in Colombia. As part of the nationwide regional elections that were taking place, the government had deployed 330,000 army troops and police officers throughout the country to "keep voter peace," even in Santa Ana. Each soldier gripped his machine gun with both hands and had bulging pouches of ammo around his belt. They looked ready to battle guerrillas in the street, which was a little disconcerting.

The negative press Colombia receives surrounding its reputation as a country overrun by drug cartels and paramilitaries is generally the stuff of stereotypes, hyperbole, and a past history, but there is no denying that political problems affect everyone in the country, even in tiny Santa Ana.

At family gatherings in the United States, two off-limit subjects are almost always put together in the same phrase: no religion or politics. While in Colombia the former was embraced ("What do you mean you aren't Catholic?"), the latter was taboo. While it may be the only reason that Colombia (or Columbia) makes the international news outside of prostitution or scandals, Colombia's political problems, drug trade, and civil conflicts are forbidden subjects for most Colombians. The FARC, government corruption, paramilitaries, and the drug trade were things I never heard much about unless I was flipping through a newspaper or brought it up with the teachers who I had gotten to know.

"Yes, there is so much corruption," Marelis would say, then she would shrug and change the subject.

"The FARC has caused so much trouble, but so has the government," Alvaro would state slowly, then lean back, pensive.

"I am going to vote, yes," Arelis said, but did not continue.

Even when the regional election day came up on October 30th, many still considered talking about politics to be taboo. Whether this was because people's opinions were too polarized, the violence and civil conflicts had taken personal tolls on friends and families that were too painful to discuss, or people were apathetic because of a broken political system, I never really figured out. Poverty, marginalization, economic disparities, and drugs in the community were problems in Santa Ana, and problems throughout Colombia.

When politics come up in Colombia, it is hard not to mention the FARC. As the most influential of Colombia's guerrilla groups, they play the part of a well-organized force that the government can use as a scapegoat whenever a problem arises. Corruption in government? The FARC is disrupting our system. Price of corn going up? The FARC is disrupting trade. Your cow just died? Those tricky FARC with their mind powers, preying on your livelihood.

The FARC (the Spanish acronym for the Revolutionary Armed Forces of Colombia) have been a big player on the scene for a long time, and living in Colombia in 2011 meant I needed to know their history.

The FARC began as a Marxist political movement, one of many guilty parties that came out of the period from the late 1940s through the early 1960s when over 200,000 Colombians were killed. It is still simply called *La Violencia*.

From 1948 through the 1980s, the FARC were trying to implement political change. At the same time, they were focused on the normal terrorist activities of extortion, kidnappings, forcing people off their land, using child soldiers... the usual day-to-day. Eventually they decided to start taxing marijuana growers, then coca growers and cocaine laboratories (like any self-respecting, wannabe government). Then, like any good entrepreneur, they thought, hell, why don't we just control everything about the cocaine trade? So began their participation in the illegal drug trade.

The United States pours money into Colombia to fight drug trafficking and this terrorist-labeled group. Since the late 1990s, the United States has spent something to the tune of $8 billion dollars trying to stop the FARC's activities as part of Plan Colombia. This highly-militarized plan involves a lot of U.S. intelligence and military goods heading to the Colombian army. Through the 1990s, the main goal was countering the drug trade and involved the highly unsuccessful fumigation of coca crops, which lead to health and environmental problems (there was also the problem of the planes destroying food and other crops indiscriminately).

When the FARC created an actual political party in 1984 and won mayoral and congressional seats, the Colombian government collaborated with different paramilitary groups and competing drug traffickers to assassinate members of the party. Needless to say, this did not encourage the FARC to abandon their armed resistance for seats in Congress and they fled to the hills (in this case, the dense jungles and mountains in the most rural areas of Colombia). Their numbers grew and violence increased. Peace negotiations in 2002 failed miserably and FARC mortars fell around the presidential palace during the presidential inauguration of Alvaro Uribe in 2002. Peace negotiations in 2013 and 2014, however, have led to some optimism about an eventual disarmament.

The FARC was by no means the only organized crime group trying to control the drug trade or armed political quasi-army operating in Colombia. In reaction to the tactics used by the left-leaning rebels, right-leaning paramilitary groups cropped up in the 1980s, and used similar tactics of extortion and violence. The alphabet soup mix of armed groups operating in Colombia included the ELN (the National Liberation Army), the Urabeños, the Rastrojos, the ERPAC (which ironically stands for The Popular Revolutionary Anti-Terrorist Army of Colombia, and was one of many groups that started with government support), and the Oficina de Envigado (the remnants the Medellín cartel of infamous drug lord Pablo Escobar).

Pablo Escobar: to many U.S. Americans, the drug lord is still perhaps the most famous Colombian, despite twenty years passing since his death and stiff competition from Shakira, Juanes, writer Gabriel García Márquez, and buxom actress Sofía Vergara, among others.

Escobar was Colombia's most successful and notorious drug lord. He got his start as a car thief in Medellín and began smuggling narcotics in the mid-1970s. Ten years later, Escobar had dozens of planes and helicopters (as well as two submarines) and controlled up to an estimated 80% of the world's cocaine trade. His rise to power came through killing anyone who got in his way and bribing, threatening, and assassinating local leaders, politicians, judges, journalists, and police officers. Escobar's men would visit or write to a politician and give them a choice: "plata o plomo?" In English: "silver or lead?" If bribes didn't work, then Escobar's enemies knew the alternative.

As well as individual murders, Escobar's cartel bombed a passenger plane in 1989, killing over 100 people, and bombed the headquarters of DAS (the immigration administration that was my introduction to Colombia back in Bogotá), killing 52 people and injuring over 1,000. In total, Escobar was supposed to be responsible for over 4,000 deaths. While Escobar was in power, Medellín had the highest murder rate in the world because of all the bombings and assassinations: 381 murders for every 100,000 people. The 1980s were not a fantastic time to be living in Colombia to say the least.

But I had to remember that the United States played a role in Colombia's darkest days. In the 1970s and '80s, demand for cocaine and marijuana in the United States grew, which is the reason why the drug trade began in Colombia at all. The millions made in the drug trade made Escobar, and the equally violent Cali cartel, both rich and powerful. The beautiful hills of the Sierra Nevada de Santa Marta Mountains became prime growing land for marijuana (known as Santa Marta Gold when exported) and the southern districts in the Andes foothills and Amazon basin could barely keep up with the U.S. demand for their coca. In 2009, an estimated 68,000 hectares (or about 153,000 football fields) were under cultivation for coca, with even more growing marijuana and opium poppies. Even after the break-up of major Medellín and Cali cartels, drugs are still a big business in Colombia.

But despite Escobar's violent rule, some Colombians remember him in a more positive light. Many claim that because he kept a firm hold on the underworld, incidents of theft, violence, and kidnapping increased after his death. Escobar used his drug money to invest in soccer teams, construction projects, and housing for the poor.

He also invested in an extravagant personal lifestyle. He considered himself above the law, and also successfully influenced (to use a euphemism) politicians, causing them to change laws to help grow his wealth. Most notably, Escobar was able to delay an extradition treaty that would have allowed the U.S. Government to capture him and try him in the United States. By the late 1980s, Escobar was worth a reported $30 billion and was even elected as an "alternate representative" to Colombia's congress. He was still living a powerful, extravagant lifestyle in 1993 when he was tracked down by police and killed in Medellín.

Escobar's notoriety, even twenty years after his death, doesn't look as if it will be wavering anytime soon. Travel agencies now advertise five star vacations where you can travel to the Medellín area and visit Escobar's old haunts. Since 2007, the Colombian government has rebuilt his estate, known as Hacienda Nápoles, creating a theme park of sorts to attract curious tourists.

You enter Hacienda Nápoles under a large archway that has one of Escobar's old smuggling planes perched on top of it. Walk around the hacienda and you'll see other remnants of Escobar's life as a drug lord. Silent guard towers watch over the gardens and trees. An old landing strip where his planes that transported cocaine used to take off from is still intact. His grand estate was mostly burned and looted after his death, but you can still explore some of the rooms that remain (locals never admitted to finding any of the money or valuables that he had allegedly hidden within the walls). Escobar's enormous vintage car collection was burned and destroyed after his death, but its remnants are still there for viewing purposes. Signs and pictures tell some of the story of Escobar's rise and eventual fall as the leader of the Medellín cartel.

Yet the purpose of Hacienda Nápoles is not to act as a sobering museum to reflect on the tragedies the drug trade brought to Colombia. Escobar essentially built himself a playground and these luxuries are now their own tourist attraction. His private zoo, pools, and bullfighting ring are now viewed by tourists as they wander through his estate. Tickets are purchased at a front desk shaped like giant crocodile, and after passing the remnants of the infrastructure needed to smuggle cocaine, you can visit a butterfly house, caged jaguars, and the largest population of hippopotamuses outside of Africa (the population thrived and went feral when the hacienda was abandoned after Escobar's death).

Cars with names of African countries drive you around the African Safari section of the hacienda, where the main attraction is a rhinoceros and the entrance is decorated with paintings of African landscapes and statues that look like African warriors, complete with shields and spears. Even the hotel there is called Hotel Safari Casablanca (and is decorated to look vaguely Moroccan, including cement camels out front). Take note: if you are planning an African safari and accidentally end up in South America, Hacienda Nápoles might be a good Plan B.

While touring the hacienda, you'll walk through the shade of leafy trees and might have to pause to do a double take. Looming high above you is a giant statue of a pink hippopotamus, posing mid-dance in a grass skirt.

Continue down a ways and the animals get larger—the remnants of Escobar's Parque Jurásico (which he built before *Jurassic Park* hit the big screens in 1993; no one said Escobar wasn't a visionary). Life-sized concrete dinosaurs tower overhead, complete with recordings of what are apparently dinosaur roars.

Then you might head to one of the seven pools to cool off with a swim. Sticking with the tradition of Escobar's strange excesses, the resort has built elaborate waterslides in and around the pools. One has a maze of platforms and bridges, multiple dinosaurs, and a wooly mammoth (confirming that the resort is in no way attempting to be a natural history museum), while another has a waterslide that is built into the flailing arms of a giant bronze octopus.

Hacienda Nápoles is now one of the mostly popular resort theme parks in South America, attracting over 50,000 people every year. Their slogan: "Enjoy a Truly Wild Adventure."

Perhaps it is a good thing that the evidence of the gross excesses of Escobar's drug lifestyle remains for the world to ponder. It does provide a physical locale to show how Colombia is moving on from how it was in the 1980s and '90s (with its violent, all-consuming drug and guerrilla culture) to become a tourist destination. Medellín has rebranded itself as the City of the Eternal Spring (which sounded very attractive after almost a year of coastal heat), and while it still struggles with gangs and severe wealth disparity like most of Colombia, it is now a major tourist and business destination. And between 2002 and 2010, murder rates in the country halved while under the administration of President Alvaro Uribe.

Who would have thought hippopotamuses would be a showcase of that change?

Yet Pablo Escobar's legacy continues—through the strangely amusing Hacienda Nápoles, and through more sobering ways in the dozens of smaller cartels, gangs, and narcotraffickers that continue to make drug-running a lucrative business in Colombia.

Even today, police estimate that 40% of all murders in Colombia are a result of turf disputes between different cartels, gangs, and *bacrims*. Bacrims (short for *bandas criminales* or criminal bands or gangs) were becoming Colombia's new power players fighting for drug territory and political power. A variety of groups (most dominantly the FARC) still control both the domestic and international drug trade.

While most reports on Colombia and drugs focus on the violent drug trade itself, around 20% of the cocaine and 70% of the marijuana that the country produces is not exported, but sold and used in Colombia. The drugs that are used and smoked in Colombia are usually of a cheaper quality and thus more addictive and more detrimental to one's health than the drugs that are exported. Selling smokable coca-base to already-struggling populations is a lucrative business for the cartels, the paramilitaries, and the FARC.

Some groups such as M-19, AUC, and EPL have disbanded since the 1990s, with some members rejoining regular civilian life. However, other former guerrillas simply joined a different paramilitary group and these successor groups have continued to commit mass murder, rape, and large amounts of extortion, as well as causing forced displacement. In 2011, the numbers of paramilitaries were estimated at around 5,700 fighters.

Still, there are now fewer major groups than there were in the past, which at least is beneficial to those who are just trying to keep up with all the acronyms. Today there remain the left-wing guerrillas with professed political motives, cartels and gangs jostling for part of the drug market, right-wing paramilitaries professing to fight these powers, and the government, which both fight and make allies with groups on every side.

If there is one thing that all the political scientists studying the civil conflicts in Colombia agree on, it is that the conflicts are complicated. As historians Michael J. LaRosa and Germán R. Mejía put it:

By the late 1990s, the FARC and ELN were fighting the military, the AUC were fighting the leftist guerrillas, the military was supposedly fighting the AUC, the FARC, and the ELN, and the drug barons were fighting the government while simultaneously fighting and collaborating with the guerrilla forces.

Politics, armed conflict, and drug running are obviously a complicated mix.

However, the once-bleak situation was improving in the years before my stay in Colombia. The FARC's numbers were estimated at

16,000 in 2001, but a decade later, the Colombian Army had killed many of the FARC's leaders, the forces were pushed into smaller and smaller sections of Colombia (which is why most parts of Colombia are now considered "safe"), and the number of members has dropped to around 8,000. Starting in 2013, the FARC and the Colombian government met for another round of peace negotiations in an attempt to reach compromise on such issues as land redistributions, drug trafficking, the rights of victims, and if there will be amnesty or political involvement for FARC guerrillas who agree to disarm.

The FARC (and the ELN for that matter) still contend that they are a political force fighting against the corrupt government and for the right of the *pueblo,* particularly Colombia's rural population. One man's kidnapping victim is another's prisoner-of-war. Some of the things they are fighting for, such as trying to shift Colombia's unequal land distribution (1% of the population owns 52% of the land), could certainly help the country. As far as other issues, such as their hold on the drug trade... not so much.

Call the diverse but related conflicts what you want (drug wars, warring cartels, civil war, the people's uprising, terrorism, anti-terrorism...) but there is no innocent party in Colombia's civil conflict. The problems and abuses continue to add up:

Twenty million Colombians living in poverty and looking for a way out. Colombian soldiers killing civilians and planting evidence to up their rebel kill totals as "false positives." Landmines placed by the FARC, paramilitaries, and the government over the past decades continuing to kill and maim both soldiers and civilians, topping 10,000 deaths since 1990 (making Colombia second to only Afghanistan in number of landmine incidents). Paramilitaries and guerrillas targeting human rights groups, trade unions, journalists, community leaders, politicians, and teachers for kidnapping and assassination. Men, women, and children forced to move from their homes because of violence or human rights abuses (more than one person out of ten in Colombia has fled or been forced out of their community, giving the country the dubious distinction of having the largest internally displaced population in the world—almost twice as many as second-ranked Sudan). Crops and livelihoods of all kind fumigated by army planes looking to destroy coca plants. Villages mowed down by machine guns and blown up by grenades.

This shit is messed up.

A year earlier I had decided to come to Colombia to explore what the country looked like beyond the stereotypes of civil conflict. I had convinced my family and friends before leaving that Colombia was a "safe" place and that the country's troubles were all in the past. While I had found that Colombia was more than its negative international reputation and was reinventing itself, the fact was that the country's troubles were not entirely in the past.

Isla Barú was not in rebel-held territory. Santaneros were not members of drug cartels. I never journeyed deep into the jungle to the sites of forgotten massacres, and I only briefly passed through land that had had recent FARC or ELN activity (the Guajira and the Santa Marta mountains made that list). And yet Colombia is a sum of all its parts, and my students and friends were affected by these problems.

Traveling between and through the neighborhoods outside the Centro in Cartagena to Santa Ana revealed Colombia's wealth disparity, which was one of the worst in the world. Of the million or so people who called Cartagena home, over 600,000 were poor. While there was a prosperous upper class, 45% to 60% of Colombians lived below the poverty line, and few owned land. This disparity, and the fact so many Colombians were struggling just to get by, underlined the myriad other problems Colombia was grappling with. Drug sales, petty crime, armed robbery, and trafficking of humans, even children, joined the selection of crimes directly affecting the poorer neighborhoods and towns like the one I was living in. As much as I loved living in Santa Ana, looking around at the struggling community and the bigger context of their poverty could be disheartening and I sometimes wondered how the little I was doing could ever improve the lives of my neighbors.

A growing semblance of a democracy was better than none at all and lines of people headed to the polls that October election morning to cast their vote, to try and keep Colombia headed down a more positive path.

For more than a month before Election Day, we had seen political advertising going up, promoting candidates for governors, mayors, and municipal council members. In Cartagena, posters with the candidate's face, political party (there were seven main parties in Colombia), and slogans were tacked to light poles, glued to walls, and put up on billboards. Out of the cities, it was common for random walls of old homes or vacant lots to be painted over with a candidate's name and slogan. We even had old concrete walls in Santa Ana repainted sparkling white and yellow to promote different candidates (painted over the chipped paint from the last election).

Car advertising was also popular, with entire private cars repainted with the candidate's message and image. Along the coast, some candidates had entire vallenato songs about them blasting from speakers in the back of their campaign's truck. The songs would go something like this (to the beats of drums and accordions): "Pedro Calderón is the choice for the people for Riohacha! He is smart, comes from a good family, will fight for you, and loves vallenato more than any other candidate! Vote Pedro for mayor! For change we can sing to!"

Okay, maybe I made those lyrics up. The songs were blasted so loudly that many of the lyrics were distorted and they used enough slang that Bogotá residents probably wondered what language the singer was using. So I didn't fare too well in trying to translate them, but what else were they going to sing about?

Many things seemed to be problematic with Colombia's elections this time around. One of the more depressing statistics was that forty-one candidates had been killed that election season, which was way up from twenty-seven candidates the last time Colombia had local elections.

But as a whole, election violence over the past decades had decreased. In the 1990 election, four presidential candidates were killed (including the front-runner, Luis Carlos Galán, who was allegedly assassinated on Escobar's orders). In the 1990s the forces in the civil conflict would usually try to disrupt the election rather than join it, increase attacks on both civilians and government troops, and boycott the vote. In contrast, during the 2011 elections, the FARC, the bacrims, and the political factions that were fighting them were all battling for control of local power and funds, so vote-buying, threats to voters and candidates, and illegal financing of campaigns was common.

In the large-scale, there were reports of bacrims buying up a few city blocks in a *barrio* for a candidate, guaranteeing this candidate all the votes in the area. How they do that probably covered all manner of crimes. These problems aren't likely to stop if the FARC gives up its armed fight and joins the political arena for good.

Independent watchdog groups identified more than 13,000 candidates (of 101,000) who were linked to "dubious interests," 447 of whom were actually facing criminal charges or had some other problem with the law that should have made them ineligible to run. Corruption seemed to apply at every level and in every political party, and while the government seemed to be cracking down on many cases of voter fraud, it was hard to imagine that the government had not also taken part in some of the more under-handed, illegal, and even vicious ways to try to gain votes so they could remain in power.

All these depressing statistics were known in part because elections were being better monitored. The government was trying to keep up appearances by fighting corruption, saying the right things, and canceling ID cards that appeared to be fraudulent. Yet corruption continued in all forms and at all levels.

In Santa Ana, I am still unsure how many of these problems were happening, but when I headed to IESA to see the voting firsthand, things looked like they were going smoothly. The usual IESA guards were helping two of the policemen organize the throng of people outside the gate. Five or six voters were let in at a time to make sure the polling place wasn't too overwhelmed, and the rest were bunched up outside, looking through the posted lists of cedula numbers to check that they were able to vote. Stepping outside his regular teaching duties, Alvaro, dressed in a rain slicker, was helping the residents of Santa Ana and Ararca find their cedula numbers and which table they'd be voting at.

It was a damp day, with muddy roads and a light rain falling, but that didn't seem to stop anyone from voting. It did, however, make the polling place more dangerous: with all the people and their umbrellas jostling to see the lists, it was a miracle no one's eye got poked out.

I smiled at the guards who I knew, gave the policemen a vague explanation that I worked at the school (they looked confused, but apparently didn't think I looked like I was going to try to corrupt voters or steal ballot boxes), slipped through the gate, and hung out to the side of our undercover, open-air multipurpose room where Santaneros were waiting in line to vote. Cardboard voting booths with the seal of the government printed on the front had been set up where people filled out their ballots. Looking at the pop-out folding parts of the cardboard, I half-expected to see numbered directions on the do-it-yourself voting booths, but I suppose the method allowed for a certain amount of portability.

Santa Ana didn't have its own mayor or council, so everyone was voting for Cartagena mayor, Cartagena council members (*consejo*), and governor of the Bolívar department. The different tables were all numbered with official ballot sheets from the federal government, designating the department (Bolívar), district (Cartagena), *corregimiento*, or section of a municipality (Santa Ana), and even table number. There were different colored sheets for each race: orange, green, and gold, which caused some confusion as voters tried to figure out what went where. One of Kassira's older students, most likely voting for the first time, flipped through the stack of papers he had just finished filling out and stood staring at the two different ballot boxes (also cardboard). Another lady in line and the man who was helping out at the table finally helped him get the right sheets in the right boxes.

I stood to the side, watching the lines of voters slowly make their way from the tables to the cardboard booths, and then go back to drop off their ballots. I waved to a few Santaneros and chatted with Oscar from Adult Class after he finished voting.

Despite Colombia's political problems, things in Santa Ana seemed to be going smoothly (not counting the confusions over which ballots went into which box). When the results came out, I even learned Santa Ana had helped elect Cartagena's first Afro-Colombian mayor. The island was small enough that it might not have been worth it for candidates to try to corrupt voters and the area didn't have much bacrim or FARC activity. I was thankful for this, especially as I continued to read the news from around the country.

I wasn't in Colombia to research the FARC, ELN, paramilitaries, or drug cartels, but that didn't mean they didn't affect life in every corner of the country. Colombia's main identity didn't consist of messy politics, drugs, and civil conflict and the effects of these conflicts were nothing like its peak in the 1990s. But even in the reinvented Colombia in the 21st century, these lingering conflicts continued to stop positive development and tarnish the thousands of other positive aspects of the country.

But at least on that one day in October, ordinary Colombians who were all touched in different ways by the history of conflict in their country got a voice, cast their ballot, and put their faith in the fact that things had improved—and had a lot of room to improve even more.

CHAPTER SIXTEEN

BEAUTY CONTESTS, INDEPENDENCE DAY PARADES, AND SPRAY FOAM

Because of the elections, the sale of alcohol was prohibited for days leading up to October 30th. The ban was lifted at 6:00 a.m. Monday morning after election day (for that early-morning pick-me-up), which was just about the time some people started to prep for festivities that were occurring in Cartagena two weeks later.

Cartagena declared independence from Spain on November 11, 1811 and throws itself a party to celebrate every year. The year I was there was the 200th anniversary and, with the speed of a cork flying from a bottle of champagne, the town moved on from politics to parties.

Like any good Colombian celebration, Cartagena's independence day included lots of loud music, dancing, and late night parties. I was relearning as the year went on how much Colombians enjoyed a good party, whether it was a national holiday, Carnaval, Afro-Colombian Day, celebrations of saints, or just the fact that it was a weekend. The eleventh of November festivo included specific celebrations: parades, beauty pageants, and craziness in the streets.

I actually don't know how many parades there were in Cartagena during the week of festivities. There were smaller parades for school-children, larger parades for the general public, a parade for gay pride, one for the beauty queens contesting for the title of Señorita Colombia, and one commemorating the route of the original march proclaiming independence in Cartagena's historic *barrios*.

I went to the last of these, which had a fun group of everyone from school kids to senior citizens dressed up in costumes and marching and dancing through the historic centers of Cartagena. We began in a small plaza in the historic neighborhoods of Getsemaní, where everyone belted out the ever-present anthem of Cartagena (which involves lots of shouts of "Libertad! Libertad!"), then there was a reading of the declaration of independence by a lady who I think was the mayor. The crowd danced their way from Centennial Park, under the entrance to the Centro through the 15th century walls, and ended up in front of the cathedral for an energetic dance performance by high school students.

On the tenth and eleventh of November, there were much bigger parades, Rio-style, with floats, scantily-dressed dancers, and bands (it was also apparently an international rule that all parades must start out with a fire truck and include a police equestrian unit).

People lined up for hours before the parade, slowly filling in the space behind the barricades on the long Avenida Santander while vendors roamed through the ever-tightening crowds, selling fried food, water, and beer. Some vendors wheeled carts full of limeade, stacked with cut-up mangos, or packed with giant blocks of ice—the last of these the vendor would set down on a corner and chip off ice cubes for chilled drinks. Homes and apartments blasted music in anticipation for the start of the parade.

People called these celebrations Carnaval, and for good reason. While nowhere near as large or elaborate as *the* Carnaval in Rio de

Janeiro (and Barranquilla) celebrating Fat Tuesday, Cartagena put on a good show. Elaborate costumes barely covered energetic dancers who shook their thing down the parade route or followed well-practiced steps with a partner. Costumed bands pounded out African-style beats on drums or played salsa or vallenato as they high-stepped down Santander Avenue, with the crashing blue of the Caribbean a mere five feet from the parade route.

The crowds surged against the metal barricades on the city side of the street, shouting, watching, or dancing along with the acts in the parade. Many wore crazy hats or wigs of painfully bright pink or green. Dozens of policemen stood on either side, watching the crowds and the simple floats slowly making their way down the avenue.

Every tiny celebration in Colombia had to have a beauty pageant, all patterned off the official national Colombian Beauty Pageant and celebrating the beautiful women Colombian was known for. The competition to see who would be crowned Señorita Colombia was an integral part of the *11 de noviembre festivos*. While the country's reputation for beautiful women is mostly due to plastic surgery and breast implants being as common in Colombia as getting braces is in the U.S. (to be fair, both are medical changes based on non-medical decisions), there is no denying that the beauty contestants deserved the hype. The women who had won their regional competitions came to Cartagena to compete in the national competition (there is no semblance of a "scholarship contest" here) to see who would be crowned the new Señorita Colombia. The current *reina* led the parade on the same float as the Señorita de la Independencia, who was wearing a 19th century suit, complete with epaulettes and a cut that revealed her rock-hard abs.

The floats made their way down the boulevard between the groups of dancers, and provided the stage for the contestants to wave to the cheering crowds. The women sported elaborate costumes, some of which should have gotten a little more honest feedback before they were worn in public. Señorita Bolívar was dressed like the Catalina statue in the Centro, with a feather sticking up from a headband (though unlike the statue, she was not actually topless) but she made a wise decision when she took off her four-inch heels soon after the parade's start. The queen from the central Colombian department of Boyacá had awkwardly placed circles on her woven bikini-type top, but even that was better than the queen representing the Guajira, who had a giant pink hat, low cut pink bikini top with tassels, and what looked like yarn balls hanging from a string around her neck. They dangled awkwardly down her chest and past her waist.

Costumes aside, it was apparent that the ladies vying to be Miss Colombia had to first go through a stringent competition of poise, talent, and debate on who had the best abs and biggest breasts to win the right to represent their department. They received lots of cheers from the crowds—and lots of open stares from all the police guarding the boulevard.

But beauty queens weren't only in Cartagena that week. Our school had our own *Reinado*, where one female contestant representing each grade, from kindergarten to eleventh, competed to become queen. After a lot of class time was missed so they could be introduced and given a chance to say a few words on the year's theme of *Santa Ana Muestra Su Raza* (Santa Ana Show Your Race/Roots), they also got a chance to walk, catwalk-style, around our multipurpose room, accompanied by loud cheers from their classmates. Earlier in the week they walked around in nice clothes, which for Santa Ana girls meant tight jeans and tank tops. During one comunidad, they all said a few words about why they were proud to participate, because there was no denying it was an honor to represent their class as their queen.

I am not sure what process they used to choose students (student vote? teacher decision? out of a hat?), but I was surprised to see Arlin come out as the nominee for the sixth graders. Certainly she was less sullen now than during the first months I knew her—and I hadn't seen her with a glue bottle since that first week—but she wasn't exactly a top student. Nor did she stand out as one of the better-looking sixth graders either.

I took her aside one day after class when I found out she was the sixth grade queen and switched out of strict English teacher-mode for a few minutes.

"This is a big honor, right, Arlin?"

She just stared at me, then nodded in agreement.

"I hope you will have pride in being the queen for all the sixth graders. I want you to keep trying and come to class and represent your classmates well."

She nodded again. I let out an inward sigh, hoping her dull response was her processing my thoughts and not due to an error in my Spanish or her complete dismissal of academics.

"Felicitaciones," I told her with a light touch on the shoulder. And congratulations were truly in order.

Our Reinado culminated in a full morning of celebrations.

We started off with our own parade around the town's bumpy, rutted, and muddy parade route. Our queens were also on floats, but these weren't exactly "floating" (or even mechanized). They came in two varieties. The first type was your standard donkey cart—pulled by the family horse or donkey of the contestant and decorated with braided palm leaves and balloons. A dad or uncle of one of the queens on the float sat on the wooden bench with the reins in his hands, slowly prodding the donkey down the parade route. The second version of a Santa Ana float was simply a wood and metal cart. Sans donkey. Older boys took turns pushing the carts in the parade over all of the obstacles in the streets of Santa Ana. One made it the whole way. Unfortunately, the cart hosting Kassira (who was representing the teachers) plus two more students, barely made it out of the starting gate before tipping. They consolidated themselves by riding other carts—floats, that is—for the rest of the parade.

Our parade navigated around puddles and motorcycles, passing pigs and donkeys that weren't fortunate enough to pull the queens around and get decorations and balloons tied between their ears.

Students in uniforms surrounded the floats their queens were on as they meandered down the street, and did everything from idly chatting with their friends to clanging tops of pots together in a do-with-what-you-got version of cymbals. They jumped up and down and sang snatches of songs praising their grade level and queen. Some grades had made signs to hold up in front of their queens' floats. Eight eleventh-grade girls were even in bright orange costumes and did a coordinated dance leading the parade down the street. Our school band, composed of about ten boys from a mix of upper grades, led the parade with more background music, banging on their different-sized drums, shaking maracas, and belting out snatches of songs.

Parents and grandparents stood in their doorways and watched the students parade past. Shopkeepers leaned on their counters, watching the festivities. Even the dogs skirting the crowds seemed curious as we looped through town. It was a pleasant link between life in town and life at school, proof that if the students and administrators really cared about something, a miraculous show of organization was possible.

After doubling back a bit on the same streets (to avoid the muddiest thoroughfares), we ended up back at the school for part two of the morning of festivities: dancing and more contestant walking.

This time the queens walked around in a traditional African costume, meaning there were lots of flower patterns and skirts of both plastic and real leaves woven into enough coverage to be considered a costume. The third grade queen was dressed in a pink fabric dress and walked around with a plastic bowl on her head like the *Palenque* women selling fruit in traditional costumes in Cartagena. Yofalis, my eighth grader, had had the same idea as the Bolívar beauty queen and dressed as Catalina (though luckily, like the Bolívar queen, she had more coverage than the statue and wore what was essentially a beaded gold bikini top with matching skirt, headband, and feather). Arlin's costume seemed mostly made from grass—which was worn over her shorts and a sports bra—and what could only be described as a nest of twigs was set carefully upon her fluffed hair. The fifth grade queen's skirt was decorated with flattened yellow Aguila bottle caps, covered in glitter. In fact, glitter was used liberally in whatever costume or float might need a little spicing up: on the leaves to make them shine, on a queen's face for a little sparkle, or on the donkey pulling the cart. Arlin had so much glitter on her body that her stomach looked positively silver.

After the whole school (including kindergarten through eleventh, plus lots of family members) crowded into the open-air multipurpose room and cheered on their queens walking around the concrete floor again, it was time for dancing.

Each grade did a dance routine, with the queen contestant in the center of a group of anywhere from six to fifteen girls (only the eleventh grade included boys in their act), all dancing to salsa, champeta, and reggaeton.

Usually unmotivated Mayerlis led my green and orange-clad seventh graders in their gyrations coordinated with music. Tiny, skinny Yofalis led fifteen of my eighth-grade girls, who were clad in pink dresses and white gloves, in a choreographed performance combining dance with cheerleading. Eighth grade was one class that had hired an adult to choreograph the dances and serious practice time had been put in. And though I still don't know how the still-sullen Arlin had become the nominee, she danced with a group of sixth grade girls, towering over everyone as they bobbed around to champeta.

At the end, the contestants were all dressed in gowns (the clothes changing necessitated another thirty-minute break of waiting around), and we crowned winners for the primary and secondary grades.

And for the secondary grades, sixth grade and Arlin had won. The screams of excitement from my sixth graders reached a new decibel level as Arlin looked simultaneously confused, awkward, and genuinely happy when they announced the winners and she received her shiny plastic crown. The rest of sixth grade surrounded her and she jumped up and down, danced with her classmates, and looked more joyful than I had ever seen her. I only hoped it would prove to be a motivating factor for Arlin as she finally moved on to seventh grade.

Along with high-pitched cheering, the announcement of the IESA Reinado winner was met by the student band beating on their drums, glitter being thrown up into the air, and loud bangs reverberating throughout the area.

Those bangs were caused by festivo regulars *buscapiés*, which brings us to the important third part of what constituted Cartagena's independence festivities: craziness in the streets.

There was of course blasting music, dancing in the streets, and crowds of people everywhere. And many ways to get yourself in trouble.

First up were the thousands of spray bottles of foam. The tall red bottles were basically regular shaving cream, but housed in a festivo-themed decorated bottle, available to buy anywhere on the street for 5,000 pesos. If you walked the streets any time after about 9:00 in the morning, you were fair game to be sprayed in the face, on your back, or all over until you resembled a strange, tropical snowman.

The spray bottles of foam might be hidden under a jacket, or people had arms extended, spraying at every person that walked by, including those on the opposite side of the street. The range of the spray was really quite impressive. If the trash left after the parades was any indication, the number of bottles emptied during the festivities reached the high thousands. The other most-common trash was the tiny yellow cardboard boxes that held cornstarch. This *maicena* was another favorite thing to cover people in as they walked the streets.

But as annoying as it was to wipe the sticky foam or powder off your clothes, it was all in good fun. Other street antics considered normal during the independence festivities got less and less fun.

Next up for the interesting/different/annoying ways Cartageneros celebrated were the buscapiés. Buscapiés were tiny firecrackers let off with annoying repetitiveness on streets everywhere. People were subtle about tossing them; you might see a group of people quickly scatter, and then there would be a tiny bright flash, a tiny explosion, and bluish smoke floating away. Buscapiés, consequently, translates to "look for feet." The name seemed to cover two things. First, they are always thrown on the ground so you look for them down around your feet. Second, after they go off you might actually need to double-check possible unwanted amputations and look *for* your feet.

I was advised to wear closed-toed shoes while walking around Cartagena's streets during the second week of November.

Other bits of the celebrations also made it advisable to wear old clothes.

Teenaged boys walked around in pairs or gangs, asking everyone for coins, their bodies painted completely black or covered in dark dye. Some carried bottles filled with dye that they were ready to splash on you if you didn't pay the 100 or 200 pesos they were asking (though perhaps less than half followed through with their threats). Others carried something that looked a bit like tar. Still others walked around with charred sticks, threatening to smear charcoal on anyone who did not pay up. It was textbook extortion and it was unfortunate that a country that was trying to get away from this stereotype allowed it so rampantly during this week.

Two boys, bare to the waist and with dark spots and smears of blue dye all over, walked up to me as I sat on a wall eating a mango during my visit to Cartagena. One boy clicked a few coins in his hand, while the other held up his water bottle full of dye. A quick internal debate took place (the factors I considered were my ability to usually talk my way out of things and the fact that I was wearing an old shirt that was already destroyed from a year of hand-washing) and I decided to give them a stare-down.

"Soy profesora," I flatly stated and tried to look bored (this was at the same time, however, that my gaze slid involuntarily to their water bottle filled halfway with dark blue liquid). "Ya, vaya," I told them in what I hoped was a nonchalant voice as I dismissed them with a hand. I must have convinced them I wasn't a normal gullible tourist (and used to dealing with similar hooligan-like behavior as a teacher) and they trotted off to find a more willing victim.

Walking through a crowd celebrating also meant people might splash you from nearby puddles, dump water on you, or smear paint on you. The worst of these I avoided. On my way back to my hostel in the heat of the afternoon, one man threatened to dump water on me, but I refused to pay him and enjoyed a cool douse of water on top of my head.

I flashed him a smile and I smoothed my hair back.

"Gracias," I said genuinely, and enjoyed being cool for at least a few minutes.

Also popular on the outskirts of Cartagena (such as on the road back to Santa Ana) was the trick of stringing a rope across a road and refusing to let it down unless the moto or car paid up, although you could get by if you called their bluff. I found this out while holding on for dear life on the moto ride back to Santa Ana as my moto driver gunned the engine, waved three boys away so exuberantly I was afraid we'd swerve and hit someone, and shouted insults at the kids as they scattered just in time.

Some of these street extortions were good-natured, such as the water being dumped on me, but others could get pretty mean. You certainly had to watch your back while walking along the street.

Not all the extra activity in the street was problematic though, because despite the extra dangers and annoyances, it was still just one big street party that went on and on for blocks and neighborhoods in every direction (all the picós were congregated in different Afro-Colombian barrios). There was random dancing in the street, even more music blasting than normal, late-night concerts and parties, decorations and Cartagena flags everywhere in town, and gallons of Aguila beers, Tres Esquinas rum and Antioqueño aguardiente consumed throughout the day and night. It was a joyful celebration of the city. Just be warned: if you ever travel to Cartagena the second week of November, you might come out of the celebration covered in foam and cornstarch, your clothes streaked with blue dye and soaking wet, and with a few battle wounds from buscapiés and young boys with ropes.

Because of the excitement and extra dangers of traveling during the independence festivos, I stayed the night in Cartagena and checked into one of the many hostels, where all manner of backpackers and travelers stayed.

I have been a backpacker of sorts in my own right and been fortunate to travel many weeks and months in parts of Europe, Africa, and South America. Yet, maybe I was already getting old and jaded from looking at these nineteen-year-old kids, or maybe I was just too full of pride about the fact that I lived in Colombia instead of being a tourist who was just passing through it on a lark, but while I enjoyed talking with many travelers, the Backpacker Crowd was one I usually tried to avoid.

The characteristics of a true traveler (whether they are backpacking or staying in five-star hotels) is to learn about new places, meet people different than yourself, and explore the diversity and scope of the world that humbles you. The main goal of some backpackers seemed to be to try to forget about real life, have as many stories of near-miss accidents and adventures as possible to brag about to friends back home, and to get drunk in as many cities as possible. Others were drawn to the cities in hopes of acquiring marijuana, coke, and other drugs supporting Colombia's civil conflicts, which they assumed were readily available and cheap.

Whether they were traveling for a few weeks or spending a gap year flitting their way through South America, few backpackers at the hostel I was at were older than thirty and they usually sat around with a beer in their hands as they discussed which discotecas were best. They always seemed to travel in flocks, swapping similar stories of long bus rides, bad sunburns, and their favorite type of beer in the various countries they had visited.

The never-ending drinking and partying aside (travelers of every type tend to enjoy nights out in new places), what annoyed me about many backpackers was the pride they had in listing off all the cities and countries they had been to. It was a competition between travelers, and the conversations would eventually end up with everyone discussing the list of places they had passed through.

"Yeah, I liked Bogotá but Lima was much nicer," one Brit might comment offhand, which could set off other travelers.

"Lima is also of course so much cheaper. I can't believe how expensive Cartagena is," says a German woman wearing what looked like a two hundred dollar jacket.

"I know," chimes in another young woman, who might have been from France. "When I was in Thailand you could get a nice hotel room for four or five Euros."

It could go on like this for a while and everyone would argue whether landing in an airport counted for your grand total of countries or not (of course it doesn't mean you actually *saw* much of the country, but this isn't a problem if your goal is to simply add another country to your list of places you have "visited"). Each backpacker in turn would try to one-up the other people around them.

"I have been traveling up through all of South America since June. Six countries."

"Last year I went to Africa and got to visit seven different countries. Awesome people but crappy buses."

"Two years ago, I spent three months island hopping in the Mediterranean. Boy, that was a great summer. Lots of cute chicks."

"Three years ago I was on the first manned mission to Mars. Talk about beautiful red rock country."

Okay, no one ever said that last one, but the way the conversations slowly built up, I wouldn't have been surprised. That these types of conversations repeated themselves the world over meant that for most the fact they braved Colombia would be at the top of the list of boasts.

I usually kept my mouth shut during these competitions, which were always friendly, but disturbing nevertheless. I was a little uncomfortable to hear people trying to boil down cultures and populations to a stamp in a passport.

But staying in a hostel also meant I could chat with travelers from around the world, and in lieu of engaging in the Who is the Most

Well-Traveled or the Who Has Had the Best Adventures competitions, I could share insights and observations from Colombia and beyond. I rode all the way back to Isla Barú with a couple from Canada who were on vacation from a semester-long development project in Peru and many backpackers showed they were legitimately trying to understand a little of the Colombia they found themselves in.

The evening of the Cartagena festivos, I sat on the balcony of my hostel in Getsemaní, joined by a lady from Norway named Ruth. Ruth, in her mid-fifties, was staring wide-eyed at the revelers who were walking by in the street down below and she seemed a little uncertain what to expect from her visit. Why Ruth had decided to come to Colombia I was not sure. It's as if some people wake up in the morning, spin a globe around, and point to where they might head next for their vacation (to be fair, I loved the spinning-the-globe game as a kid, although it was always disappointing and a good geography lesson considering how many times you ended up in the ocean).

"What are you planning to do while in Colombia?" I asked Ruth.

Ruth had no clue, and rubbed her gray hair nervously. She also started asking me about the FARC and which parts of the city were safe (which was ironic since the hostel we were staying at was located in prostitution and drug-heavy Gestemaní, outside of the safer Centro). I heaved a sigh and began chatting about the different museums, sights, and beaches Cartagena offered, all the time begrudging her for her lack of knowledge on the place she had somehow found her way to.

But was I really much different when I decided to apply to be an English teacher in Colombia? I shouldn't have judged her. When I first came to Colombia, I hadn't done much to find the truth behind the stereotypes either and had arrived just as blind. And if I was perfectly honest with myself, I had also relished the idea of boasting a bit about braving Colombia, about living and surviving in a dangerous country. What I had found instead was that Colombia had moved on from that label. Living in Colombia *could* be an adventure, but a few remote jungle areas aside, it was also just a place no more dangerous than any other. No longer was traveling to Colombia only for U.S. Marines or Indiana Jones wannabes.

Ruth bade me a goodnight and I stayed on the balcony for a while, thinking, writing, and watching the revelers down on the street. Eventually I turned in for the night, going to bed at my usual 10:00.

Ten o'clock was well before any of the nightlife even started in Cartagena and my bedtime would always elicit strange looks from everyone in the hostel. When I assured whichever roommates I had that I wasn't sick but just didn't have plans to go out, they would shake their heads, confused. What was I doing in a hostel if I didn't plan on going out? Many would get concerned looks in their eyes (looks usually reserved for giving condolences to someone who has just lost a parent) and tell me I could join them for the night.

"No, no," I would assure them, "I am going to get up early, but thank you." I'd usually eventually come up with an excuse ("I have to get up early for a long bus ride..."), but I could tell the average backpacker didn't really understand.

I'd wake up in the middle of the night as my roommates stumbled in, and slip out of bed in the cool morning not long after they came back. I would take my morning walk, grab a tinto and arepa con huevo, sit by the wall, and be back to pack up my bag and head to Santa Ana usually before any of the comatose figures under the sheets had stirred.

Of course during the Cartagena festivos, I couldn't really fault backpackers for their late-night partying. After all, they were just doing what the locals were doing, the bicentennial being another excuse to party.

Most of the craziness (the parades, the beauty contest, the extortions, fireworks, foam, and the multi-day street parties) happened every year on the week around the eleventh, so it was hard to tell what parts were special for the 200th anniversary and which were traditions that continued year after year. I was sure some of the processions around town, meetings, and speeches had a little something extra for the bicentennial, because after all, it wasn't every day you got to celebrate something like that, especially on such a cool date as 11/11/11.

But as the Cartageneros (and everyone visiting Cartagena that week) proved, you didn't need to wait for the calendar to flip to all those ones to start celebrating. If the music is blaring and your neighbors are wearing hot pink wigs, grab your can of foam, cheer on your favorite beauty queen, and join in on the celebration.

CHAPTER SEVENTEEN

LIFE ON A CARIBBEAN ISLAND (DID I MENTION WE HAD A BEACH?)

Colombia, and especially Cartagena, was an increasingly popular tourist destination, and not only for backpackers looking for good photos, clubs, and adventures. Business conferences, cruise ships, even the Summit of the Americas (which also brought Secret Service agents and their not-so-secret dalliances with prostitutes) convened on Colombia's northern coast. Tourists of every ilk filled the streets and hotels of Cartagena, enjoying the exotic beauty of the historic Centro and the prime Caribbean location.

It was always a shock to return to the city after a couple of weeks in Santa Ana and on Isla Barú because of the number of tourists and Cartagena's hustle and bustle. However, while you won't find Santa Ana on any lists for potential tourists, the island did have one of the main tourist attractions in the area: Playa Blanca, or as Pedro liked to call it (to prove he did know some English), White Beach.

Playa Blanca was about twenty minutes outside Santa Ana as you continued south on the island and was *the* tourist beach to go to if you were visiting Cartagena and wanted to get in your Caribbean beach time and work on your tan.

Playa Blanca was almost exactly what I envisioned a Caribbean beach to be and was correctly named for its pale sand (though the name could also refer to how many very white tourists were there). The beach had soft, bright sand and tall palm trees blowing in the gentle Caribbean breezes. Dozens of small wooden shacks and houses were set up, offering all sorts of restaurants and places to string a hammock or sleep on the soft sand.

During the quiet mornings, pelicans fed on fish in the surf as the sun rose at your back. The pelicans would hurtle towards the water with startling speed and land bill-first with a satisfying splat, then sit in the warm water, bobbing up and down with the waves. Yellow crabs bounded up and down in the uneven sand, their oval black eyes raised above their head, and their claws fading to white.

Mid-morning, the pale waters turned brilliant blue-green and a famed turquoise azure that draws thousands of shivering New Yorkers, Londoners, and Berliners to tropical waters during the Northern Hemisphere winter. Patches of coral, rocks, and different colored sands turned the waters into patchworks of different shades: some teal, some an opaque light green, others a deeper blue. The modest waves were edged with white as they crested, bringing foam and a new layer of sand and shells to the beach. In some places the waves worked tirelessly to smooth out footprints from the shoreline, while in other places the waves crashed against sharp rocks that were covered in seaweed and algae. The air was heavy with the smell of salt, and the saturated sea left crusts of white on the shore, boats, and towels.

Tourists swam in the calm surf or lay with too little sunscreen on newly-purchased sarongs or rented beach chairs, sometimes under small lean-tos providing shade from the fierce midday sun. Other tourists, already with painful-looking burns, walked along the sand, adding to a bustle of dogs and the occasional cow or donkey, boats, vendors, and birds. Tourist-watching was always a favorite pastime of mine and never got old (though some of the tourists were, and I can't say I approved of many of the choices of bathing suits... what is it with European men in bikini-worthy bottoms anyhow?). When tourist-watching got repetitive, there was always some other entertainment—one morning I was sitting watching the surf when suddenly a pair of horses appeared out of nowhere and galloped down the beach, scaring a couple of tourists so badly they jumped into the water.

And it was always nice to greet fellow Santaneros, whether it was one of our students or someone we recognized from walks through town who were also at the beach for the day to enjoy the water and cooler breezes. You didn't have to be from a chilly big city to appreciate the beauty of Playa Blanca.

Tourists came to Playa Blanca in a number of ways. The most common was to take one of the four or so daily boats that left from downtown Cartagena for the forty-minute ride through the choppy Caribbean waters. Tourists also frequently came as part of a tour of the Parque Nacional Natural Corales del Rosario y San Bernardo, of which Playa Blanca was technically also a part of. The visitors swung by Playa Blanca for a few hours for some serious sun tanning and then they returned to Cartagena around four o'clock in the afternoon, usually with an uncomfortable red color.

Of course, I came from the mainland or Santa Ana by mototaxi, although one cool morning, I enjoyed the hike of around four miles to the beach from town with Alyssa, Shannon, and TL. Many Colombian families, especially on weekends, came in their shiny cars, driving onto the Pasacaballos ferry and parking at the beach for the day before heading back to Cartagena in their now dusty and muddy vehicles.

For adventurous backpackers, guidebooks laid out the bus/ferry/motorcycle taxi route, but failed to mention the two towns they needed to pass through along the way or anything else about the island besides the fact that the route was a bit of a mess after it had rained. It was true the turnoff leading from the main road was potholed, slick, and wet after rain with puddles of pond-like depth. However, the guidebooks also dismissed the beach as a "two-hour nightmare" and complained about the number of vendors and "peddlers" selling their wares on the beach.

First of all, two hours is really only enough time to get a sunburn and not much else.

Certainly vendors were a large part of the identity of Playa Blanca. And yes, they were making a living by selling food (including fresh fruit and *cocada,* a sort of a firm, chewable version of Easter coconut dulces, which meant I could rarely resist it), great artisan carvings, necklaces made from shells from the shoreline, bright sarongs, cold water and beer, and much more the average beachgoer might be interested in. Vendors of every age, from elementary school kids to ancient abuelos, with Styrofoam coolers slung over their shoulders wandered the sands. Some stacked a dozen straw hats on their heads, draped sarongs on their shoulders, or carried large boards full of hand-made necklaces, bracelets, and earrings. Many of our students sold fried corn balls or necklaces or were otherwise left to their own devices as their parents worked.

Granted, I didn't like getting interrupted from a nap, a good book, or viewing the blue vista stretched out in front of me either. I would rarely buy a bracelet or a drink, never got a massage (another popular item offered), and I only occasionally bought fruit or ice cream. But after a friendly smile and a polite "no hoy, gracias," the "peddlers" would move on.

The island relied on tourism dollars, even if tourists never gave a second thought to the fact that people lived in the places they were passing through. Most tourists didn't stay the night and took afternoon boats back to their Cartagena hotels to shower, put on aloe, and get ready for a night on the town. So after around four o'clock, the beach would transform again into a quiet place of relaxation. The sun would set as boys played soccer in front of the orange globe that was sinking beneath the water. A fishing canoe or two would slowly drift by on its way home, the fisherman paddling against the magenta waves. For a few precious minutes all was quiet and all you'd be able to hear was the wind in the trees, birds calling goodnight to the beach, and the soft breaking of the waves. After a while music would start: champeta, reggaeton, and vallenato blasting from speakers all along the beach as the residents and tourists alike stayed up to drink, dance, and relax in the cool night air.

There was one part of the beach that was distinctly private. The Isla Barú branch of the Decameron Resorts and Hotels chain was new as of a few years before my stay. A far, but doable walk down to the end of the beach was the all-inclusive resort, which would set you back about $1,000 for a three-day stay (though this did include all your food and drink while you were there). It ruined the view a little but certainly wasn't an eyesore and did bring some benefits to the area. The Decameron employed 300 people with steady wages and maintained the road through town so their giant charter buses wouldn't get stuck while bringing in tourists (or at least they wouldn't get stuck too often).

But Playa Blanca was not just a postcard you could drop into on vacation. On the backside of the beach was where real life took place. Dozens of people actually lived at the beach, adding to the dozens more who commuted to the beach from the nearby towns. Young men carried heavy crates of beer and soda, and mothers standing at charcoal stoves slowly fried up the coconut rice and fish that would head out to a tourist lounging in a beach chair.

While we might have looked like tourists as we swam through the salty waves, people knew we were the teachers from Santa Ana, so they were just as likely to try to start up a conversation with us to practice their English as they were to try to convince us that we needed a massage. We hung out with the people at the beach who we knew, and bought snacks from the families of our students. We saw the beach on its clearest days, during storms, when it was empty, and when it was buzzing with tourists and vendors.

I got to know Playa Blanca, but the truth was Isla Barú was much bigger than one town and one beach. I decided that before I left the island (the year was speeding near its close) I needed to do a little traveling around the Colombia that was close to home.

In the north of the island, I usually sped past the homes and farms on the back of a moto as I traveled to and from the ferry and the road to Cartagena, never stopping between Santa Ana and the canal. In the other direction, I had walked and taken numerous motos all the way to Playa Blanca, but never past that point in the road.

I finally did walk around the town of Ararca, which was a blink in the eye on the way from the ferry and smaller than Santa Ana, but with the same ramshackle collection of concrete shops and houses lining its rutted streets.

The actual town of Barú was on the southern tip of Isla Barú and I knew little about it. No volunteer from the year before had ever made it down there and residents of Santa Ana didn't head there often. It was like Barú was some distant jungle town a couple of days' journey away. But it was only about eleven miles to the end of the island and a couple of moto drivers who we knew went every once in a while, so in November fellow volunteer TL and I paid for an expensive motorcycle ride to very tip of the island.

For the first five or ten minutes after we passed the turnoff to Playa Blanca, the landscape and road looked a lot like the road I had gotten to know so well after ten months of living on Isla Barú. The views fluctuated between open forests with lush green vines climbing up trees, a few houses and farms, banana trees, cows, and the occasional crop of corn or pineapples flashing by. The hard-packed dirt road linking the island may not have been the thoroughfare maps made it look like, but despite the spots that got muddy after it rained (and of course, The Puddle), you could safely speed down the dusty track without problems.

And then suddenly something unexpected happened: the road turned into asphalt.

Roadwork was always occurring on Isla Barú and there was an ongoing debate about whether or not to pave the road in Santa Ana. The pluses of doing it included the fact that road crews wouldn't have to continually bring in more dirt and rocks every month or so and that buses and cars wouldn't get stuck in The Puddle. Minuses included that the runoff might flood nearby streets and that asphalt is significantly hotter to walk on in bare feet than dirt.

That there was already an asphalted road came as a complete shock to me. If you had told me Isla Barú had a road that wasn't made of dirt and rock, I probably would have snickered and asked how many Aguilas you had just drunk. However, apparently someone had won the "to pave or not to pave" debate on this part of the island, probably thanks to a small resort called Punta Iguanas that was just off this road. After the turnoff to the resort, about five minutes later, it was back to dirt again, and we passed open marshes and little traffic. We forded a small stream emptying into the ocean and suddenly the road ended at a narrow beach.

"Ended" might be too strong of a word. If you were in a car larger than a small Jeep, then it was time to turn around, but deep tire imprints in the sand revealed it was passable for motorcycles. As we neared the edge of the beach, my driver, Wolfrido, and TL's driver, Lorenzo, stopped.

"La arena es profundo aquí y no podemos tener dos personas en la moto," Lorenzo said. Since the sand was a bit deep, we couldn't have two people on the motos and we'd have to walk a bit.

TL and I got off the motos so our drivers could navigate the soft sand with more ease and we enjoyed a ten-minute stroll along the thin beach. Pelicans stared at us as we went by and the large Decameron Resort was visible in the distance. It was clear the road had not always reached the edge of the beach. A telephone pole stuck out of the water maybe twenty feet into the surf—obviously the waves and sand had overtaken the road and mangrove groves that were just inland, reducing the shore to the current thin strip of sand.

Then a road miraculously appeared again. And after shaking sand from our sandals, swigging some water, and swinging back onto the backseat of the motos, we continued along the road.

The route was now much narrower, just wide enough for one car, although we didn't see any. It seemed even fewer vehicles ventured out this way than in Santa Ana. We only passed two motos the whole time and we gave the drivers friendly waves as we zipped past. There were a few pedestrians and we stopped and talked to one of Lorenzo's friends who was walking around in board shorts and snorkel gear, carrying three freshly caught octopi strung up on sticks.

The well-surfaced road was soon replaced by a muddier, wooded lane. The ocean wasn't too far off on our right, and a few hotels and farms sported tall walls and gates among the trees. On the left was forest. Long-limbed trees with wide leaves bent over the lane, providing a natural archway. Vines and creepers covered the trunks of a variety of other trees, and a few feet off the road, it was difficult to find any bare forest floor.

I asked Wolfrido about the forest, whether there was anything on the eastern, inland side of the island.

"Solamente selva," he replied. Only jungle.

An earlier contention from a Santanero that ocelots roamed the island didn't seem so strange now as we passed in the shade under the trees. After all, we were passing through what was (on a map anyhow) part of the Islas Rosarios National Park. Of course, on that same map it looked like a normal road the whole way, the yellow line confidently cutting across unbroken jungle, even at the part where the road had disappeared at the beach. Looking at satellite images later, I saw a maze of tiny bays and inlets cutting the island almost in half (the reason the road had not been rebuilt further inland was clear: the island in that area was only around 300 feet wide).

Because of the shade, this part of the road was much muddier. Our drivers had to balance themselves continuously with their feet as we slipped and sometimes slid along the bumpy tract. For the most part, it was a fun ride and I was able to enjoy the new scenery with a warm breeze in my face. For the most part, we navigated the mud and mayhem quite well. After all, our moto drivers did this for a living.

So I wasn't too worried as we entered an even-muddier section of the road. I reached back to grab onto the backside on the moto and we slowly made our way around one puddle, then into another. We hit the puddle going maybe only three miles an hour, then we slipped a bit and completely tipped over into a calf-deep mixture of mud and water.

The good news was that we avoided possible burns by falling to the left, not on the muffler. The bad news was that the mud was a lot deeper on the left side. Both Wolfrido and I landed with a squelch and the moto tipped on top of us, trapping my left leg under Wolfrido and the machinery.

After a moment of confusion (*wait,* I thought, *how am I sitting in a mud puddle?*), we started to unravel ourselves. With a heave, we pushed the moto off of us, Wolfrido then successfully stood up, and I—who had been at the bottom of our moto and mud pile—steadied myself in the slippery mud.

TL and Lorenzo came running up, first looking worried, then they laughed as Wolfrido and I looked at each other, both splattered and soaked in the earth. When I got my bearings and attempted to step out of the suction-like mud pot, I discovered I wasn't going anywhere. Try as I might to pull myself free, my right foot was completely stuck. Unable to move or fully twist around, I simply looked down to where my leg had disappeared into the gray-brown froth, which looked like some sort of sci-fi swamp creature who had crept out of the earth to turn me into mud.

Bracing herself on more solid ground, TL offered me her arm, and after a few tries, I pulled myself out, removing my leg successfully with a satisfying slurping noise. My leg got free, but my trustworthy Chaco sandal did not, despite being tightly strapped to my foot when I had entered the deep mud. So there I stood—one shoe on, one foot bare, my left side covered in mud, my right leg darkened up to my knee—and only really had one choice: I would not let the mud eat my sandal. I slid my arm elbow-deep into the mud, feeling around for the lost shoe. My fingers slid into the earth, touched a stick, a few rocks, pockets of water, and something that I swear moved away from my hand as soon as I touched it. I finally did find my Chaco, and after a decent amount of tugging and slipping into yet more mud, I successfully extricated my sandal, which was now a shapeless grayish-brown blob.

Wolfrido and I cleaned off in a small trickle of a stream, returning my leg to its gringa-white and my sandal to something close to its original black color. I had a few cuts and bruises from being on the bottom of the moto sandwich, but luckily all the mud had provided us with a soft landing and we were mostly unscathed. Only a few scrapes on my leg and a strange brown design on one side of my once-green capris served as a testament of the accident.

With all the moto rides I had taken—on Isla Barú and around Colombia—it was perhaps surprising that this became my first and only moto accident. Alyssa may have slipped into a puddle as well on the way to Playa Blanca one morning and Adam may have burned the side of his leg on the hot muffler, but it was amazing how lucky we all were considering all the things that can go wrong while riding on a motorcycle. With the mix of dirt roads, giant buses, wandering pigs and cows, billowing clouds of dust, pond-worthy puddles, and Colombians' love of speed, there was obviously some saint of motorcycle passengers that was looking out for us. While I always enjoyed the air rushing past me as we streaked by green hills (it was as close as I got to air conditioning many days), I also always wore a helmet to avoid tempting the gods of rutted roads. Every few months there was an accident on the main road, and shortly after I left I was saddened to hear that a recent graduate of IESA was killed when his moto collided with another.

Gray streaks of water ran down my leg as I washed the last of the mud off and I was thankful the accident wasn't worse.

We finally got on our way again, and ten minutes later, we were on another muddy path, passing houses on the outskirts of Barú. We went down a tiny hill and the path opened up to the town square and sports field, which was a mess of green, brown, and gray mud, with blooms of algae and moss growing every few feet. We decided to get off the motos and skirt the mud before heading into town.

Barú was smaller than Santa Ana. It had around 2,500 people (no one seemed to know the exact number), was still pretty poor, and was also comprised almost entirely of Afro-Colombians. A lot of Barú looked the same as Santa Ana: rutted streets, a few donkeys passing by, a smattering of small stores.

In Santa Ana, almost every building was constructed with concrete, which was cheap to use and cool in the ever-present heat. However in Barú the residents seemed to have taken advantage of the forests that surrounded them and built many of their houses out of wood. It added a little style and variety to the homes, but I am not sure how they held up in the torrential rains and penetrating sun. Quite a few had tall columns on a wide front porch, which reminded me and TL of houses in the Old West in the United States. Someone could have gotten a hold of a copy of *Butch Cassidy and the Sundance Kid* and started the architectural trend for all I knew.

We walked around, creating a small sensation. Santaneros had gotten used to us and we were always greeted by students, parents, and shopkeepers as we went through Santa Ana's streets. Here in Barú, reactions was a mixture of unabashed stares ("Dios mío, there are white people in Barú!"), many looks of confusion ("Wow, these tourists are really lost if they were looking for Playa Blanca"), and a few sales pitches for tourist trinkets ("Amigas, we have beautiful towels for the beach").

We sat with Wolfrido and Lorenzo and ate sancocho for lunch while watching the movement of goods and people from the main dock in town. A thin donkey with a wooden saddle pulled a cart loaded with crates of Aguila. Bags of what looked like rice and beans were piled next to wooden siding. A half dozen canoe-like boats, their motors hanging in the air, attested to the fact that the Caribbean was the main route to get in and out of Barú rather than the treacherous road that we had taken. Boats from Playa Blanca and from Cartagena came and went with regularity and most groceries and goods arrived into the town by the ubiquitous canoe-like motor craft. Across the water to the west, we could see different hotels and resorts, which were small but expensive affairs each on a different island of their own.

In Santa Ana, hopping over to the mainland may have sometimes felt inconvenient, but in actuality it was pretty easy. Santa Ana (and Ararca) felt much more connected to the wider world than sleepy Barú, but I could have gotten used to the tiny town on the tip of the island.

We left after lunch and made it back to familiar roads without incident (so as to not tempt the fates, we walked past the mud hole that had claimed my perfect driving record as a motorcycle passenger instead of driving through it).

And soon we were back to speeding along the smooth dirt track towards the land of cars and trucks and giant Decameron buses. My thoughts were split—contemplating the complexities of what it meant to live and work on a Caribbean island, while at the same time concentrating on my surroundings to make sure I stayed safe, unscathed, and upright on my moto.

CHAPTER EIGHTEEN

AFTER THE STORM COMES THE CALM

According to the official IESA schedule, December 16th was the last day of class.

However, like the ambiguous nature of when my first day of classes actually was, trying to decide on what was my official last day of school was complicated. A half dozen days could be considered my last day of school (and the sixteenth was not one of them) as my year teaching finished up.

One possibility for my last day was November 18th (yes, almost a full month before the "official" date) since this was my last day of real teaching and including new material for each grade.

November 28th was the last day in class to review materials and the last day with an actual semblance of regular class periods. This day of class randomly fell on a Monday, mainly because of rain, meetings, and exams that canceled classes for the rest of the week. So the school schedule was until the end.

November 30th was the day of the English exam and could also be considered the last day since the exam was the last assignment given to most students and the last time I was in the classroom with all of them.

December 1st was our last day of comunidad (which started a full hour and a half late), when we had the last singing of the school anthem, gave out behavioral and academic awards, and listened to some end-of-the-year announcements.

When all the announcements and such were over, Arelis read off the names of the students who had passed all their subjects for the year and thus could officially call their school year over.

"Carlos! Marianela! Luis Kevin! Maria Angelica! Katia!" I heard the names of most of my best students and tried to catch their eye as they left, waving a quick goodbye to each.

One by one, they fell out of their lines, sometimes with shy self-congratulatory smiles, sometimes ducking away and hurrying to the gate, sometimes with a whoop, a yell, and a little dance before sprinting out the door and to their vacation. About half of the sixth graders and at least two-thirds of my eighth graders got called, but only about one-fifth of my seventh graders heard their name and headed off into town. A fairly substantial student body was still there after all the names had been called (especially for seventh and tenth grades). These students had more work to do to pass the year and had to come back the next day, December 2. All the students who had not been called the day before came and milled around the schoolyard while waiting for a new list of names to be posted. Arelis came out of the computer lab, where the teachers were compiling all their data, and she was mobbed as she stapled up the lists. The students crowded around, looking for their name.

The students fell into one of three categories: (1) their name was on the passing list with an X and they got to leave, (2) their name was on the failing list with two to three courses and they needed to stay to do extra work before they could move on to the next grade, (3) their name was on the failing list with an X, which meant they had failed more than three classes, got to go home, but failed the year and would have to repeat.

There was a good mix of cheers and tears as students crowded around to find out their fates (that there were so many students who were unsure of how they had done up to this point also reflected some of the problems with Colombian schools).

I watched the reaction of certain students who were still unsure whether or not they would be repeating the grade. Claudia and Luz Daris craned their necks, trying to see around the backs of ninth, tenth, and eleventh graders who were much taller than them.

And then a cheer erupted and I couldn't help but grin as they both leapt into the air with jubilation and gave each other a hug. And it was a well-deserved show of emotion. From the first two periods until the last one, Claudia had raised her test scores from twos to sixes and Luz Daris had raised hers from fives to nines. I knew they had passed English and was happy to see that their improved work meant they would be going on to seventh grade next year.

As they hung onto each other in a prolonged hug and dance, both of them looked my way.

"Ganamos!" they shouted at me with joy. I could translate their happiness to either "We passed!" or "We won!" and I gave them the biggest smile my face could manage. I passed on my congratulations, we exchanged high-fives, and they danced out the gate of the school.

But of course not everyone received good news, and I started talking to other teachers about what sort of *recuperación* activities we needed to do for those who had failed English but still had a chance to pass the year. Most seventh graders had failed too many classes to move on to the next grade, so no recuperación for them. Most eighth graders had passed (in fact I only had one student who needed English to move on—the rest would have to repeat the grade). Arlin was one of the sixth graders who had sneaked by in most of her classes, but her poor effort on her homework and terrible exam scores meant she still had work to do to pass English.

December 6 was another candidate for the last day of school since I gave the last assignments to the few students who needed to do the extra recuperación work. I gave a new exam to one eighth grader and wrote out a four-page recuperación worksheet for her, Arlin, and a few other students so they could complete the work over vacation in order to pass English and thus their year. Arlin yet again needed a little extra push to get her motivated to actually work, but I was gratified to know that she would finally graduate to seventh grade. Luckily, the head of our English department, Arelis, was returning the next year (unlike many other teachers who tried to move to a different school as quickly as they could) and Arelis promised to keep my recuperación students accountable for the extra work during vacation—because yet again Pedro was nowhere to be found.

I said a final goodbye to students and teachers and wrote out the worksheets without Pedro's input (the last time I had seen him was the week before). In fact, the next day he was back at IESA was the following January, so there was no goodbye, thank-you, or criticism from him about the year to provide me with closure.

I never heard from him again.

The final candidate for the last day of school was December 7: the day of graduation. IESA had two graduations: one for *transición* (celebrating the end of kindergarten) and one for eleventh grade (celebrating their last year).

Kayla, Alyssa, and I waited with the kindergarten students in a classroom and chatted with students and parents. Of course, the graduation was running over an hour late. The students were wearing their school uniforms with burgundy graduation hats perched on top of their small heads. It was obvious that their parents had made their hats and the tassels looked like they came from everything from window cords to sweatpants strings.

In the ceremony, they all sang the school song and national anthem (turns out kindergarteners weren't much better at singing the school song than anyone else), and the coordinador said a few words (of course, the principal, Alaberto, was nowhere to be found). Beaming parents applauded for their children as each one went up to the front shyly to receive a certificate and a kiss on the cheek from the two kindergarten teachers.

The eleventh grade graduation took place in a large conference room at the Decameron Resort, which meant I finally had an opportunity to get inside the place and look to see how the other half lived—when I had walked to the entrance earlier in the year, I couldn't convince the guard at the gate to let me in for a quick look around. Two of the ubiquitous charter buses with the Decameron palm tree logo had been scheduled to pick everyone up outside the school for the afternoon ceremony, but for one last time, circumstances beyond our control delayed and switched the schedule.

At the time when the buses were supposed to be there, the street was empty of vehicles, then we were delayed further when a torrential downpour started (Kassira, Kayla, Alyssa and I were glad to have made it to school before the street turned to mud, since we were in dresses and heels for the celebrations). We chatted with students and hung out in the principal's office and an empty classroom as eleventh graders in gray robes and purple sashes and families who were dressed in their nicest clothes arrived.

An hour and a half later, the rain had let up and we all headed out to stand in the street and wait for the buses. It had been a year of delayed starts for everything from parties to classes, but I still couldn't get away from the feeling that I was going to be in trouble for being late. Of course, I knew the ceremony couldn't have started since all the graduates were still standing in the muddy street with us, but there were some parts of my culture were so ingrained in me that spending a year in a different country couldn't change them. I could understand being fashionably late, but was I supposed to arrive to a Colombian gathering thirty minutes late? Or an hour? Did a Colombian's vocabulary even include the word "late?" These were a few of the questions that I never found answers for during my time in Colombia.

The buses eventually arrived, we all boarded, and I stood in the packed aisle as we safely crossed The Puddle and sped along the Decameron road to the polished white gate of the resort. It was strange to be wearing a nice dress and heels as we entered the resort moments after driving on a bumpy dirt road, passing cows, an ancient-looking man riding a donkey, tiny ramshackle homes, and farms.

The resort was clean, with potted plants, two-story white buildings, more tile and stonework than I had seen for a while, and large pieces of artwork. It certainly did not look like Santa Ana, though I recognized a few of the workers who walked past. Besides some of my students from Adult Class, we would sometimes see the Decameron staff waiting in town for the bus to the resort or they would pass on motos during one of my walks.

We settled into the conference room, which had been decorated with red and white balloons, and the graduation ceremony finally started.

The ceremony began with the singing (for the last time, *finally*) of the school song, followed by the Colombian national anthem and Cartagena anthem, featuring both our old and new principals. Jorge, who had been principal for ten years, received a much larger cheer than Alaberto, the current administrator—many students actually had to ask who he was. They didn't even know he was the current principal. Ouch.

In many ways, the ceremony was similar to my own high school graduation. The graduates walked into the room to music before taking their seats. Both principals gave speeches, along with one of the teachers and a selected student. There was a slide show of photos taken at IESA throughout the years. Students were called up, one by one, to applause so they could shake the hand of the principals and teachers, receive their certificates, and get their photos taken. Once the names of the forty or so graduates had all been called, we all toasted their future successes with fruit punch.

Norman, the homeroom teacher to one section of eleventh grade, raised his glass. "A sus futuros. Suerte!"

"Salud!" we all responded with glasses raised high, and drank the sweet juice before we walked outside.

Outside on the foyer, friends and families collided in hugs, and the graduates walked around with big grins on their faces. Flashes went off as graduates and relatives snapped pictures.

After passing on congratulations to some of the eleventh graders who I knew and getting a picture with Arelis and a few of the other teachers, I ducked out of the conference area to take a quick peek at the ritzy resort. I walked past some of the three-story hotel buildings that had been painted a sparkling white with bright red trim and greeted some of the workers as they swept a performance area. Oscar threw me a quick wave as he passed along the way, his teeth flashing white in the moonlit evening. Lamplight glowed out of the hotel rooms overlooking the ocean, where the almost full moon shimmered. Although I could hear the nearby crash of waves, the breezes rustling the thick palm fronds overhead, and the usual evening insects and frogs, it didn't sound like Isla Barú. Without lowing cows, barking dogs, honking donkeys, and crowing chickens, it was as if the resort was located on its own island far from Colombia. In Santa Ana, the shouts of Santaneros, blasting TVs and radios, and the rhythm of champeta and vallenato connected the island to Colombia and the real world. Inside the walls of the Decameron, wealthy Colombians and international tourists could ignore the outside world with ease.

I headed back to the conference room and followed the IESA crowd out of the foyer area and into the parking lot. The Decameron staff were giving us a gentle nudge out the door. After all, the resort had been nice enough to host the graduation, but they didn't relish the idea of dozens of high school students (or gringa teachers) wandering around. We waited about forty minutes in the dark for the buses to come and finally rode back to Santa Ana.

We returned to a town buzzing with graduation excitement (Barbacoas' graduation had been the same day), with people wandering the streets and sitting on their front porches with food and beer. Strains of Strauss's "Blue Danube" were discernible between the vallenato and champeta—the waltz was a tradition for graduations and *quinceañera* birthday parties, although I never saw many people doing the box step. I headed back to the Villa, navigating past the mud and puddles, which reflected twinkling Christmas lights.

The school year was officially over.

My final grades were in and I had finalized my contract obligations with IESA, the ministry of education, and WorldTeach. The school year was over for both the volunteers at Barbacoas and the group of us at IESA.

The eight of us who had taught and lived in Santa Ana had each taken a different journey as the year progressed. But we had stuck together and lasted out the year together, unlike many other volunteers in more developed areas of Colombia. We had survived the classes, the heat, the bugs, the days without power and water, and all sorts of tropical diseases. And so we decided to celebrate our year by spending a last night out in Cartagena.

A night on the town in Cartagena always began with some cheap street food, maybe *ceviche* (which on good days was the local shrimp cocktail and on bad, a sort of sushi in tomato sauce), pizza, hamburgers, hot dogs, or roasted chicken. That night I ate my last Cartagenero hot dog, which, as always, came with onions, crispy bits of potatoes, ketchup, pink sauce, mayonnaise, mustard, pineapple sauce and—sensibly—lots of extra napkins. We sat at plastic tables that were in front of a dozen food stalls and watched the full moon rise as it got dark.

An hour or two later, we strolled through the bustling streets, past a vallenato band playing on the corner, restaurants with outside tables filled with patrons sipping drinks, and rows of vendors with key chains, paintings, and carved bowls that were laid out on large pieces of fabric. Horse carriages rattled past us on tours of the Centro, the clip-clop of the hooves adding to the accordions and maracas of the bands, the salsa music drifting from restaurants, the chatter of couples sitting at tables outside cafes, and the beats of a group of teenage street rappers and amateur beatboxers who roamed the tourist-filled streets, hoping to earn a few pesos.

We ended up at the wall, where we joined Colombians and foreign tourists on top of the stone bulwarks, which were lit up in yellow from lights set around every corner. A restaurant on top played music and the warm wind coming off the Caribbean whipped our hair about as we chatted and sipped our drinks.

Music, tropical breezes, a mixed drink, and good company. In some ways this was the ideal Colombia—a mix of the historic and the modern—and it was easy to imagine that all was well in the world as we looked out on the crashing waves of the Caribbean.

I looked down the wall, past tables, past a family walking, and past a group of friends like us who were drinking and chatting, and I saw a group of tourists. They were laughing as they leaned against the stonework and chatting in English as they passed around what was obviously a joint.

And all the realities of Colombia came flashing back.

What those tourists were passing around wasn't just some marijuana that had been grown in a friend's backyard back in the United States. Somewhere in Colombia, people were loading trucks that were headed to Cartagena with a mixture of marijuana and cocaine packed and hidden in the back. Somewhere, people were helping to run a cartel, bringing drugs to the coast so they could be shipped out to the United States and Europe. Somewhere, a person was making deals with politicians, armed paramilitaries, and soldiers to make sure there was land to grow marijuana and coca.

Back in the United States, that group of tourists would probably buy Colombian roses in the supermarket, sip on Colombian coffee, wear a ring made with Colombian gold or emeralds, fill their tank with Colombian petroleum, and maybe even listen to Colombian music—but despite everything else that was redefining Colombia in the 21st century, the equation of Colombia = Drugs was one that many people were still helping to propagate. I just wished the group of gringos would realize what they were a part of, who they were financing, and who they were harming with each not-so-harmless puff.

Even as we headed to a discoteca, the image of this group stayed in my mind, even when we agreed to dance salsa with flirtatious Colombians and moved to the beats of reggaeton until the early morning. We finally walked back to our hostel on the cool dark streets of Cartagena.

The image of the group of gringos stayed with me the next morning as I sipped tinto and walked the bright, balmy streets watching pigeons, locals, cruise tourists with nametags, and ice cream vendors slowly meandering through the shade of Plaza Bolívar under the watchful eye of El Libertador.

The image stayed with me as I finished a last tall glass of fresh fruit juice and rode back on the rocky road headed back to Santa Ana.

While I was leaving Colombia soon—as were the tourists—all of us had affected the country, for both good and bad. I prayed to St. Ann, to San Pedro Claver, to every god and saint of travelers, educators, politicians, and farmers that our effects and the changes happening in Colombia would continue tipping in a positive direction, and that Colombia could come out of its stormy past to a new and prosperous calm.

In my last week in Colombia, there was a last minor flood to ford through, a last meal at Barú Grande (I must have become a little bit Colombian during the year, since I got seconds on the coconut rice), a last dedito to savor, a last stop by the store, and a last handshake to Gabriel, Alejandro, Bleidis, and the other workers at Barbacoas and IESA. I chatted one last time with Carlos and Marianela at The Pan, got to see Katia as she was walking back from Barú Grande and got a big hug, gave Luis Felipe a fist pound as I passed him in the street, and gave Ubadel a firm handshake and a kiss on the cheek after he drove me to the ferry on the back of his moto, and I headed off to Pasacaballos, Cartagena, and the airport beyond.

As small and seemingly insignificant as Santa Ana was, it was a part of Colombia's continuing history, connected to the pulse of the world regardless of whether we like it or not. Maybe Luis Felipe was just joking when he shouted out all those months back that he wanted to be president, but no one knew the limitations of Colombia's future.

Were there problems I couldn't solve at IESA? Certainly. Were there circumstances I couldn't improve in Santa Ana? Definitely. It turned out that I was not a great teacher. It turned out that the system still ended up winning most of the time. It turned out that Colombia was still on a long, slow process of finding a new, more optimistic identity for itself as it journeys further into the 21st century.

But it also turned out that there were days in and out of the classroom when I made a positive difference just by being an awkward U.S. American talking about English, geography, sports, and life. It turned out that there *were* days when students just seemed to get it, when individuals cared about their education and classes, when my smile was returned—perhaps tentatively at first, then with genuine warmth.

I'd like to think that my students can now successfully spell a few English words (after all, I internalized the difference between Colombia and Columbia), but even if they forget the specific orthography of my complicated language, I believe they'll still be able to translate a friendly smile into something that can better their world, their country, and their community.

That's a language the world really does need to learn, no matter where in the world we might find ourselves.

And despite all its ongoing challenges, I discovered Colombia certainly had a lot to smile about.

EPILOGUE

When I was in Colombia in 2011, the official slogan of the Colombian Ministry of Tourism was *el único riesgo es que te quieras quedar* or "The only risk is wanting to stay." It was witty and almost entirely true (though the tourism board might still want to warn tourists of the risks of sunburns, mosquito bites, and undrinkable coffee). However, I still hoped that there would be a time when Colombia wouldn't have to talk about risk at all.

Colombia—and Isla Barú—were far along in the process of reinventing themselves and going through constant change. Since 2011, Bogotá has banned the once-ubiquitous horse carts (which should at least help with traffic problems). The FARC and the government attempted a new round of negotiations. Different drug cartels were dismantled and new groups sought out power. A different WorldTeach volunteer teacher has taught in my place each year since I left.

The sun was shining just as strong. The humidity was just as stifling. The food was just as delicious. The faces were the same. But when I returned in December 2013, it was clear major changes had happened in Colombia and Santa Ana in the two years I had been gone.

I had gone back for a half-month visit to explore new regions and visit my old haunts. I wanted to see what students I could find (few, since they were on vacation), meet up with colleagues (Pedro was still at IESA—and was actually at school the day I visited—though hadn't changed his teaching style much), and enjoy again the country I had gotten to know so well.

The easiest change to spot in Santa Ana was that The Puddle had completely disappeared under a small culvert and four feet of rocks, dirt, and asphalt: the main dirt road from the ferry to the beach had been completely paved. Some side roads into Santa Ana now featured pavement and concrete, and a few had redone sidewalks. And the biggest change had yet to come: a bridge connecting the island to the Pasacaballos mainland was in the works, scheduled to be completed mid-2014.

The paved road brought with it the strange sight of taxis and other cars on the road, and large billboards lined the small highway advertising, among other things, expensive apartment spaces for condos being built by the beach.

My visit back of course had to include some beach time and I was happy to see Playa Blanca hadn't changed much, though there were a few more thatched tiny hotels, huts and restaurants, and the boats bringing tourists from Cartagena were more numerous and more crowded. The road brought in more tourists from the mainland as well, along with a Postobón soda truck delivering refreshments to the place where before motorcycles, boats, and donkey carts had ruled.

But larger changes still might happen, and already Hilton hotels had one attempt blocked to build a new resort on the beach. Because no one seemed to actually own the beach, the government was finding that selling off the beach property was an easy way to make a bundle of money and attract more tourist dollars to the Cartagena area. That wouldn't be so good for everyone who worked at the beach. Not everyone who made small carvings or offered coconut drinks could suddenly shift to working at a hotel. And it would be a shame if they built on that piece of land that was blessed with such natural beauty. The crabs scuttling around the driftwood, the pelicans bobbing on the waves, and the fish flitting around the patches of coral wouldn't know what hit them if a multi-story building grew out of the sand instead of trees. Hopefully giant resorts would be absent from the beach for years to come.

In many ways, the Santa Ana and Colombia I knew was already gone. Part of me was glad—I had moved there to try to add to the change that was happening in Colombia—but part of me will always be nostalgic for the rickety canoe rides and for navigating The Puddle on a bumpy mototaxi.

A week after I re-explored Isla Barú, I stood on a windswept hill, looking down on a green valley punctured with tall palm trees and dairy farms and fell in love with Colombia for the second time. In the emerald coffee-growing region and the towns of Manizales and Salento, I fell in love with a Colombia that was familiar but distinctly different from the Caribbean coast I had gotten to know so well. Everyone still greeted everyone else with a smile, everyone still snacked on arepas and fresh juice, ate too much rice, drank too much aguardiente, and talked soccer, and yet here was a Colombia where the tropical heat had been reduced to a warm summer breeze, and where tourists and locals alike drank water out of the tap. As I rediscovered *agua panela* and enjoyed the piping hot tierra templada version of the drink, I remembered why I had wanted to come back and why also I would have to return again: there was simply too much of this country I hadn't explored.

When I returned to Colombia, I found their tourism slogan changed to "Magic Realism." The phrase fit.

Colombia's problems might be real, but the country also has a special magic to it; from its landscapes (the mountains, oceans, deserts, and rainforests) to its passions (music, fried food, and being late) to its people (from the master of magic realism, Gabriel García Márquez himself, to studious Katia, friendly Otto, committed Arelis, and the dozens of welcoming Colombians I met around the country).

While I may have once stereotyped Columbia as a country full of violence, drugs, and a bleak future, I now knew that Colombia is a country full of friendships, happiness, and optimism for what is to come. The future looks bright.

ABOUT THE AUTHOR

In 2011, author Bryanna Plog spent a year in Colombia as a volunteer English teacher through Harvard-based WorldTeach and Colombia-based Volunteers Colombia. Originally from western Washington, she is currently an educator and park ranger with the National Park Service. She continues to write and blog about traveling, Colombia, and other favorite destinations at bryannaplog.com.

Made in the USA
Middletown, DE
08 November 2019